MANIC MAMA

MANIC MAMA

Dysfunction Sucks

A. J. IRWIN

Copyright © 2023 A. J. Irwin.

All rights reserved. No part of this book may be reproduced, stored, or transmitted by any means—whether auditory, graphic, mechanical, or electronic—without written permission of both publisher and author, except in the case of brief excerpts used in critical articles and reviews. Unauthorized reproduction of any part of this work is illegal and is punishable by law.

ISBN: 979-8-89031-697-4 (sc)
ISBN: 979-8-89031-698-1 (hc)
ISBN: 979-8-89031-699-8 (e)

Because of the dynamic nature of the Internet, any web addresses or links contained in this book may have changed since publication and may no longer be valid. The views expressed in this work are solely those of the author and do not necessarily reflect the views of the publisher, and the publisher hereby disclaims any responsibility for them.

CONTENTS

Chapter 1	DYSFUNCTION INGRAINED	1
Chapter 2	PERSERVERANCE FOR EMANCIPATION	11
Chapter 3	BRAT SOCIETY	20
Chapter 4	COAXING COMPANIONS	32
Chapter 5	PARDON GRANTED	39
Chapter 6	TOUCHDOWN	45
Chapter 7	FAIRY-TALE TRANCE	48
Chapter 8	GRAND BALL	51
Chapter 9	RETURNING TO PURGATORY	55
Chapter 10	FOREBODING	58
Chapter 11	THE PENDULUM SWINGS	62
Chapter 12	TO AND FRO	64
Chapter 13	TO AND FRO … TO AND FRO	66
Chapter 14	SWITCHING ROLES	68
Chapter 15	PLAYING HOUSE	72
Chapter 16	MENTOR	75
Chapter 17	BRIGHTEST PLACE	77
Chapter 18	RESTLESS	83
Chapter 19	NEW THINGS	87
Chapter 20	TOPSY-TURVY	93
Chapter 21	MAMA'S INSTINCT	97
Chapter 22	CONTEMPT	101

THE LIONESS PROWLS

Chapter 1	IN THE BALANCES	109
Chapter 2	WEE HOURS	114

Chapter 3	A MIRACLE	122
Chapter 4	ELUSIVE STATE	135
Chapter 5	NORMAL	143
Chapter 6	BONDING	147
Chapter 7	LACKING	159
Chapter 8	NEVER THE SAME	162
Chapter 9	INTANGIBLE	169
Chapter 10	BUTTERFLIES	175
Chapter 11	WARNING SIGNALS	178
Chapter 12	DISTURBED	181
Chapter 13	QUEEN'S WAVE	190
Chapter 14	OPPORTUNITY KNOCKS	202

CRACKING FOUNDATIONS

Chapter 1	WITHOUT LOOKING BACK	215
Chapter 2	CHANGE OF PACE	224
Chapter 3	TRANSFORMING	236
Chapter 4	ROXY	244
Chapter 5	TOP OF THE WORLD	248
Chapter 6	STATE OF AFFAIRS	253
Chapter 7	MANIPULATION	257
Chapter 8	NEWFANGLED THINGS	265
Chapter 9	ANTICIPATIONS	274
Chapter 10	BLINDERS	281
Chapter 11	SUGARCOATED	284
Chapter 12	DREAMS OF FATE	287
Chapter 13	CROWNING	291
Chapter 14	KINGDOM	294

✘ HIGH STAKES ✘

By A. J. Irwin

*Hollow holes exist,
where bonds should be fond.*

*Though for a lifetime, I wanted to embrace you,
all I got was
frantic commotion, flatline emotion.
A result of your lack of
devotion.*

*Place your bet.
Spin the wheel of your insanity
among the innocence of humanity.
Push them to the edge
of your dysfunction.*

*Spin the chambers in Russian roulette.
Take a chance at glancing the heart.
Spew out the muck,
that never promised much luck,
Of ever finding
the real
YOU!*

CHAPTER 1

DYSFUNCTION INGRAINED

On Roxanne's eleventh birthday, her present was to be given during the court procedures, where she would receive her current daddy's last name—Brown. She then would become a part of the family of her sister's natural father and her mother's current husband. She gave a giggle of excitement that turned sour. "However, this would be the third daddy for Roxanne!" The judge stated loud enough to spear her in the back and spin Roxanne's anticipation toward her pregnant mother's direction with a look of discrepancy as the judge waited for Vanessa's answer. Roxanne felt ensnared in a world controlled by her mother as Vanessa Rose opened her mouth to reveal the name of Roxanne's natural father, but not before clutching her daughter's ears with a sound-blocking pressure that muffled everything except for the screams of Anxiety that coursed through every fiber of Roxanne's shivering body.

A few short years later, Roxanne had been molded into the governess of their cute happy family, had already become frayed and bitter. It was a cold winter day. The sky was gray and threatening to wreak havoc on the Truckee Meadows while Vanessa screamed vulgar threats in Daddy

Browne's direction. He took up all his material belongings and went away. Vanessa went back to doing the casino stroll, dealing Blackjack and hustling for big tips while finding comfort from the opiate cough syrup, which cushioned all the demands that controlled a single mom's world.

At the age of fifteen, Roxanne had been chastised into taking charge of her siblings and being castigated for their crimes. "The perfect little siblings, could do no wrong!" Roxanne mimicked Vanessa's assured attitude while attempting to console her withering existence that had been forced to take on the responsibilities of governing the home, the children, work, and being a half-decent student. Above all, she fretted over her mother's pleasures. While attempting to be loved and accepted by her mother… or anyone!

"I've learned to silence my cries!" Roxanne reflected on the visions of when "Mother felt the need to beat me!" Her voice cracked with sarcasm that shook the following thought from her feeble mind. "I've learned not to complain!" came from the cracks in her soul. "Not even about the noise growing inside my mind?" uttered from her dry throat as an uneasy feeling darkened her destiny and caused her soul to scream for release from her perdition. It was in that perdition that Roxanne lived out her sentence, envious of her storybook mentor while desperately hoping and praying to find a Prince Charming who would take her away from all this pain.

"Cinderella's Prince Charming put her on a beautiful stallion and bravely carried her away from her entrapment!" Roxanne mumbled, quivering in despair. Shaking herself from the on-going daydreams during the long, hard summer, the beatings became more frequent. And her siblings grew obstinate due to Roxanne's all-day, everyday authority over them. The siblings knew that she would be to blame for whatever happened. And they found it to be a convenient weapon in their armory. "Of the Brat Society!" Roxanne assessed firmly as she contemplated Vanessa's second child, Isabella, a curly-blonde-haired little cutie—a princess to most, but to Roxanne, she was "a spy sent to encumber my entire life!" rumbled Roxanne's tolerance.

Isabella would purposely whirl through the clean house, destroying all of Roxanne's efforts. Her sadistic laughter taunted and teased Roxanne, who frantically tried to re-clean Mother's house. "Spotless!" Roxanne chastised her efforts. "SPOTLESS, spotless ... spotless!" Isabella mimicked as she danced around her fretting, sweating Cinderella.

It has to be, perfect! Roxanne's mind screamed, forcing her to scrub and wipe even harder.

"Missed a spot!" Isabella's words cracked a stinging whip into Roxanne's flesh.

"Just the way…Mother, likes it!" Roxanne chanted the chastisement of frustration and anxiety. Anxiety glanced at the clock, with the consideration that dinner also had to be prepared. *You're not going to make it. Not with those squabbling siblings!* Chorused through Roxanne's mind, demanding that she speed up with another crack of the whip, tearing her flesh to a bloody pulp and introducing the overwhelming desperation that taunted her efforts.

Roxanne tried soothing the crowd of contending emotions by explaining how she had tried locking her siblings out of the house once, but that resulted in a double-bloody beating.

"One, for locking the kids out!" Roxanne frolicked, repeating the offense. "And two, for causing Isabella to break the window!" she somberly recalled from memory as she talked over the vacuum cleaner.

"Maybe that is when my head began to fill with static?" slid past her lips, with a definite consideration in her tone. "The chattering noises behind the curtain of static that have taken up residency way off in the depths of my mind. Sometimes louder than others, but constantly, they accompanied me for at least the last two months now!" Roxanne concluded in a methodical tone as the garage door opened and Vanessa entered the dining room.

Mother usually came home early enough to relieve Roxanne so that she could review her homework or other things she needed to complete after she returned from work.

Nevertheless, tonight Vanessa came in late and staggering from the substance that had attempted to drown her reality. *Opiates chased with alcohol!* Echoed from the furthest depths of Roxanne's mind as she cringed from her Mother's somber mood when she stepped into the kitchen, trapping Roxanne in the corner as Vanessa pushed her slim hips against the kitchen counter to reach for a bottle of beer from the icebox. Roxanne stood erect with electricity warning her senses to disappear as she watched Vanessa stagger into the icebox. She struggled to force the door shut while attempting to pull the magnetic bottle opener from the front of the spotless icebox.

Suddenly, a rush of courage picked up the tatters of Roxanne's disappointed heart and dashed past the brooding Vanessa. Quickly, Roxanne prepared for work while Anxiety clashed with all that was expected of her. Roxanne shot a nervous look at her mother, who usually, attentively tended to her youngest children while Roxanne got ready for work. But tonight, she was following her oldest around with a bourbon in one hand and the other clenched so tight that her fist was turning white, except for the index finger, which stuck out as an accusing pointer blaming and threatening Roxanne for all that had gone wrong during her day… and in her life.

"Please, Mother, I'm sorry you had a bad day!" Roxanne attempted to appease Vanessa. "I will try harder, to make your days easier!" Although Roxanne sugar-coated her words, still a warning singled Roxanne's spine, telling her to choose her words wisely. "Right now, I have to go to work?" she pleaded while harnessing every ounce of her self-restraint to keep from bolting for the door and escaping her misery.

Roxanne bravely stood her ground while apologizing to her belligerent mother before she calmly took that sixth and final step toward the door, reaching for the doorknob.

Vanessa suddenly pounced in front of her daughter and blocked the escape passage, causing Roxanne's hands to come up in a natural gesture of self-defense, blocking her mother's sarcastic words that sprayed into her face.

"Well, if you're so damn eager to make my day!" She slurred her words as she fumbled in her pocket and retrieved the monetary note necessary before she continued spewing her demands in blistering terms. "Stop at the damn store!" Vanessa's eyes rolled her into leaning against her timid daughter as she shoved a five-dollar bill into Roxanne's hands, which were still held up in front of her face in a defensive position.

"Oh-oh-o-kay Mother!" Roxanne stuttered with her remaining courage while closing her fingers around the money, clutching it tightly in her sweaty palm before leaning in to kiss her Mother.

Vanessa turned her head with a habitual expression of revulsion smeared across her face before taking on a nonchalant stance that carried her away.

It was Roxanne's heart shriveling and sinking into the abyss of her existence where she had been formed by the familiar emotions of terror, humiliation, and neglect.

Roxanne had been holding her breath since she tried to kiss her mother. And now, the cascading waves of her emotions crashed into her already-swirling mind, pulling her violently into the gloom of melancholy before she could open the door and rush out of the house into the late-afternoon sun. A cool breeze blew gently into her face, beading her nervous sweat into goose bumps that iced the tension in her knotted muscles. Her lungs finally agreed to a few deep breaths that began rejuvenating her heart. Her senses welcomed the sun, which had begun defrosting the glacial sentiment that frequently had its way with her.

Roxanne began pushing and stuffing her mother's threats and defensive body language into any crevice of an already-overstuffed existence, consumed by the nagging static.

Although finding space for a load of offensives was difficult, Roxanne fluttered from the anguish with a long sigh as she slipped into the relief from reality, where pleasant daydreams found her skipping through the daffodils of life.

Until she was alerted by a stinging sensation, the vines that supported her inflictions, had grown thorns. While Roxanne inspected the wound, she noticed, tiny droplets of blood, trailing to her. And when she looked down the trail, she could see damnation bearing down on her. She quickened her pace, attempting to outrun the chastisement that began penetrating her protective seclusion with the boiling substance that was packed deep inside the cavity of her stomach.

"Nothing you do is right!" slammed into her, nearly piercing her heart on its searing path to her already-traumatized mind.

"Never good enough!" shook loose a burst of sarcastic laughter that trailed up the burnt path and exploded into Roxanne's heart before engulfing her mind.

"You know I loathe you?" hissed from the abyss of her existence, causing Roxanne to clasp her ears with as much pressure as possible while Vanessa's words taunted tears to stream down Roxanne's face as she tried to squeeze the drama from her mind. "No ... No! Nooo!" she protested.

"Stop ... Quiet!" Roxanne demanded as she squeezed her ears tighter, attempting to quiet the noise that held her captive, devouring her completely.

Roxanne began mumbling over the destruction of her Mother's words while perspiration beaded the blanket of goose bumps. She fought for control over the isolation of insecurities that attempted to singe her until she internally combusted and left only a trace of charred DNA, to be blown away by the aftermath of Vanessa.

She found herself rebutting the insecurities, louder and faster until her mouth grew dry from screaming at the top of her lungs with conviction. Suddenly, Roxanne stopped dead in her tracks. She struggled to release the pressure that was applied to her attempts to squash what was vexing her. Finally, she was able to drop her hands from her ears. She stood with her arms straight at her side. She spun in a three-hundred and sixty-five degree scan of the area. Her heart began to beat with the signal; *"Nobody's watching!"* Shaped her lips into a smile as she began humming a rhythm and mumbling the words.

I got sunshine… on a cloudy day.
When it's cold outside… I got the month of May!

Roxanne continued to hum until the calmness put the buoyancy back into her stride and carried her back into the land of daydreaming, where confidence massaged her while determination recalled a letter she had received from her friend Erica from Southern California explaining in detail the weather, beaches, boys, and parties with boys. Erica's words enticed Roxanne's soul while attempting to convince her to muster up the courage to ask her "warden" if she could come down for a visit. "That was nearly a month ago!" uttered Roxanne as she mentally revisited the letter that had been previously opened and inspected by her Mother.

Roxanne had considered many times to ask for permission, but confusion faltered her with doubt. "Mother had read the letter!" Shook Roxanne with a feeling of invasion. "Mother knew the offer had been made!" seeped from Roxanne suspiciously. "However, she never said anything about it." Her words pushed out vigorously with a strong burst of unfamiliar emotions that could only be expressed as fortitude, charting a path up her spine, igniting her indignation at the same time, she contemplated every scenario that would prevent her from getting away. Those scenarios flashed through her mind over and over until her serious contemplation left her with one undisputable decision. "To wait for the perfect opportunity!" She bravely stated out loud as she began to contemplate exactly when that would be.

"When she isn't drunk and angry!" Roxanne again confirmed out loud as she reached her workplace where the tasks were simpler and less stressful than the responsibilities at home.

The hours quickly slipped by while she served charbroiled hamburgers and French-fries to some happy; some not so happy, some friendly, and some rather rude and indecisive people Roxanne recalled as she collected her tips and waved a shy good-bye to the cook before clutching her arms around herself and went shoulder first into the spring-hinged door that creaked with resistance as she passed through into the darkness. The wind snatched the door from Roxanne and slammed it shut, firing a warning shot into the silent street.

The temperature had plummeted, and the wind whipped and bit at Roxanne's exposed flesh as she walked an extra hundred million feet in the opposite direction of her captivity. Until she pushed through the doors of the only store open after ten o'clock at night. Roxanne walked aimlessly up and down the aisles, trying to focus her thoughts on the items her mother wanted. She shoved her hands into her pockets and pulled out the contents. There in her shaking hand was a five-dollar bill, but no list. "Oh, great!" escaped in a small, unsure voice, Apprehension coursed her veins and pumping her heart with the fear of guaranteed doom, while tension secreted pungency into the air about her, insulting her sinuses. "How am I to know what she wants?" quivered Roxanne's voice, signaling the release of the rumbling locomotive, departing from the pit of her stomach on a targeted course, straight to her brain.

When the thundering rumble reached its destination, it exploded into a screeching static. Roxanne stood in the aisle, clutching her ears, her heart refusing to beat. Suddenly, the next locomotive penetrated the wall of muddled static, allowing the seepage of faint words to puddle in her mind. She attempted to make out the message, but the distortion only confused her as she walked the aisles, afraid to pick up anything for fear that it would be the wrong item.

Abruptly, her mind found clarity, with a vivid image of her Mother holding the product up while fire shot from her eyes, roasting her daughter in the fire of contempt and chastising her in a shrill voice, shattering Roxanne's tender state.

"Can't you do anything, right?" Vanessa's voice thundered with a loathing venom. Her hostility grew with each striking word and caused droplets of blood to spill from Roxanne's ears. "What made you think I wanted this?" completed a mental checklist of the entire kitchen and selected the items that they didn't have, hoping she couldn't get it wrong.

Apprehensively, Roxanne stood in front of the clerk while she again contemplated the household inventory. Her indecisive mind attempted to pull her back down the aisles for any items she may have forgotten. But when the clerk smiled at the end of his task, the register rang up six dollars and five cents. Anxiety nipped at Roxanne as she considered putting items back, but the indecision of which to keep and which to put back, forced her to use all her mother's money, plus some of her own tip money, to pay for the excessive purchase.

Roxanne's mind taunted her as she bundled up, managing to wave a polite goodbye to the clerk with her arms carrying the heavy box of her Mother's wants, and stepped out into the cold, unforgiving winds of the Sierra Nevada Mountains.

On the extra-long journey toward her damnation, she contemplated with manipulation how to escape her hell. Roxanne huffed a sulking disposition as she reflected on her Mother. "Who has to have a buzz before she could come home and deal with her commitments!" Roxanne panted with frustration as she continued to grumble. "The leftovers from false hopes and wishful thinking!" Roxanne protested out loud. "Mother's dreams of happy homes and white picket fences were all false!" Roxanne wanted to chuckle over Vanessa's poor luck. "The best she could hope for now is that her new man loves her enough to accept the children!" pushed puffs of hot steam into the cold night air as Roxanne dragged her physically and mentally exhausted existence down the dark empty streets.

Although numb, her ears hummed with a droning static that pounded her heart with the rhythm of pain that insisted her emotions disunite.

"Like a fetus torn from the wall of the uterus dies!" she moaned in contemplation. "So had she felt since the last beating her mother had ordered her third stepfather to deliver to her," she mumbled into a mental flashback of the coaxing Vanessa, slurring syllables, demanding Eldon to pummel Roxanne's entire body until she lay lifeless on the bedroom floor.

"God... please!" Roxanne pleaded for comfort over the flood of memories. The ones that flowed in the direction of overwhelming desperation blanketed her with a conceived plan of pleasing her mother into guilt. "She won't be able to say no!" Roxanne stated out loud while the fingers on each hand crossed, refusing to give power to the haunting negativity that iced her goosebumps.

CHAPTER 2

PERSERVERANCE FOR EMANCIPATION

Roxanne frantically ran from the voices that chased her until she stood on the edge. It was there, the forbidden ones tempted her to step over the edge. In turn, the good forces blew their trumpets with a warning, pleading for her to turn back, "Stay on the sane side!" bounced off the walls of static as her thoughts hungover that fine line, where she teetered with curious anticipation.

"It was there, she was in control and nobody else mattered!" Roxanne defended the qualities of the edge as the good forces trembled with disapproval. Hysterical laughter of the forbidden wrapped around Roxanne and spun her like a top, spinning her uncontrollably over the edge.

Roxanne's body exploded with pain when she hit the bottom of the abyss. She lay on the floor next to her bed, recollecting the passion she had in her dream for the things that were in the abyss.

"What was over the edge?" she searched but found no recall, as she twisted for the time. A rebelling moan volunteered itself and demanded that she rub her hip before turning her attention back to the hands-on the clock, which stood firm at four o'clock in the morning. The starting gun fired an exhilarated rush of energy that pulsed through her and pulled her up from the floor.

By the time twilight had popped its head up in the east, Roxanne was tying her hair back as she headed out the garage door. With her spirits held high above the bag of collected trash from the house, where all the trash cans had been washed, and the refrigerator had been cleaned out and wiped down.

Beads of sweat glistened in the early-morning sunrays as Roxanne swept, wiped, scrubbed, washed, shook, mowed, raked, and watered every material and living thing on the outside of the house. Roxanne inspected her work with a white glove while Anxiety began stirring awake. *Missed a spot!* chastened her companions. Roxanne polished the car's hood to a higher shine before retrieving the freshly beaten rugs that were airing on the fence.

Are you sure they are good enough? Bit at her, as she inspected the rugs. Roxanne flinched, an attempt to shake the monkey from her back, as she pushed through the door, with her nerve-dashing annoyances following right behind her. "Stop!" she begged. "Not now!" Roxanne pleaded as she came face-to-face with the unexpected presence of Vanessa. Roxanne's lungs expelled a deflating wheeze before they shriveled and choked out the last of its life support. Roxanne struggled for perseverance when she attempted to speak. Still, only a croaking frog leapt from her throat, leaving her with only a nervous smile to greet the suspiciously growing impatience of Vanessa while Roxanne attempted to fill her lungs with air and clear her throat. "G-g-good morning, Mother?" was delivered to her mother's back. "Would you like me to pour you and Eldon some coffee?" Her words trailed in hesitation while Vanessa rubbed the rush of her daughter's words from her eyes, while Roxanne turned to retrieve the coffee cups from the cupboard.

"Maybe, some breakfast?" Roxanne offered with kindness. "Maybe... breakfast in bed?" Roxanne suggested as she closed the cupboard and turned to meet Vanessa's snarling lip.

"Why are you making so much noise!" she barked, "So damn early in the morning!"

Roxanne's courage threaten to abandon ship, but not without her attempting plan B first. Roxanne passively stroked her mother's disposition, not wanting to give her secret away. Quickly, she changed the conversation. "Would you like me to run you a bath?"

Vanessa shot a glare of suspicion at her daughter and held her in an eye-locking trance while she calculated her daughter's intentions. Vanessa continued to hold her daughter's actions in contempt. As Roxanne slid almost to safety, "Clean the tub" cracked the whip, tearing at Roxanne's already-scarred flesh.

Hot daggers prodded at her self-esteem while the tub began filling with water. "The perfect temperature!" Trenched Roxanne's mannerism.

Just the way she likes it! cracked the whip that dug into her already bleeding soul.

What did you expect? consoled the voice from inside her as she stood up.

We are not going to let her be our dictator forever! forced a rush of courage to straighten Roxanne's back as she spun around to see a wink of satisfaction and a smile of approval in the reflection of the mirror.

Vanessa Rose reviewed her troublesome ward's actions while sipping her spiked coffee in the spotless tub, heated to the perfect temperature. "I know that girl—she's up to something!" Vanessa muttered while she washed away the layers of replenishing cold cream from her face. "Well, she won't win. I always have the upper hand!" Vanessa teased with determination to throw away the key that locks Roxanne in perdition.

Roxanne was in a trance of eating humble pie as she waited out the last minutes of her homemade breakfast, which included fresh-squeezed orange juice, still needed, to be made. She heard Isabella and Spencer enter the hallway with their stomachs pulling them toward the aroma that led them to the kitchen.

"I'm hungry!" Isabella's screech caused rippling waves of emotions to flood Roxanne's bloodstream, forcing her to spin around, with her finger pressed up against her lips.

"Me too, I'm starving!" Spencer protested against his sister's warning in a loud nerve-racking bleat of a persistent goat. Roxanne's natural reaction was to reach out and squeeze the breath from his neck. But she fought for restraint, knowing that would be her deadly wound.

Instead, Roxanne's face masked her manipulation with a shrewd smile as she escorted her siblings to the table with a tray of bartering items. Each of the siblings recklessly flopped onto their chairs and began demanding their orders. Roxanne's shrewd smile widened to devious, as she dangled frosted glasses of orange juice, out as bait.

"If the two of you are good!" grabbed only part of the siblings' attention while they watched Roxanne wave a glass in front of them. Isabella began wavering for the drink with a disputing tone that forced Roxanne to land the glasses with a thud, atop a recently placed napkin. She purposely fixed an eye-locking stare into each of her half-attentive siblings' eyes. Roxanne picked up a homemade biscuit, smothered with sweet blueberry preserves, made from the blueberries that grow wild by the Truckee River, during the right seasons. "I will pay!" snagged the siblings.

Roxanne began reeling them in as she placed a biscuit on the saucer-sized plates in front of each sibling. "For the both of you, to go to the movies!" lit up their eyes and turned their heads in her direction, and began bobbing in agreement, before Roxanne disappeared into the kitchen.

When she returned to the dining room with the main-course plates in hand, she was greeted with an agreement. "OK, it's a deal." Spencer's words rushed out to his oldest sister (governess/slave) as Roxanne placed his plate in front of him, suspiciously examining his motives and integrity before turning to her sister.

"Both of you have to be really, really good!" caused Roxanne to lock eyes with her sister's innocent *Who me?* expression.

"Really good, okay." Roxanne stabbed at her challenges as Isabella's eyes darted to her plate in defiance.

Suddenly, Roxanne felt like a politician, losing ground in the Hometown, fighting to remain in control of her cupping hand at the end of her arm; that was extending towards her sister's throat. Roxanne could hear through the static in her mind, voices that insisted, she stop.

Come on, girl, just chill! pulled back Roxanne's reigns.

"You're going to ruin everything," forced her hand into a fist that slammed down onto the table, just inches away from Isabella's plate.

Daringly, she leaned into the demon's eyes while connotation made her voice quiver, possessing a threat of its own.

"I will kill you!" rushed through Roxanne's lips before she could slam her mouth shut, in front of the shaking teary-eyed siblings, their eyes wide and in full attention to the stranger that swore to devour them.

"Really good!" came in a stuttered whisper from the siblings' lips. Allowed Roxanne to finally breathe as she watched the siblings, heads bob, in an up-and-down movement of conformity. Roxanne's black eyes shot back from one sibling to the other until a smile softened her eyes to a mocha brown.

"Okay, pinky promise?" Thrust Roxanne's fist out, with only the pinky finger, extended. A smile smeared Roxanne's face as she watched the siblings comply with the pinky swearing that straightened their posture and removed their elbows from the table. Relief, smeared a smile across Roxanne's lips with a positive thought, giving her a feeling that she had regained her ground. She dared allow a relieved whisper to pass her lips.

"This plan, just might work!" Blew wind into the sails of her confidence as she turned toward the kitchen, where she prepared plates for the remaining occupants.

Anxiety was expecting trouble at any moment while Roxanne put the prepared plates into the oven to keep warm. Suddenly, noticing an extended period of quietness caused panic to mix with Anxiety's Pessimism. Together they began dancing around Roxanne until she grunted and pushed past the skeptics, rushing into the dining room with her companions, close in tow.

A pleased smile shaped Roxanne's lips as her companions circled the table and stood behind the siblings, sitting in front of plates that had been licked clean. Silently, her brother and sister glided paper airplanes back and forth across the table. A soft smell of tranquility danced around Roxanne as she watched with interest, amused by their child's play, while Anxiety caught a second wind and pushed out the next responsibility. "Will you please quietly, change your clothes?" Spencer shot off like a bullet, but Isabella's head snapped around, shooting icy daggers from her cold blue eyes.

"No!" expelled from her burning inferno. "You … don't tell me what to do … when Mom is home!" Isabella protested.

Roxanne rushed around the table, contemplating strangling the spoiled little brat. Instead, stronger forces stuck her hand in her pocket and pulled out a handful of change, with the intent of bribing her sister.

"Isabella?" Roxanne said firmly as she leaned into her sister's shoulder. "If you get dressed, very quietly, I will give you a nickel!"

Isabella offered the sly toothless smile of a well-seasoned swindler, who had years of experience conning desperate people when she held out a chubby hand and extended it into her sucker's direction.

"Two nickels!" the child said with experience.

"It will cost you … two nickels!" Roxanne shot her manipulator an evil-eye from the black abyss of her once-almond eyes.

Why don't you kill her? Anxiety circled Roxanne, encouraging her. *Enough is enough!* stomped on Roxanne's toe before she dropped two nickels into the palm of her rival's hand and patted her on the head while Roxanne fought to ignore the less tolerant, sinister side of her companions, who were telling her what to do more often than not.

Roxanne shrugged the companion off to watch the young, ruthlessly evil girl stick her tongue out before she turned and skipped away, humming a repetitive melody that sounded like "Sucker, sucker, sucker!" Which rose into a higher pitch than Roxanne's companions. *Oh, what a sucker you are!* The companions chastised Roxanne as she exhaled a mental note.

STIPULATE AGREEMENT …
BEFORE … MAKING A PAYMENT!

"Hey, that's not fair?" stabbed Roxanne in the heart as she watched Spencer storm out of his bedroom, his face glowing a mad red.

"Mom, Roxanne gave Isabella two nickels!" he shouted as he pounded on the bathroom door. "She gave me none!" he moaned like a record player turned to slow speed, blasting through the closed door.

Distress polluted Roxanne's bloodstream with the threat of ruining everything, she had planned and worked for. She forced her hand into her pocket while rushing toward Spencer, hoping to appease him before Mother opened the door.

But as her bad luck would have it, just as she reached her brother with change in hand, her heart became encased in fear as the door at the end of the hall opened. "What the hell is going on?" thundered in the presence of Eldon, who was viciously snarling like a rabid dog as he rushed up to Roxanne and towered over her. "Why the hell are you always starting fights?"

Roxanne couldn't breathe; her heart vigorously pounded in an attempt to take flight. But Vanessa closed up the back, sealing off any hope of escape.

"I'm not trying to start a fight!" Shook Roxanne's confidence, rattling her voice of defense as she opened her hand, exposing two shiny nickels for her defense. "I just ... haven't given Spencer his yet!" Her words expounded from her severed heart on its way to the acidy pit of her stomach.

Roxanne thought about changing her composure as Eldon and Vanessa looked her over for evidence that would support their doubt, but she was frozen in place. *Great!* The cynics roared in her mind as her body flinched when Eldon reached out and patted the young siblings on the head with approval as he spoke in a soft, monotone voice.

"If you can't please them, and at the same time control them"—Eldon's smile widened as he playfully poked Spencer in the side—"it will be your hide I beat, not theirs!" Eldon turned his dagger toward Roxanne and shot her a warning sign before returning to his bedroom where he finished preparing himself for work.

Roxanne weaved in the static of her mind, dodging the shadows that passed by as she stood in blinding fear.

"I love you!" pulled Roxanne from the depths of despair, providing the courage to open her eyes. Through her distorted vision, she saw Vanessa's smirk, painted in a bold-red lipstick, a biscuit in hand, as she walked out the garage door.

Roxanne's heart leaped into the frenzy of missed opportunity that fired a shot into the space of her entrapment, startling the only contender to rush after her opportunist, but Vanessa continued to back out of the garage with a quirky clown-like expression, painted red, just for Roxanne. Who kept pace with the car until it reached the street as Vanessa stabbed a be-good pointer at her daughter and pulled away before Roxanne could ask for a brief pardon and caused an emptiness to swallow Roxanne, numbing her senses and prohibiting words from forming in her mouth while she fell to her knees, clutching her ears, in the static that flooded the chambers of her mind?

CHAPTER 3

BRAT SOCIETY

Spencer was shaking his sister's arm while Elizabeth was chewing on their subject's ear. She could only see the siblings' moving lips. "What are they saying?" Her questioning mind was the only sound that could be heard while engulfed in the world that lives over the edge. Roxanne desperately began forming her lips, mimicking the siblings own lip movements. "Roxanne ... Roxanne?" came through in waves as her brow sweated, with a last-ditch effort. She fought against plunging into the abyss that exists over the edge.

Spencer's concern and Isabella's skepticism were masked with life-or-death charts that were dictated, by the beating rhythm of their lips. Roxanne's soul could feel a magnetic pull that gravitated her toward the beckoning calls of her siblings while distorting the edge. Mimicking over and over again, until she could hear her own words.

"Hello ... are yah alive in there?"

Spencer turned a concerned look to Isabella, who had become bored with annoyance. "Roxanne, let's go!" commanded Roxanne's blue-eye rival, president of the Brat Society, shoved Roxanne. "Come on, before it's too late!" she barked orders in her sister's direction.

Roxanne sat there on the ground with her knees pulled up to her chest, rocking back and forth, her black eyes staring into another world.

"Roxanne ... Roxanne?" Spencer blared into his sister's ear.

"Hello ... is there, anybody in there?" the siblings questioned as they coaxed her to her feet, encouraging her step-by-step. As Roxanne began focusing, she stumbled over her foiled attempts. "Sabotaged by her two greatest adversaries," she mumbled as she stuck her hand in her pocket and pulled out what little money she had left. "Shoot, with what I have already given them, they could go to the movies every day, for a week!" Roxanne assured herself while pushing coins around in the palm of her hand and tallying their scores.

"After all, they had broken the pinky promise!" she thought, as she assessed Spencer's underhanded guilt. Roxanne's eyes quickly shifted to Isabella, burning her with flames of condemnation for antagonizing the whole thing.

"Hey, let me pay up for my part of the deal!" stopped her young siblings in their tracks and spun them around with bright, eager eyes.

Roxanne gave her sister a critical smile as she dropped a nickel into her evil clutches. She then turned a flaccid look at Spencer before dropping a dime into his little-boy hand. "Hey, that's not fair!" Isabella's protest caused a lethal shot to be fired in her direction. "You, my dear sister, broke the promise!" Roxanne pronounced the judgment clearly. Isabella stood scorched from her sister's dragon words as her mouth opened to scream her objections. But she decided it was not important enough, to risk her life over. *Besides that, would be admitting guilt*, the demon girl thought as she spun around and skipped away, humming that repetitive song. "Sucker, sucker, sucker!" Roxanne shook the evil rival off and turned a bleak smile toward Spencer that sent him shooting off like a bullet in Isabella's path.

"You two, can stop and play at the park, on your way home!" Roxanne called after them as they darted up to the doors of the cinema.

A ton of weight spilled from Roxanne's shoulders as the cinema door closed behind the disappearing siblings. She lifted her wrist to retrieve the time as she walked back to the house. Baffled by the late hour, she raised the watch to her ear to find it was still ticking, affirming, she had lost almost two hours.

Roxanne contemplated those missed hours as she pushed through the door of the house where the rest of the day sped by, while she rushed to get done all she had planned, and with a lot of coaxing from the companion's voices that had penetrated the wall of static. Roxanne decided that if she heard another *Missed a spot!* she was going to scream.

She collapsed on the couch, exhausted and out of breath, in the spotless house. Her mouth was parched when she sank into the plush sofa, too tired to move. She let her mind drift into a dream of sunsets on the beaches. "In sunny Southern California!" she sang in her fantasy world while mentally sailing into the tranquility of her dream.

Without warning from the weather broadcast, her day trip was suddenly foiled by a tornado of muddy children. That slammed its way through the door and landed in the center of the front room. *Oh, that's it… Just kill those brats*! A voice hissed from Roxanne's core as Isabella stood in front of her, covered in mud from head to toe. Her face was a rich brown color, except where her tears flowed—glowed with a mad-red color, fueled by the anger that burned inside her.

"Spencer pushed me in the mud!" Isabella bellowed as a combustion of laughter rolled Roxanne onto the couch; washing the look of regret from Spencer's face, he began to howl with laughter. Roxanne pushed herself up from the couch to find Isabella shaking, with her hands balled up into a tight fist. "Shut up! Shut up!" she raged. "It's not funny!" Isabella screamed into Roxanne's face before she swung around and hit Spencer smack dead in the nose.

Horror shot through Roxanne as Spencer screamed and blood splattered everywhere. "Son of a bitch … I can't believe this!" Roxanne shouted as hysteria tormented her with feral thoughts.

Kill them! erupted in the abyss.

They're spies! raged the companions. Roxanne's head felt as though it was going to explode, leaving her unable to resist the coaching.

Sent to destroy her every plan! Caused Roxanne to fly off the couch in a rage that was coaxed by her companions.

The two of you ruin, every damn thing! Spouted the companions as Roxanne snatched her siblings by their arms and pulled them down the hall and into the bathroom. Both Spencer's and Isabella's eyes were wide with shock, fearing the intruder who had possessed their sister. The intruder began filling the tub with water and aggressively stripping the clothes from the Brat Society, as she spewed loathing words at them. "Ooh, I'm telling Mom!" the evil she-thing taunted the invader, which caused a cynical laughter to bubble in the abyss where the destructive companions competed to emerge from Roxanne first, rumbling to the heights of a maniacal rage. "Who cares?" spewed from the acidy pits of the abyss.

"Not you … or him?" Roxanne ranted as she shot daggers at her brother.

"Go ahead, tell Mother. My ass is dead already!" slit Roxanne's throat.

The siblings watched the intruder with faces that displayed false sincerity and innocence while tears flooded Roxanne's face. Her lips quivered as she mumbled, "Maybe she will do us all a favor and just finish me off, for good!" stabbed at Roxanne, who was compressed under the direction of the only ones that ever sided with her. The companion named Aspiration, loathed the Brat Society as Roxanne reached out for the shaking, flinching children. She methodically encouraged them into the tub while resisting the desire to hold them under the water until they stopped.

Just stop talking! Anxiety insisted.

Stop making messes and breathing! Her mind screamed with premeditated deliberation. Roxanne fought for the strength to subdue her feral desires. "Hurry up and bathe!" Roxanne said in a demonic tone as she turned away. "Mother will be home soon!" sounded with a meticulous ring. She turned her back to the Brat Society and faced the ones who churned inside her. They chorused in an agreement: *Away with the Brat Society!* Scorched temptation. But Roxanne fought with resistance in defense of the Perfect Ones!

Why shouldn't we demand their heads? The councilors questioned with an annoyance that exploded Roxanne's ground and began shaking things over the edge. Roxanne looked about the room for any flies on the wall before she leaned in close to the council and whispered, "If we take the heads of the Brat Society—" She stopped her words with consideration before she continued. "It will surely be the end of me!" Before she forced herself to turn away from the council and walked away.

Roxanne slid a pot roast into the oven while considering whether she had the strength to make it out with her life, let alone with her sanity? Her thoughts physically swirled around her as she rushed out to the garage, to put the children's clothes in the washer. Her heart skipped several beats before submitting to a weak flutter when she found Isabella's white dress spattered with blood.

Oh, that's typical! Spouted Pessimism, who was riding on the coattails of Cynicism as Roxanne ran into the house and grabbed a bottle of club soda.

Better work! Chastised Anxiety while Roxanne prepped the dress with the soda and a scrub brush. *What about Spencer's clothes?* Rushed Anxiety's fret into Roxanne's nervous system. Hesitantly, she inspected Spencer's clothes.

Relieved to find no blood and hardly any mud on Spencer's clothes; shook a rush of laughter loose that had been buried in the abyss. Knotted in her chest before rumbling with an explosive power that produced Isabella's warning. "It's not funny!" played back in slow motion. Isabella's fist, pulling back from Spencer's face with the splatter of blood.

"God… please?" Roxanne pleaded while nausea swamped her bloodstream. She began dumping bleach into the washer as her companions bickered and fretted over Spencer's clothes. *Hide them!* was the final choice, insisted by the contempt of the companions. Roxanne rolled up her brother's clothes and placed them in a temporary hiding place while she worked on getting the blood out of her sister's favorite dress. She had broken a Nervous sweat while dabbing and scrubbing that dress. *What about the mud trailing into the house?* Fussed the problematic companions, the ones that placed doubt in Roxanne's plans and caused her to fear even breathing. Roxanne could see part of the world that existed at the bottom of the abyss where the companions come from. And as she teetered on the edge, she viewed the set-up of her fall, from the top of the master plan.

Roxanne collected the items needed to scrub the trail of muddy footprints from the sidewalk up the driveway and into the house. Anger and Frustration helped push and pull the vacuum cleaner over the dry mud. *It's getting late*, cried all those that helped lift her despondency.

"Shut up," she fought back with the fortitude of a queen as she headed toward the hall, with vacuum in hand.

The Weary noted the huge wall clock quickly, ticking time away. And for the hundredth time today, Roxanne exaggerated. She had lost count on how many times today her heart skipped a beat rather than fluttered. Giving her good cause to think her heart would surely drown in the pool of dread that had swamped her chest cavity.

Dread flooded Roxanne's senses as the companions imagined a toe tag wired to her toe that read, DROWNED… IN A POOL OF

DREAD. Her body drew cold and withered. Sadness creased her face. "Oh man!" escaped Roxanne and quickened the pace of her heartbeat.

"They will be home soon!" pushed from her as she first shoved the vacuum into the front closet, then flew down the hall and swung the bathroom door open. "Come on, out of the tub!" Roxanne commanded as she clutched her siblings in unison, pulling them from the soupy brown water.

"The countdown is on!" she warned as she quickly towel-dried her charges. "I want you"—Roxanne huffed for oxygen—"to put on the clothes I put, on your beds!" Roxanne finished her orders in the face of Isabella's stance of insurgency, which died quickly when Roxanne's face turned a deep purple and fire shot from her eyes.

Isabella slid her small hands around to cover her naked butt while balls of fear kept a fresh breath from expanding her lungs. Her blue eyes grew as wide as silver dollars and began shivering in rhythm with her body. Isabella couldn't move, but at the same time, she didn't dare release the words that fought to spill from her mouth in a tattling formation. Instead, Isabella's eyes darted for a long moment, side to side as she planned an escape route. When suddenly, Roxanne's hands came up in a strangling gesture and she took a lunging step forward, Isabella took that route, escaping with her body parts and her life intact.

Roxanne gave a sinister smile as she watched her little sister scamper like a frightened rabbit, dashing in a quick zigzag, away from its predator. An evil chuckle came from the abyss and spun Roxanne toward her brother, who raised his hands in a surrendering motion, as he slid past the transformed stranger.

Roxanne stood erect in the swirling emotions as she tried to recollect the acts, that made her siblings flee, but the answers remained elusive while she cleaned the bathroom for the third time today. "Spotless— the way M-O-T-H-E-R likes everything!" She labored and squeezed out each letter, spelling *mother*.

Suddenly, Roxanne noticed the reflection in the mirror had its tongue sticking out at her conformity. Roxanne stumbled back from the retorting reflection that cascaded her into an abyss of perplexed Skepticism. Unsure whether or not she imagined it, signaled a Nervous laughter to Shake her confidence and spin her into the kitchen, where her mother's favorite meal rested in its own juices. "Cooked slowly to perfection!" she basted with melancholy. "Only to be devoured!" she said methodically.

"Just like my existence!" brought a sudden visit from her most loyal companion, Anxiety. Roxanne's eyes shifted as she calculated the time remaining until the showdown began. "Fifteen minutes until dinner is done!" she fidgeted, noticing a spot she had missed. She wiped the top of the kitchen window frame.

"Twenty minutes, until Mother gets home!" caused Roxanne's heart to skip a beat again as she recalled the toe tag: POOL OF DREAD. She listens for a minute, hoping to hear the voices of those she was trying not to recognize. But when the companions' hampered her search for approval, she carried on, wiping and polishing everything over and over again.

A complete and excellent report was a prerequisite for a pardon! The companions clamored while debating the quality of the duties, Roxanne had performed. *Not that it would work, but it couldn't hurt?* continued the other companions in sarcasm while Cynicism, rode gracefully high, on the waves that were crashing in Roxanne's mind.

When Isabella stepped into Roxanne's peripheral vision, she had on a pastel-blue dress with white tights covering her knobbed-knees, and black patent leather shoes adorned her feet. Isabella held ribbons that matched her attire in one hand and a brush in the other. Her lips were pressed into a puffy pink pout. When Isabella's eyes met Roxanne's black eyes that exhibited the invader was still smoldering internally.

Roxanne turned away from the blue-eyed fiend, she couldn't help think, how cute she was.

"I'm sorry, for being a brat!" Isabella's words froze Roxanne.

"Huh, never ceases to amaze?" passed inaudibly over Roxanne's lips as she turned to face the one who had never said sorry.

"That's okay!" Roxanne said passionately with a forgiving smile.

"I'm sorry for getting mad" left a strange silence in the room.

Like the calm before the storm! Roxanne's companions predicted from the distant part of her mind. And what was that blaring sound, a warning signal? Roxanne wondered as the sound vibrated from the fog house that Anxiety had set off, bellowing the best advise!

Stable girl, Don't let your guard down! Echoed through Roxanne's existence as she put Isabella's hair into pigtails and tied a bow to each one. Suddenly, a vision of Isabella's bloody dress still presoaking in the washer caused a wave of nausea to slap the panic button.

"There, you look beautiful!" rushed from Roxanne as Isabella turned with the sweetness of a curtsying angel into Roxanne's offer of an impatient smile.

"Please, check if Spencer is dressed!" Isabella shrugged her shoulders before signing off with a disastrously smile, skipping toward the hallway. Roxanne was having second thoughts, giving Isabella authority, but she had to tend to the dress. The fret of Anxiety rushed over Roxanne's thoughts as she began walking toward the garage door while finishing her orders.

"If he is … the two of you can play a game until dinner is ready." Surprise warmed her into a smile of satisfaction that encouraged Roxanne, as she watched Isabella pounce into Spencer's bedroom.

Roxanne swam through the mixture of sirens that blared warning and waded in the satisfaction of hopeful thinking as she reached out to open the garage door. "You're not the boss of me!" kicked Roxanne in the back of her head as her brother's screams crushed what little optimism, she had just basked in.

Feeling mortally beaten, Roxanne decided it was imperative that she get that pardon *ASAP!* insisted the companions, just as the door opened and Vanessa stood face-to-face with her daughter.

Roxanne was grasping at syllables. "M-m-mo-mo-ther!" Roxane's Legs felt heavy, fitted in cement shoes. Her heart fluttered, then stopped as Vanessa stepped deeper into her safety zone.

Roxanne wanted to raise her arms in self-defense, but they too were cemented in place, when Vanessa stopped long enough to give Roxanne an audible snarl that curled her upper lip before she maneuvered her way around Roxanne and made her way to the easy chair where she plopped down and slammed her eyes shut.

Roxanne sucked in a deep breath, trying to imprison the remaining courage that desperately hung on her companion's frayed optimism while she carefully assessed the temperament of her warden's current mood.

The sure sign came when Vanessa placed her long, thin fingers to the center of her eyes and squeezed the bridge of her nose, causing the chatter of Roxanne's companions to rise drove the static in Roxanne's mind, with enough force behind their wings, to fan the flames that scorched her attempts and threatened to burn down any chances of ever being pardoned.

Roxanne silently slipped past her irritated, hardworking, resting mother and walked down the hall to Spencer's room. The siblings sprang up for their inspection in front of an almost frantic Roxanne, who stumbled over her unfocused, words of warning: the information received was, "Mother looks as if she has had a really bad day!" Shook Roxanne in front of the unchanged expressions of her siblings. Violently whipping at Roxanne's rapidly shedding tree of hope, she pleaded with them. "I want the two of you to be really, really good!" Roxanne's almond eyes seemed to roast to a dark brown while the siblings looked to each other for a lead of action. Looking like a princess, Isabella shook her head in agreement with her servant but Spencer gave a sly smile with a look of a dare.

"It's going to cost you!" he said with the confidence of a seasoned blackmailer. Roxanne grabbed him with one hand and stuck the other into her pocket until she was clutching the first piece of currency and pulling it out.

"Here, you little f———n' brat," Roxanne fumed as she stuffed a fifty-cent piece into his small hand. Spencer's eyes grew big as the half-dollar, while the mischievous smile of an experienced con man crossed his face as he tossed the huge coin into the air. "What's f———n' brat mean?" he asked in a slow, condescending tone.

His words increased the threat of never-ending panic attempted to coagulate the life force that pumped through Roxanne's veins.

Restricting the oxygen supply caused her head to spin than to pound with excruciating pain.

"I want one too!" spun Roxanne into Isabella's direction with another payment of bribery while her lungs screamed for air.

Finally, she drew in the desperately needed breath, which pushed out her next words on the exhale. "Both of you had better put smiles on your adorable little faces," found Roxanne, molding Isabella's lips into a point that turned blood red. Roxanne imagined them spurting blood before she squeezed them just a little bit tighter. "Watch what you say, and no whining or fighting!" rushed from Roxanne's mouth as Irony shook her hand in anticipation of a good show.

Roxanne nervously smiled and nodded her head, cueing her acting crew into motion, she released her hold of the leading performer's bloodstained lips.

As she watched the siblings turn toward the hallway and begin the assent, Roxanne realized her heart had ceased to beat as she followed them into the grand performance.

Roxanne crossed her fingers in hopes of being impressed by the siblings' ability, to fake smiles and cheery attitudes, with the grace of the experienced as they acted out a lifetime performance, in front of Roxanne's greatest critic.

The performers stopped directly in front of Vanessa, remaining in a curtsy as they stole peeks of the most important client in the room. But the prestigious elite's head remained clutched in her hands. The fingers of her right hand now pinched her eyebrows together; she didn't bother looking up at the hardworking entertainers, nor, did the majesty mention all the work Roxanne had done.

The crossed-in-hope fingers began to crack and throb while Irony began hackling as the acting crew looked to their instructor for a cue. Roxanne could only offer a displaced smile before placing an index finger to her lips, giving the cue for silence, not only to the performers but to the loudest person in the room, the hackler.

Roxanne turned a critical eye from the heckler. With a hopeful eye, she looked to the audience; still, there were no interested attendees. Only the continuing taunting of Irony's howling laughter at the expected spoiled attempts, flowed with choked-back tears, while Roxanne waved her surrendering hand and motioned her confused actors off the stage.

CHAPTER 4

COAXING COMPANIONS

Roxanne pacified the performers with a basket of warm bread and a jar of honey before rushing back to the kitchen, where she served four plates of nearly gourmet cuisine: the crux, nicely finishing the presentation of a fully prepared table, adorned with flowers and silver candlesticks. Sweating in nervous contemplation of failed attempts and laboring her last-ditch effort while listening to the coaxing of her constant companions, who attempted a prep talk, and to stroke the self-esteem of their unsure and reluctant chief executive.

Come on, girl. You can do this! broke through the walls of static. *If you don't, we will be trapped in this hell forever!"* sparked the fire to the rebellion that set-in council, way in the back, of Roxanne's mind.

Hell ... trap ... die ... here! screamed Anxiety while the anticipation of failure was being heckled by Pessimism's doubt.

"Die here ... trapped in hell!" smoldered the survival instincts of Roxanne's soul, which was demanding, blaring over the heckles, almost drowning them out completely. *FIGHT, FIGHT. Stand up for your rights!*

Fight for emancipation! pierced her indignation while beads of sweat rolled down her entire body.

"EMANCIPATION … EMANCIPATION!" sounded over and over until she was in sync with the companions.

"I have to get out of here!" caused a rush of urgency to flood her senses as the voices of the companions continued in chant, *E-M-A-N-C-I-P-A-T-I-O-N*, they called out in big, bold letters. As the beading sweat turned to ice, her vision came into focus. Roxanne was stepping in time with the coaxing chant, she muddled with her companions. "Emancipation, emancipation!" over and over until they added perseverance.

Perseverance for emancipation! pulled Roxanne's shoulders back with determination. "PERSEVERANCE for EMANCIPATION!" swung a bold Roxanne around with a surge of poised confidence. *Okay girl… here we go!* Assured Roxanne before pushing her through the swinging doors as her face cracked into a faint smile that ached from the force of the forged etching.

You can do this! encouraged Optimism.

Just keep on smiling! roared a sarcastic Persistence.

Roxanne found her brother and sister, sitting at the dining table, locked in children's talk. Without their notice, she slid the plates in front of her waiting siblings. Whom are purposely mischievous, with underhanded trickeries, but her true emotions for them secreted to the surface and pooled in her eyes?

Come on, girl. You can do this! The companions encouraged when Roxanne's etched smile turned sour as she swallowed the pain and wiped at the tears. *Where's that carved smile?* coaxed the companions, who demanded ratification for the courage they supplied for Roxanne as she approached her mother with that mannequin smile.

Vanessa's demeanor polluted the air with agitation, threatening to choke out any that dared to come near her. Roxanne shook from the discerning qualities of past experiences when she stepped into her rival's territory.

"Mother, are you ready to eat?" Roxanne whispered in a humble tone. Vanessa waved her off with a well-manicured hand before her voice snapped.

"Would you just give me a minute?" trapped Roxanne's breath under that patronizing lump in her chest as the ice of courage quickly melted, leaving her drenched and cold while the companions voiced their demands for recourse with their blaring static. But when Pessimism burst out with heckles, Roxanne's senses short-circuited, causing her to wobble and creak under pressure as she staggered in blindness. Fearing as a marionette when its strings have been severed, she too thought she would collapse to the floor before grasping the back of her dining room chair and sliding cautiously into the support of the seat.

It was there in that chair that she rode out the violent storm that raged with her emotions and created a force field of static, blocking the voices that tried to console Roxanne. Their last word, Roxanne received was, *Keep trying!* as the tidal wave of foiled attempts washed away any life preservers that may have been available. Roxanne's head swayed and rocked with the cascading waves as she searched for the conviction to carry on. Although she felt lifeless as a wrung-out rag doll, Roxanne forced one eye to peer through the cracks between her fingers. To have reality rush up and surprise her with Embarrassment. Her hands fluttered nervously to her throat before she dropped them onto the table as she forced an etched smile, attempting to provide her brother and her sister the comfort they seemed to need.

"Let's pray?" Roxanne suggested as she held a hand out to each of her siblings, who returned a confused look in exchange for their sister's strange and uncommon request. Suddenly, Isabella sensed Roxanne's desperation, which caused her own cautious nerve to smack Spencer on the elbow, alerting him to follow suit as she reached out for her sister's trembling hands.

Spencer giggled along with the heckles of Pessimism after Roxanne said the prayer out loud for all to hear. But when the siblings tried to release their hold, Roxanne hung on for dear life. Her eyes remained closed as she mumbled under her breath, "Please, Lord. I'm dying here!" Almost immediately, a sense of self-confidence allowed Roxanne to release the desperate hold she had on her sibling's hands and open her eyes as the static subsided. But it did not take long for Frustration to deliberate the constant annoyance of Vanessa's imprisonment of Roxanne, who sat hopelessly numb while the heckling of her unsupportive companions backed her mother with the power to stab Vanessa's disgust into Roxanne's eye and cause irritation to tear up and run down her face.

Loathing's exasperation tore into Roxanne; Contemplating, how the second part of her plan had been derailed by Vanessa's nasty disposition.

"We could try cheering Vanessa up!" caused laughter to crackle from the Pessimistic, because they knew her chances of achieving that was *none to none!* agreed Roxanne's crowded mind.

Abruptly, the room came back into focus to find Roxanne sitting all alone at the dining table in front of the candle that had melted down to nothing.

Melted down to nothing! hissed from the depths of the abyss, where Roxanne's existence churned into scolding molten, liquefying everything that fell over the edge.

With a breath that felt like her last, Roxanne managed to lean forward and blow out the flame that sat inside the silver candlesticks. Habit picked up the plates that seemed to take on the weight of the world. As Roxanne carried them into the kitchen, she noted how exhausted she felt. But there was also a feeling of deadness, a disconnected feeling that had entered the colosseum of emotions that circled Roxanne as she scraped and rinsed the plates, she had been laden to carry.

Methodically, she did the task she had done a million times: put the leftovers into the icebox and prepared some dishwater before turning to the swinging door. *We'll never make it out alive!* The cynical companions wailed as she pushed through the swinging doors to finish cleaning up the spoils of her efforts. That's when, suddenly, Anxiety slapped the warning button, alerting Roxanne to spin on her heels and retreat from Vanessa, who was sitting at the dining table with a bourbon in hand and a smirk of contemplation masking her disposition.

Distress stole the breath from the shaking Roxanne as she retreated to the corner of the kitchen, where her heart pounded from the near-unexpected confrontation. Her soul ached with fear and confusion, swirling her in the dance of her chanting companions. *Perseverance for emancipation!* Accompanied by the native drums that pounded courage into Roxanne's bloodstream. *Perseverance for emancipation!* Insisted the assured ones.

PERSEVERANCE for EMANCIPATION! grew louder and louder until the courage pushed Roxanne toward the doors as the tribal drums pounded faster and louder, while all the companions sang.

FREEDOM … FREEDOM … Winning freedom! struck a nerve and created a renewed energy to surge through Roxanne, warming her face and pulling her shoulders up and back with her head held high. She noticed a calmness in the static. She could only hear the voices insisting, *you can do it!* They encouraged Roxanne to pull her mother's plate from the warm oven and carry it into the dining room and placed it carefully in front of her brooding mother, who continued to pull sips of bourbon from her glass.

"Mother?" Roxanne asked for Vanessa's attention with a calm, steady voice. But her mother's response caused Roxanne to quiver as Vanessa's hand rose into a stopping position to silence her daughter.

With her tongue slashed and her words cut, Roxanne thought she might die before being able to speak as she watched Vanessa pull another sip from her glass. Roxanne's spirit wavered as Vanessa pulled the last sip of bourbon from her glass and then smacked her lips with pleasure before wiping the rim with her finger and smearing her lips with the bourbon's flavor.

Only then did she speak to Roxanne's trepidation without raising her eyes from the empty glass. "So, what is it you want to do before school starts?" Vanessa turned the floor over to Roxanne, who was attempting to restrain her jaw from hitting the floor as shock waved through her body. She resisted a schoolgirl's scream and struggled to remain unemotional as she took the opportunity that had presented itself.

"Erica has invited me to California!" Roxanne said in a manner that didn't suggest that Vanessa already knew. "I would like to go?" caught Roxanne's breath while she searched for the strength to push out the next sentence.

"Would it be... okay?" weaved Roxanne in anticipation while she watched her mother attempt to pull droplets of bourbon from her empty glass.

"Yeah, you can go!" Vanessa spoke her slurred words from the rim of her glass before she willingly turned her eyes toward her daughter's direction for the first time today. "That is, if you can afford it!" released the tension on the tightly twisted possibility that dangled in Roxanne's stomach, tickling her into laughter as the tension began to unwind.

"Oh ... thank you, Mom!" Roxanne nearly shouted into her mother's ear as she wrapped her arms around her. "Don't you worry—this trip won't cost you a thing!" Roxanne assured her mother as she pulled back to a straight stance and squaring her shoulders as a sign of conviction.

Vanessa examined her teenage daughter with the intent of crushing her dream anytime, between now and the day she was to leave. But right now, Vanessa decided to play with her when she winked a deviant eye and pointed to her cheek, allowing Roxanne to kiss it.

CHAPTER 5

PARDON GRANTED

It was during the planning for her trip to California Roxanne reflected on how she had never known unconditional love from anyone. "Surely, not by a man!" she whispered in her daydream, where she desired a Prince Charming to love, honor, cherish, and protect her.

"Just as Cinderella had!" Caught Roxanne's breath with anticipation that came in short, quick gasps as she visualized her Prince Charming, sweeping her from her feet and riding into the tranquility of happily, ever after.

Her daydream found her at the grand ball, where she was to be the guest of honor, on her first night in California. A giddy laughter flushed her cheeks a rosy pink as a heightened sense of importance grew in her when her Prince Charming, that she hoped to meet, danced her into the bliss of happiness.

Roxanne focused on her fantasy, hoping, for an everlasting escape instead of all the stress and anxiety that was eating away at her stomach and buzzing in her head like flies while she tended to her regular responsibilities and eagerly prepared for her trip.

Secretly, Roxanne had been saving money for at least seven months before she was granted her pardon. "So that wasn't a problem!" she confirmed out loud as she finished counting. "Seventy-two dollars and eighty-three cents!" she confirmed inaudibly while smiling at her money purse before slipping it back into her private hiding spot.

Anxiety continuously fretted over the promised freedom being revoked, while Roxanne did everything possible to appease her mother and Eldon. She broke a sweat every day with her physical and mental labor as she evaded any unforeseen disaster that might spoil her plans. Her great extent had gone as far as to pay her brother and her sister, not to fight, and to be really good. They had drawn up a contract where stipulated conditions were scribed. Number 3 on the list stipulated, a lump sum would be paid, the day Roxanne left.

"I don't want anything to ruin this opportunity!" escaped from her lips when she was alone. *Don't dare speak of our weaknesses in front of those who have the power to crush our hopes!* chorused the companions. But as the date drew close with everything arranged, the harder it was for Roxanne to control the enthusiasm, mixed with feelings of anxiety.

Roxanne knew she was standing on a carpet that could be yanked out from under her at any moment, causing her to hide the giggles that fluttered with the butterflies of anxiety in her stomach, as the parting date grew close.

Anxiety had been watching the clock while Hope crossed the departing date off the calendar with a big red X. As the last minutes ticked by, approaching the last hours, trepidation sailed into the room with a load of mixed emotions. "*Why hasn't anyone else, talked about it?* Blew the trade winds that powered the boat, set on a coarse that circle Roxanne. *Maybe, you were dreaming?* heckled Pessimism from the boat as Anxiety, quickly swam up to Roxanne, who stood on the beach of uncertainty."

"You're probably right. It all seemed too easy!" took a huge bite out of Roxanne's confidence, causing her to fear that at any minute, she may wake up from a blooming dream.

Roxanne's voice shook with Skepticism's doubt. *What if Vanessa really hadn't approached Roxanne with permission, to go to California?* Cynicism pushed Roxanne out of bed, demanding that she check and recheck her luggage and her airline ticket for concrete evidence that the nearing adventure was true. Before she again slipped between the blankets of her bed, where she tossed and turned all night, checking the clock consistently every twelve-minutes and counting down the last ten seconds.

Just like on New Year's Eve: you throw away the old, embrace the ones that you love, while ringing in bigger and brighter things.

"Finally, 4:30 AM!" Roxanne expelled from her dry lips as she spun out of her bedclothes and into her traveling attire, grabbed her bags and her ticket before rushing in to kiss her mother goodbye.

Vanessa only moaned a warning as she rolled over: "Be good!" faded into the sounds of the sleeping while attempting to challenge the young girl's dreams. Roxanne stopped in the bathroom light that shone, just inside Spencer's room. She pulled the stipulated contract from her right pocket, consulting the notes that dictated the conduct of each sibling. She turned the contract over, to find they had agreed on four cents a day, without infractions. Subtracting one cent per infraction, Roxanne calculated the contract: nine days. Times four. Equals thirty-six cents per client, without infractions. She flipped the contract over and did the math, subtracting for Spencer's three infractions "leaves thirty-three cents!" Roxanne whispered as she pulled the money purse from her bosom and counted out six nickels and three pennies, and placed them in a pile on top of Spencer's nightstand before tucking him in and tussling his hair. As Roxanne turned to walk away, she felt a special love for her brother, and for that, she pulled out her money purse and placed a bright silver dime on the other side of the nightstand, all by itself.

Roxanne stood just inside Isabella's room, calculating thirty-six minus nine infractions left twenty-six cents as she stood at the foot of her antagonist's bed. *Smother her!* suggested the companions. Roxanne shook her head, protesting even the thought of coming close to Isabella, fearing, waking her. Knowing she would ruin everything at the last minute.

On cue, Isabella let out a hard exhale as she rolled over and faced the startled Roxanne. The lungs of the timid rabbit that wanted to run were already holding a breath. But the lungs gasped at more air while Roxanne wished she was invisible. *Steady, girl!* vibrated from the abyss, coursing every crevice of her soul. Why the strong-willed companions held her ground until it was safe to leave fifteen cents on Isabella's nightstand before silently skating out of her greatest danger zone.

Roxanne's heart raced as she paced back and forth, expecting the warden's posse to crash through the airport doors at any minute to shackle her and drag her back to the chastisement of her purgatory.

"BOARDING FLIGHT: 778 TO LOS ANGELES," the airline attendant announced in a loud, clear voice. Roxanne fervently pushed through the gate and sprinted her way across the tarmac, rushed up the stairs of the airplane without looking back. Her heart shook with trepidation. Her legs began to lose the muscle control necessary to carry her as she approached her seat next to the window.

Roxanne slid down in her seat and nervously propped an airline magazine up in front of her face. Her heart threatened to explode behind the magazine that hid her from the posse if they came looking for her.

"Oh my God, please!" she pleaded just over a breath. sweat beaded her body, while her heart began swarming with the frantic motions of the chatter of her pessimistic companions. A flashing sign read, Fasten

Seat Belt, drew the attention from the hammering commotion of guilt feelings, telling her, to surrender. Just as the turbo engines combusted and the plane began to taxi down the runway. The butterflies in Roxanne's stomach took flight ahead of the airplane that gracefully lifted into the air. She giggled at the idea that the next time her feet touched the ground, she would be four hundred miles away from the clutches of her Mother.

According to the pilot, they had reached a cruising altitude as the belly of the airplane became parallel with the horizon, while a ding of a bell, turned the seatbelt sign off. Roxanne exhaled the breath she had been holding for the last nine days. She sucked in the untroubled humorous atmosphere on the airplane while being amused by the people she assumed, would visit or lived in California.

The couple that shared Roxanne's adjoining seats were showing acts of admiration for one another. Roxanne's eyebrows knitted with confusion while a big warm smile touched her heart as she bashfully studied the couple's acts of admiration. White teeth beamed a reflection of their smiles, in to one another while their healthy tanned skin showed their age, to be her mother's age. It was obvious that they are very much in love and most likely very happy, Roxanne decided, as she watched the man take up the woman's hand and slowly drew it toward his lips. He gazed passionately into the woman's eyes until her face glowed red and she giggled.

"Oh ... Frances!" she breathed with appreciation as she leaned into his chest, they melted into a mutual gratification. The man she had called Frances passionately kissed her hand, long and hard while his beauty placed her other hand on the back of his head.

"He must be her knight in shining armor," Roxanne told herself, while she listened to the laughter that bestowed the proud stories of the loving couple's children inside their happy and content home.

They seemed to have a genuine love for their children! Roxanne silently thought through the smile, she gave the couple. *Someday, my Prince Charming will gaze into my eyes like that!* Roxanne concluded before turning her eyes out the window, waiting for a concurring sign. But the only sound she heard was Pessimism chuckling, possessing the power to turn Roxanne's smile to a doubting frown.

Roxanne opened her teary eyes, to see a sunbeam illuminating from the Pacific Ocean. It brightened her spirits, knowing that her adventure was right down there and caused her to giggle out loud and wiggle in her seat until Enthusiasm stepped up to dance with her between the buildings that had grown so big, they blocked the view of the ocean and the sun.

"You could fit a hundred Renos and Sparks in this one city!" Roxanne exclaimed in a rush of marveled words that rode the roller coaster of Elation as the plane descended safely into the LAX airport.

CHAPTER 6

TOUCHDOWN

A warm, fuzzy covering blanketed Roxanne's flesh while tears that belonged to elation clogged her throat as she stepped into the blinding sun, to disembark the aircraft that had taken her away from her purgatory. Out of the blue, a riveting shrill swooped the emotional girl up, bursting through the sunspots, and guided her down the stairs. "Roxanne … Roxanne?" shouted Erica from the gate, where she was waving madly. The girls raced toward each other, embracing one another, for their own longing needs. Erica held her shaking friend tight while Roxanne choked over her tears. "Why are you crying?" caused Roxanne to wipe away her tears of joy.

"I can't believe… I'm really here!" She coughed to clear her voice.

"I must be dreaming. Quick, pinch me!" she pleaded with her longtime cherished and missed childhood friend from Reno, which had become even more dreary, since Erica's parents divorced and she moved to California with her mom.

Erica reached out and pinched Roxanne.

"Ouch!" Roxanne protested as she rubbed the stinging area of her arm.

Erica laughed as she gently shoved Roxanne. "See … you're not dreaming. You're really here!"

Roxanne's eyes lit up with the relief that grabbed a hold of her friend and began bouncing in a dance of jubilation through the airport and out into the parking lot.

The freeway that took them from Los Angeles that would eventually lead them to Pomona, acted as a massive circulatory system, feeding the city and different counties. They twisted and turned through the metropolitan area that was so enormous it spread out like an ocean, lit up by the lights of houses that held families. Buildings that housed businesses. Graveyards that kept the deceased. Zoos that caged the animals. Jails that held the dangerous. Trains that carried the commuters, in all different directions.

"I can't believe … all the people … in this town—city!" Roxanne spoke in astounded syllables. "The buildings, reach the heavens … The stores, are bigger than any store in Reno!" She said, as she stuck her head out the window, tracking the different directions available, with the help of the freeway signs.

Erica laughed with delight as she watched her friend take in all that flew past, with an excited expression. Fixing her eye's wide open, for the first time in her life, Roxanne inhaled the humidity in the air, Feeling alive as the wind blew into her face while she eagerly waved at the drivers in the other cars.

Roxanne slid back down into the seat while fixing her hair. "Yeah, it is a lot bigger than Reno and it's always warm!" Erica, assured Roxanne as she downshifted the Volkswagen Bug and exited the freeway.

"The people, are nice! There are so many, cool things to do!" Erica excitedly expressed as they made their way through a neighborhood street that blossomed with exotic-colored flowers that mantled the outline of the plush green lawns where ivy stretched its clawing vines to the rooftops of the houses.

Erica pulled into a large parking lot that led up to a gigantic grocery store while they bopped to Jerry Lewis during the Wolfgang show. Roxanne's eyes were wide open with all the awesome sights as she flipped her ponytail with the beat of the piano that Jerry pounded out. The best of girlfriends laughed, hugged, and talked all through the store and back out to the car; filling it with party supplies, chatter, and schoolgirl laughter. They howled along with Wolfgang and sang along with the popular hits of the teenagers while slowing down to flirt with the boys in the other cars before taking off on the power of exhilarated liberation that had begun to make Roxanne's senses tingle. For the first time in her life, she was doing the things that normal, teenage girls do! She thought as her smile beamed at her best and only friend in the whole world.

Erica's expression suddenly turned pensive as she turned down the radio. "So, how's the family doing?"

Roxanne shot Erica a peculiar look before answering. "Please, I just want to forget all about that world!" Was all Roxanne offered on that subject before her somber look returned to a smile when she leaned forward, to turn the radio back up.

Erica shot a smile at Roxanne as she reflected on her childhood friend's predicament before she had moved away, recalling Roxanne pleading with her not to leave her alone. She had begged with an ocean of tears.

"Please, take me with you!" Had been Roxanne's, ultimate idea of a solution. That was nearly, four years ago! Erica thought as her shoulders shrugged voluntarily with the sudden decision that things had gotten no better for her friend, and most likely than not, things were much worse.

CHAPTER 7
FAIRY-TALE TRANCE

Erica chattered as she weaved in and out of traffic on the boulevard in Pomona, and after making a couple of turns, she told Roxanne to close her eyes. "No peeking!" she demanded just before she pulled up to their destination. "Keep your eyes closed!" Insisted Erica before she slid out of the car. Erica walked around the car and opened the chariot door for her guest, who had peeked between the spaces of her fingers. An implausible expression was plastered on Roxanne's face when Erica giggled. "Okay, open your eyes!" She beaconed Roxanne as she waved her arm, in an ushering fashion, for her friend. Roxanne stood there: Her eyes, traced everything. She sucked up the scents, of such a wonderful place. Leaving her mouth gapped, with pleased amazement. "This is it?" Rode on the breath Roxanne had been holding since, she turned the radio back up.

Roxanne, slipped her long slender legs out of the chariot expecting to wake up from this wonderful dream, she stood erect with the enthusiasm of a child's thrill-when entering the animated world of Disneyland for the first time. "Oh my God ... this place is so beautiful!" Roxanne breathed in the bustling life of vivid-colored flowers and plants grown in temperature-protected houses in Reno, grew abundantly, outdoors in Southern California. A warm gentle breeze teased Roxanne into a dance, with wildflower fragrances, in the abundance of sunshine that created a fairy-tale tranquility. "Hurry … pinch me!" Roxanne ordered Erica, who had cradled her guest's arm, and began escorting her longtime friend up to the kingdom of her seven days of Heaven.

As the best friends giggled and teased each other's hair into a half-inch lift, the week of festivities for Princess Roxanne was planned. The agenda was set with the promise of laughing and grooming, talking and laughing, going to parties and laughing, going to the beach and playing, watching boys, and giggling. "As girlfriends do!" Roxanne shouted. Just before the girls howled in laughter, their hands slapped a high five.

Erica first gave her longtime friend a grand tour of the castle to familiarize her visitor with the surroundings. Erica told short anecdotes of her friend's that smiled back from her yearbook. Envy pouted into the pictures of the happy smiles that made Roxanne ecstatic that Erica's life in Southern California had provided the normalcy necessary to bring up a well-adjusted individual.

"Now you will recognize some of the faces that will be here tonight!" Erica said as she swung the book closed, sealing her memories for a lifetime.

Roxanne's face was painted with a lack of self-confidence when she walked out of the bathroom with a dark-green wool dress on her slender body. Erica looked into Roxanne's reflection of doubt and smiled.

"Appropriate enough for the Sierra Nevada Mountains?" Erica chuckled with distaste. Roxanne's head rocked in agreement with her fairy-tale provider. "But, not for the sultry, sunny California!" Erica stated as she spun around to her closet, pulling out a pair of faded hip-hugging jeans and a white T-shirt.

Erica tossed the appropriate attire to Roxanne while explaining the evening's entertainment as Roxanne slipped on the snug T-shirt. Erica continued explaining there would be all sorts of diverse activities. A drinking and a wet t-shirt contest would definitely start the evening. Roxanne giggled shyly with inexperience as Erica signaled the thumbs-up approval from the experienced. With a wink from Erica, Roxanne shook the jeans out with the fairy dust that sprinkled magic into the air. Giddiness swarmed around Roxanne as she slipped into the perfect-fitting jeans with a patch on the right butt cheek that read, KEEP ON TRUCKIN' courted the happy dust.

CHAPTER 8

GRAND BALL

The doorbell created a girlish shrill to bounce off the walls as Erica clasped Roxanne's hand and ran to open the kingdom so people could come and go in the escapades of their choice. A fervent desire burned inside Roxanne as she laughed in small-talk conversations while she filtered through the rooms.

She began to sweat as time ticked away on her wristwatch. The hours grew long. Roxanne had yet to see any sign of the man who would sweep her away. But she consoled the angst of Pessimism that began growing in her chest, with a good-luck shake of her leg and slapped the patch on her ass before she continued to search for her prince charming during this once-in-a-lifetime opportunity

Never before had Roxanne been to a party so diverse, yet everyone seemed to enjoy one another's company. The girls cheered the guys on as they participated in the competitive sport of arm wrestling, filling the air with a pungent smell of sweaty men. Promiscuous jokes were told, causing most of the group to bellow in laughter and make the inexperienced blush.

"Body painting, in the kitchen!" was offered by the nudist that flew by in pastel colors. "LSD in the basement!" according to the man with the sugar cubes.

Roxanne chose to watch the men challenge and defeat one another in their heated competition. "Surely, my Prince Charming would be strong and daring!" she spoke her thoughts out loud as if they were a prerequisite. No sooner had she finished her words than a handsome man stepped up next to her, smiling with a winking eye as he offered a glass bottle containing a transparent liquid to this beautiful stranger.

Roxanne reflected a nervous smile of the inexperienced while considering that she had never before tasted alcohol. Nevertheless, with an encouraging caress to her back, she raised the bottle to her lips. Slowly, she tilted the bottle and allowed the substance to scorch her mouth and force her throat closed. Sweat beaded Roxanne's body while tears swamped her eyes.

"Go for it!" Erica encouraged her inexperienced friend.

"Yeah, baby, try it. You'll like it!" the man said.

Roxanne closed her eyes as she forced the alcohol past the barriers of her body's natural defense. Instantly, a rush of warmness clouded her mind, swaying her body to the sound of Alvin Lee and Ten Years After.

"I'd love to change the world!" Spun her in a circle with the tantalizing substance swaying and wooing Roxanne, causing her to lick her lips, into the shape of a beaming smile. She slowly opened her eyes, to find Erica returning a smile of bad influence.

"Good stuff… hey, sweetie!" the handsome guy said as Roxanne dabbed at the tears in her eyes while her head rocked in agreement.

"This is my cousin Steven!" pledged Erica as she put her arm around her friend and leaned into her. "He thinks you're adorable!" Erica giggled as Roxanne bravely pulled another mouthful of the transparent liquid; swallowing hard, as she pushed Erica back. "Stop…

it!" Roxanne gagged out, seductively hot, the heat of the spirits. Her face turned beat red, searching for the courage to speak the words, pronounced in a whisper. "Hello," was all she managed to say before she held out a delicate hand with long, luscious fingernails painted a seductive red.

Intrigued by this beautiful young feline, Steven's loins growled with hunger while he stretched her arm out and spun her into him. Roxanne caught her breath, anticipating his next move as she shot an innocent smile into his winking eye. Steven spun her into a forward bend, exposing the patch on her ass as he leaned over her and put the mouth of the clear bottle to her lips.

"The name of the game is chugging all the way!" he said into Roxanne's unsure expression. "Keep on Truckin'… Baby!" he enticed as he swatted the patch on Roxanne's ass, causing her to burst into nervous laughter as she put her lips to the mouth of the bottle and chugged into a tiptoe stance that any ballerina would be jealous of. Steven's eyes grew big so as not to miss a single move of this inexperienced beauty. He was completely engrossed with her as she swallowed, inhaled, then exhaled again with the blare of a steam whistle.

Steven roared with laughter while Roxanne did a jig that ended with her licking her thumb and placing it on the "Truckin'" patch as she created a hot hissing noise. Unable to resist his desire, Steven swooped the guest of honor up, and by the stroke of midnight, he had charmed her into bed, where he continued whispering sweet nothings into her ear. Roxanne cooed and giggled into the special feeling Steven gave her, but when he said, "I want to make love to you!" gave her the illusion of being swept away on the white stallion. While tears of euphoria streamed down her face, he deflowered her, over and over.

Roxanne woke in the morning with a sluggish feeling of a hangover when she rolled over to see her Prince Charming. But he had escaped without waking her. "Maybe you were dreaming, hallucinating, or something?" She attempted to brush any thoughts of him from her aching mind as she flipped the blankets back to find her virginity staining the sheets red.

CHAPTER 9

RETURNING TO PURGATORY

Melancholy hampered the next six days with thoughts of him while she tried to enjoy the beach and others she was introduced to, but Steven crowded her mind. "Were his words sincere... or devious lies?" Forced to chock out the words of her companions. *So he could get, what he wanted?* Interrogated her. A sickening pain mixed with a need to vomit consumed her entire body. The disappointed voices that showed up a few days after her encounter with Steven chastised her through the curtains of static while she was on her way back to her purgatory. *Without your Prince Charming!* the companions ridiculed. *Or without love!* caused Roxanne to moan with a sickening pain in her heart "I gave him my everything!" she pleaded with a trembling voice. "My virginity!" she displayed as exhibit, hoping to prove her good intentions. However, the companions treated her like a tramp as they rebutted.

To a man who was looking for a good time! they scolded.

No commitments ... no promises ... no white horse did they ride off into the serenity of true love! The critics thundered viciously, causing Roxanne to hang her head and sob while sentencing for her shortcomings was delivered.

She was to return to her purgatory with desperate loneliness chewing at her spine. To endure the abusive life where her stepfather beat her at the warden's command.

Roxanne performed her duties as cook, housekeeper, governess, student, and breadwinner. For what, she wasn't sure. Nothing she did was good enough to please her mother, who seemed to be even more short-tempered these days. Not only with herself but also with Eldon. Vanessa barked and snapped at him with disgust that only the flies on the wall knew the story, and they weren't talking. Although Roxanne could see the change that inflicted the family's disposition, she could only push it under the rug where all secrets were kept.

Roxanne began to fear this was the extent of her existence, with the torment all around her. Boxing her in with the warnings that attempted to filter through the static, clogging every thought as nausea crested her mornings. Denial eased the rush of fear from penetrating her instincts the first time her stomach turned early in the morning. But when her anticipated date came and went, without any sign of her monthly. She knew deep inside her heart, she was pregnant.

Being scared to death of her Mother's reaction, Roxanne secretly made a doctor's appointment before splitting her tips into three envelopes marked "Sibling bribery," "Pregnancy," and "Escape fund." The escape fund envelope had the most money compared to the sibling bribery envelope, which she was always dipping into.

Then there was the newest addition, the pregnancy envelope, which she had just started. "To pay, the doctor's bill!" Hissed between her lips, unexpectedly.

Roxanne crushed the envelope to her chest and cradled it as she picked up the escape fund envelope and robbed the contents while adjusting her priorities, and slipped ten bucks into the pregnancy fund. Roxanne attempted to cover all her steps so there would be no trail, finding it's way back to Roxanne's warden. who continuously smoldered in deep thought while plotting and anticipating her next order of sentencing. *To the torture chamber!* chanted the companions while Roxanne cried herself to sleep.

CHAPTER 10

FOREBODING

Roxanne strolled off the school grounds with a bad omen gnawing at her spine since the banging gavel, ordered the crackling of the companions, *she missed her monthlies!* Her companions offered as they gathered around Trepidation in chorus. *Missed her monthlies ... monthly, missed her monthlies!* Roxanne released the cradling position of her hands from her belly and raised her hand to her face, wiping at the heated embarrassment that flushed her cheeks while receiving chastisement for her crime. Roxanne would not admit her actions verbally because all those in the council knew well what she had done.

We have to protect the baby! Anxiety cried.

Right ... Roxanne's a stupid piece of shit. She can't even protect herself! slammed Skepticism's fist.

Now, extra care must be taken to survive! Dread choked out.

Maybe the rabbit won't die? stated Optimism in a room full of pessimists, who burst into cackling and the banging of the gavel.

The redundant sound of the crackling and the banging gavel sounded during Roxanne's escort, of the companions accompanying her, to Vanessa's control, where they expected to lounge on the couch with their opinions as Roxanne performed her Cinderella act. But as they turned the corner, dread grabbed Roxanne's heart, freezing her in place as the entourage realized; the warden and her deputy were in the office.

Run ... Run away! the entourage screamed.

Roxanne frowned at her ill-prepared items, knowing she only had her book bag instead of her envelopes. And while Scrutiny stepped up to announce the sure outcome of Pessimism defeating Optimism, Roxanne paced back and forth.

"I know something is wrong!" Roxanne stated before bravely stepping into the street and crossing the line that might hold her annihilation.

When Roxanne walked into the house, she wasn't surprised to find her mother intoxicated, with an empty bourbon glass in her hand.

"Oh, look, the whore is home!" Vanessa shot her daughter a smug look as she turned to pour herself another drink. Sarcasm sliced at Roxanne as Vanessa finished pouring the last drip of bourbon into her glass and turned to Eldon for support. Instead, her traitor took a stance as an unbiased referee between the mother and the daughter, which caused Vanessa to viciously snarl at her husband for his lack of respect and his typical lack of parental participation.

"We've got to do something." Vanessa snapped before she sidestepped Eldon and chucked a wadded piece of paper at Roxanne as she began screaming obscenities at her. "You're a whore!" Vanessa screamed at her daughter. "You little fucking, tramp!" her mother raged in a fit.

"I knew you couldn't be trusted," Vanessa slurred as she staggered and danced around the referee with her eyes full of disgust and loathing sprays of venomous chastisement landing all around, singeing Roxanne. Vanessa's lip's curled into a frown of pungent taste that lingered in her mouth while hate consumed her. Suddenly, she stabbed a sharp, manicured fingernail just under Roxanne's chin. "God as my witness, you will do the right thing!" Vanessa said in a spray of bourbon-laced words.

Roxanne's heart plunged with despair for the unknown, but the one thing she knew for sure, was the results of the crumbled paper. While nausea swarmed the pits of her stomach, Anxiety rampaged through Roxanne's existence while the other companions began their familiar chorus.

Perseverance for emancipation. Perseverance for emancipation, they screamed at her until Roxanne's brain began to dislodge from the violent shaking her mother provided as she screamed words that Roxanne could no longer understand. Even though she felt each word shredding her to pieces. Every smack into her body and each shaking, slashed her soul. And without recourse, Roxanne's companions abandoned ship. Except for Anxiety, who played captain of the sinking ship, withstanding the storm alone as the rest washed into the white-capped waves that crested and slammed in the pit of Roxanne's stomach. *Man overboard!* Anxiety screamed just before the boat swirled in the tide pools, before going nose up and being sucked underwater with the companions.

Anxiety shot the flare gun off, which lit up the waves enough to see that they had created a toxic mucky soup. Roxanne wobbled in her mother's hands like an uprooted tree, just as her eyes rolled back and her eyelids slammed shut. The static attempted to protect Roxanne by turning up the level until it was all she could hear.

"Vanessa, stop. She is with child!" Eldon shouted with a tone of compassion that broke through the static and stopped Vanessa's hand in midmotion from hammering her daughter in the lower abdomen with the intent of expelling the unwanted fetus.

Vanessa spun in her husband's direction with a look of reprehension while searching for the words of damnation. "How can you defend this whore?" she shouted as she reached back and snatched a handful of her daughter's hair. "She is a disgrace!" She shook her daughter's head with the force of revulsion.

"I can't even stand to look at her!" Vanessa sprayed venom into Roxanne's face with the power to physically paralyze her and leaving her for easy pickings.

Roxanne was hopeless when Frustration heated the resistant tears. As Vanessa slapped her about the face, head, neck, arms, butt, and legs, no longer could Roxanne control the floodgates; when the wall of tears busted open, built-up tears of Depression and Anxiety gushed out with Steven's name surfing the waves of Guilt that tainted Roxanne while the other companions floated in and flooded her world.

CHAPTER 11

THE PENDULUM SWINGS

During Vanessa's interrogation, Roxanne couldn't reveal the man's last name or phone number, no matter how many times her warden scorched her with injurious words. "Well, isn't that typical of a whore!" howled Vanessa with disgust, spitting venom into Roxanne's face as she grabbed a handful of Roxanne's hair and proceeded to pull her down the hall and into her bedroom, where Vanessa slung her onto the bed like a bag of discarded trash.

"You stay here, until I figure out what to do with you!" Vanessa's loathing demeanor slashed across the remaining piece of Roxanne's heart, leaving her there alone in the despair of the unknown, almost sure if she couldn't escape before sentencing ...

It surely would be, at the gallows, she would hang for her crimes. The companions fretted.

Vanessa made a series of heated calls before connecting with Erica, setting the girls' ears on fire from the loathing anger that seeped into the phone line. "What's the selfish pig's family name and history?" Vanessa demanded the information with threats for the damage done to her daughter.

Erica began mumbling, stumbling over the molten secretions that scorched her mind. "Steven's my cous—"

"How old is this, Steven?" Vanessa cut her off. "How do I get a hold of him?" She fired at Erica, causing her to dodge in and out of Vanessa's words, trying to get a word in edgewise. But when Vanessa heard the number twenty eight, the line went dead. Erica could only hear Vanessa breathing hard on the other end of the phone line.

"What's his number?" the exasperated Vanessa's words slimed the phone line with a revulsion that lapped up Steven's phone number before the line went completely dead.

Erica's heart ached for her friend, recalling a frantic Roxanne informing her about a month ago, that she had missed her monthlies!

"Damn, Roxanne must be pregnant?" gagged Erica with regret as she frantically picked up the phone and dialed Roxanne's number, waiting a lifetime for each number to spin back on the rotary phone, only to be met with a busy signal.

CHAPTER 12

TO AND FRO

On the third ring, a woman picked up the line from the number Erica had given to Vanessa. The woman barely got out a "Hello!" before Vanessa severed her tongue.

"Is Steven there?" silenced the woman on the receiving end.

A moment later, the confused woman taped her tongue back on but found it difficult to say, "No . . Steven, doesn't live here!"

"Who is this?" demanded an answer.

"This is ..." The receiver of the phone call hesitated before offering, "This is Steven's mother!"

The words sliced through the phone line, sparking Vanessa's indignation, which cut off the lady's name. "Well, Steven's mother ..." She paused long enough for a cold breeze to frost the phone line. "Your son molested my sixteen-year-old daughter!" The shrill voice of an angry woman seemed to drag on forever. "Now she is pregnant!" stabbed Steven's mother in the gut, causing her to stagger, for ground while the vicious woman informed her, the news of the unwanted, bastard pregnancy. "Well then ...," Vanessa fumed bellows of smoke into the woman's ear.

"Let me leave him a message!" announced the vengefulness of the following threat. "If he doesn't make it right, it wouldn't be only Roxanne's head that rolls!" Vanessa finalized with a sharp razor cut, underlining her words and severing the phone line.

CHAPTER 13

TO AND FRO ... TO AND FRO

Steven smirked with irony as his parents relayed the message that he was in big-trouble, the irony being, he could barely remember that night. He admitted only to himself, in defense, as he attempted to recall that night.

Having just been divorced at the age of twenty-seven by his estranged wife and their children. Steven was working in an orange factory at night, and found himself alone during the solitary hours of the early morning. When it's the darkest, coldest, and the loneliest point of the night, just before the sun began to crest the horizon and all the liquor stores are closed. Steven smiled with some comfort as he pulled his date from the glovebox he had purchased in advance.

"She's only a fling," he insisted as he pulled her toward him and began to softly caress her clear-glass body. "Just to pass the time!" he spoke softly while loosing her top.

"It meant nothing!" Steven said as he raised the only lady in his life to his lips. "Help me relax, baby!" he said with assurance as he lifted the mouth of the bottle to his nose, smelling her intoxication.

"Mmm," he exhaled. "Makes me want to have a real good time!" He whooped it up as he slid the edge of the bottle across his lips. No longer could he resist the temptations of her impurities. Only then could he admit to himself, the reasons for the frequent visits with his "good-time girl!" During these days of loneliness, when he should be at home with his used-to-be loving wife, tucking their children into bed, instead he was bandaging his pain with alcohol while filling his time working and parting with any one-night stand that would have him. By the time he pulled up to Erica's house that evening in question, he had opened his second "good-time girl" for a quick splash that rolled him into bed with a pretty young lass from Reno.

Suddenly, a fervent memory heated his scrotum as he recalled tearing her innocence, which caused him to hesitate for only a moment before plunging his drunken manliness deep into her vulnerable young body.

"She was a virgin?" kicked him in his family sack and pushed out his next words in protest. "I couldn't be … her only lover!" he assured himself. "Nor the father of her unwanted conception!" Those thoughts coagulated Steven's arteries and short-circuited his senses as he searched for an acquittal. But all he could find was an expression of disapproval on his father's face; his lips moved, but Steven couldn't hear the words that rushed from his father's mouth as he began standing up, turning a fist out, and cold-cocking his son under the chin.

Steven's heart pounded with fear. He could hear only the waves of regret flooding his entire existence as the power of his father's disapproval sent him staggering with stars.

CHAPTER 14

SWITCHING ROLES

Roxanne found herself on a Greyhound bus with all her personal belongings in one steamer trunk a bun in the oven, and a receipt for a one-way bus ticket, on the turning of seventeen. Which she did turn, the day after the pregnancy results ... *Found its way... to Mother!* grumbled her companions. *Headed back to not-so-sunny Southern California to marry a man who doesn't love her and doesn't believe he's the father of her child!* The companions continued to mock Roxanne.

Roxanne was baffled by the pounding in her head that quaked her body, motioning her to run for the bathroom and relieve the nausea that consumed her. While the companions stirred the current events and situation into a chastising laughter that boils rapidly inside her.

The cresting waves of her reality forced toward the exit, insisting on spewing out with her entire insides. Beads of sweat dotted her skin, making her damp and chilly, as she leaned against the wall and wiped the perspiration from her forehead.

"This isn't what I wanted when I wished for a Prince Charming!" Roxanne choked out as she wiped the tears from her eyes and took a deep breath. Mustering the courage to carry her back to her seat while she gently cradled her stomach. A smile curved her lips to see that her belly had begun to pooch. Roxanne exhaled, "Don't worry, baby!" she heard herself coo. "I promise to love and protect you forever!"

Roxanne felt her cheeks turn hot with a blush as the words passed her lips, and she experienced her first maternal emotion. "I wonder if Vanessa had made the same promise before I was born, or ever?" Roxanne rubbed her small baby bump, warmly caressing what she needed so bad. "A baby of my own ... to love and cherish!" Tears welled in her sinuses until she was choking on sobs of uncertainty while cooing to her unborn child. "No matter what, baby," she assured the fetus, "we will survive!" Roxanne testified as she slid out of her chair and turned toward the restroom. She pushed through the crowded aisle filled with judgmental eyes that shook her nerves. Nevertheless, she straightened her back and raised her head with confidence as she offered a smug smile back at all the peering eyes while she assured herself and her unborn.

"It couldn't be any worse than what we just left behind?"

Roxanne peered out her window to find that there was no ticket parade or smiling faces to greet her when she arrived at the bus depot in Pomona. Only a hesitant Steven and an older couple stood outside the depot.

Roxanne's body perspired with the heat that smoldered from her anxiety and embarrassment when she stepped off the bus, to be greeted with a nod of Steven's head as her feet touched the blacktop. Steven turned his back to Roxanne and began walking toward the middle of the bus, where the older couple stood in front of the baggage compartment.

Roxanne staggered like a whipped pup as she followed Steven, feeling the thickness of the air squeezing her throat as Steven painstakingly introduced her to his mother. Who accomplished testing

Roxanne with a clicking of her tongue against the roof of her mouth. And with judgment passed, Mother Blakley shook her head.

"We'll have to put some meat on your bones!" was all she had to say as they watched Steven and his dad manipulate the trunk the bus driver had pulled out of the compartment. When it came to rest on the flat cart, they each wiped their brow before turning their eyes to Roxanne.

"Sure, is a cute young filly!" were Steven's father's only words before he tipped his cowboy hat, nodding his head, he slipped his arm around his wife's shoulder. They started walking toward the parking lot.

Steven grimaced an acknowledgment to Roxanne as he picked up the rope and began towing the trunk while motioning Roxanne to follow them to the truck. The men lifted the trunk onto the bed on the truck and slid it up against the back window. Steven jumped onto the bed of the truck and sat next to the trunk as his dad walked around to the driver's side of the '58 Ford pickup and slid in next to his wife, who sat in the middle of the bench seat of the truck.

Roxanne wasn't sure what to do for a good long minute until Steven's mom stuck her head out of the passenger door. "Roxanne? Let's go!" ushered the way for the lost girl into a distant land, accompanied by those she and the companions considered to be hostile natives.

Roxanne held her breath while the baseball game filled the space, void of conversation, broadcasted from the transistor radio. The woman next to her looked her up and down before she shook her head in a distasteful matter and ticked her tongue on the roof of her mouth.

A rush of damnation swarmed Roxanne's head with a nauseous static that secreted her mind with hopelessness while she sat silent. Most of the companions chanted *Judgment!* While the others attempted to throw her a life preserver during Steven's mom's obligation to oblige the review of wifely duties. Then added that a baby shower had been planned, with a bunch of strangers except for Erica. "That would be Tuesday, at noon!" Steven's mom confirmed without looking at Roxanne as Steven's dad pulled off the road and came to a stop in front of the courthouse. "We'll get the marriage license now!" she said. "And the shotgun wedding is scheduled for Friday!" she finished while encouraging Roxanne to get out of the truck. With her spirit spinning with emotions, Roxanne met Steven at the back of the truck. To find him stuffing the exact same kind of bottle he had shared with her almost four months ago into his pocket. He gave her a challenging look that caused Roxanne's eyes to cast downward. "You know what to do, boy!" pushed Steven toward the courthouse with Roxanne in tow.

CHAPTER 15
PLAYING HOUSE

Roxanne sat on the edge of her marital bed, twisting the simple gold band that encircled not only her finger but also her heart. Tears fell from her eyes as she recalled the wedding vows that bound her to a man who was being punished for having a lustful heart.

She recalls the phone conversation to her mother, begging her to let her come home. But the line went dead, probably fifteen times before the exchange date came, and now gone. The pain of the rejection squeezed Roxanne's heart as if it were a ripe lemon, the juices laden with pulp ran down her face, stinging it with its acids. The acid burned into her lonely and abandoned soul-filling Roxanne with a sudden desire to call her mother, but she knew it was too late. "I now have a new warden!" spewed and echoed out loud as she stuck her hand into her sweater pocket and pulled out a piece of paper Steven had given her before he went to work.

She hoped it professed everlasting, unconditional love for her and their baby as she unfolded the letter. A gagging reaction presented itself when Roxanne found a woman's script behind sequential numbers and titled "Wives' Duties." Roxanne's mind screamed while her companions shredded the note with indignation when Roxanne realized what was scripted is what she had been doing for her mother for years. Only now, her charges were Steven's visiting children from his first marriage. And upon consummating the marriage where Steven pounded her deep and hard, *Like, he had a score to settle!* her companions insisted.

"Wives are to be submissive!" was under the title of the paper Steven's mother had given to him to give to her. Roxanne pondered that sentence for a moment, focusing on the word *submissive* before she went searching for a dictionary. Not that she didn't know what *submissive* meant. But she wanted to see if her name was physically listed as an example.

Roxanne gave a small chuckle that belonged to the surprise that knotted in her chest when she did not find a picture or her name mentioned. But she learned she had been submissive to everyone in her world for as long as she could remember!

She reminisced, on her existence. A slideshow of pictures visualized the haunting scenarios. While looking down at the words, she considered the definition: a condition of being humble; submitting to another's authority; surrender, boiled, hissed from the abyss as a rumbling began shaking Roxanne, but her thoughts were stuck in a puddle of quicksand. A scream frayed Roxanne's nerves, causing her to drop the dictionary in fear of being caught cheating or something. She took strides with her long legs to the bedroom she hoped to fix up for the child she was expecting, to find Steven's children fighting over a toy. Annoyance stepped up and snatched the object from the bickering siblings and tossed it into the toy box. Steven's children stood with wide eyes and their mouths shut. *That's better!* Annoyance suggested. Roxanne offered a nervous smile to the children, attempting to cover for her companion's shortcoming. "Let's go outside?" she said to the timid children. Roxanne hung laundry on the clothesline as Steven's children played about the backyard while her chorusing companions cluttered her with overwhelming feelings of insecurity. *That comes from never being loved!* Anxiety stepped in to remind her of that. Resentment and Shame rode high on the roller coaster of emotions,

The companions yelled on the downfall of the track. Fretting over the possibility of Steven ravishing her while riding up the incline of the track. *Until death does them part!* Roxanne's body trembled from the turbulent ride as waves of nausea crested the highest point of the ride. And on the downfall, *Without, love or sincerity,* Trepidation screamed with Pessimism in harmony as Roxanne hurled.

CHAPTER 16

MENTOR

Over the last eight years, Roxanne had befriended the lady who lived across the street. Although Lisa was seven years older than herself, they had developed a relationship that Roxanne could compare to no other. Lisa was a prudent mother of three and the wife of a mechanic. She stood tall with strong cheekbones incasing her brown eyes. And when she allowed her brown hair to shimmer around her olive complexion, it created a captivating visual of deep chocolates, blended into a fine-looking woman.

Lisa had become Roxanne's best friend and mentor, as they shared everything; from pregnancies, clipping coupons, barbecues, birthdays, babysitting, and other things that filled their lives in the quaint hick town of Norco, where Steven and Roxanne managed to develop a compatible relationship, in which Roxanne had sat in many hours of council with Lisa to develop. And although Roxanne has done everything she had been counseled to do, including taking Steven's boots off when he got home from work, she could still feel Steven's resentment.

Her thoughts turned and reflected on Steven's demeanor when he was with their children. She sensed the strain on Steven's part when it came to his relationship with Scarlet, compared to the gleam of pride when he interacted with his boys.

A heavy coating of contrition brushed Roxanne's face with a warm blush as she shared her concern with her mentor. But Lisa found Roxanne's secret to be void of any real evidence when she stated. "Fathers value their sons … their prodigy of sorts!" Lisa briefly chuckled into Roxanne's twisting eyebrows. "Although, both parents are very important to each sex!" untwisted Roxanne's expression of doubt a bit. "There are things only a dad can teach his sons!" placed a question mark over Roxanne's head.

"And a mother teaches her daughter!" Retwisted Roxanne's eyebrows even tighter as Lisa's words fell on foreign ground. By the time Scarlet was six years old, Roxanne had absorbed years of mentoring, feeding on the highs and lows of Lisa's voice. Needing her like an addiction, at other times, resenting her.

Being the elder, Lisa thought she was always right. In comparison, Roxanne considered herself to be the queen! concurred the companions of domestic duties, nodded tiresomely. *Having earned her title, by being a slave, all her life! added the companions.* But out of a genuine respect, and receiving no instruction from her own mother, Roxanne would give in to her mentor's advice, from cleaning the oven to disciplining the children. Roxanne learned to smile with interest while nodding her head with thoughtful consideration and tolerance for her trustworthy friend. However sometimes, she didn't feel like hearing it in that quaint little hick town where she had switched roles.

CHAPTER 17
BRIGHTEST PLACE

From being the oldest, unloved sibling and child slave to being a submissive wife and the mama of three, in less than five years! The companions sarcastically applauded while chewing her ears. She swatted at the buzz like it was a fly. The negative connotation swarmed about her, imprisoning her tear ducts while she scrubbed the kitchen floor her way!

Feeling like she wanted to cry, but over the years, her tear ducts had dried up. Giving her cause to fear the flood of tears that pooled in her chest.

Making her heart feel it would surely drown in that pool of dread once again.

Optimism moved in close and began caressing the fretting Roxanne with encouraging words. *You've given them what you lacked!*

Fortitude stepped in. *The best of mothers, wives, friends, and example!* stroked Roxanne as Resilience joined the band of supporters. *You've created a perfect world where children are showered with love!* signaled the Trio into chorus.

Treated others, with respect and consideration! stirred the discontent companions. *Just the way you needed to be treated!* caused the flood of tears to continue pooling in her chest, threatening to break the levee.

The flustered Roxanne lit a cigarette, smoking half of it as she rounded up the kids and headed across the street. She was finishing the long white addiction as she stepped up on the curb, into the yard of her cherished friends.

Marty was tinkering with his mechanic projects in the garage. Roxanne politely stood there with a look of interest as he explained the mechanics of an engine, with his head under the hood of a truck, his dark hair, slicked back with VO5 to prevent his hair from getting in his way. Roxanne held an attentive disposition while Marty explained how to disengage a carburetor. But she was sitting in judgment as to which was more slicked and stained, his hands or his hair?

Marty suddenly stabbed a stare at Roxanne with his glass eye as Roxanne smiled and decided, "Too close to call," and considered the vote a tie.

There was no doubt that Marty desired to operate a garage of his own someday! *He'd fit the part!* chuckled the companions, what with a grease rag tucked in the back pocket of his grease-stained coverall. His stature was of medium height, stocky build, and the smell of dirty oil.

"Unless you're going to help, the wife, she's in the house!" Marty smiled and nodded his head toward the door that connected the garage to the house. Roxanne smiled and offered, "Good to see you, Marty!" as she walked past him.

Roxanne stepped into the kitchen to find Marisa in the spotless room, eating a banana, with her schoolbag and pom-poms at her feet.

School hadn't started yet, but football had started up and Marisa was the captain of the cheerleading squad. She was the oldest of Lisa's and Marty's children—a tall, slender girl with ash-blonde hair and green eyes. She didn't talk much, but she did read and study a lot and was very responsible.

"Reliable!" Roxanne mumbled over her lips while considering asking her to babysit this Saturday.

Scarlet came running into the kitchen with Carolyn hot on her heels. Suddenly, Carolyn's engine sputtered, just before running out of gas and coasting to a stop. While her prey howled with laughter as she circled her mama, passing by Carolyn without even a scrape. Carolyn pushed her dead engine up to Roxanne, wiping the sweat from her brow. She placed her hands on her hips, and with a frustrated look on her face, she huffed and puffed. She was a thin, fragile child, the second-born of Lisa and Marty.

"Scarlet did what my momma told me not to!"

Roxanne only smiled at the girl, who was quick to please her parents and even faster at tattling. Roxanne started down the hall searching for Scarlet, who had escaped while Roxanne tended to Carolyn when she ran into the boys in Carolyn's room, where Brandon and Stevie stood in dresses.

"It was a dare!" the embarrassed Stevie said as he peeled the dress off, his face painted in the color of heat. Brandon continued curtsying and doing a confident queen's wave until Stevie socked him in the arm. "Stop it!" he demanded.

"Ouch!" whined the true cross-dresser, the youngest of Lisa and Marty, the prodigy of his father. But Marty hadn't the time to haul around a little "sissy-boy who would rather go by, the name of Toma, and play domesticated games while wearing an apron!" Roxanne had heard Marty tell Lisa at the end of a heated argument. Sweet, cute little Brandon. Toma did love to clean the playhouse and take care of the baby dolls when the children played their childhood games, Roxanne thought as she retrieved a camera from her purse and snapped a picture of Steve screaming in protest as Marty again preformed a perfect queen's wave.

These were extraordinary, delightful years: laughing, playing, and loving one another on the cul-de-sac, "Where the sun shone brighter than anywhere else in the world!" Roxanne sang to herself in the house, where she had taken up her role as a dedicated young mother and supportive wife. Her home was spotless, and the children were clean, polite, and content. Although Steven's other children didn't come around much anymore, it had opened a wider relationship with Mark and Stevie and their father. But there was still a strain on Steven's relationship with Scarlet, and Roxanne feared that the boys could also sense it.

Roxanne contemplated, while she finished ironing Steven's uniform for a career position, she encouraged him to take, at the local fire department. She found herself frowning at the twenty-four- hour shifts and his schooling in Fresno, which took him away for most of each week, which in turn left Roxanne alone with only the children most all the time.

One rare evening, when Steven came home to what had become so routine and dull for Roxanne, she had been wearing on him for a few weeks now. "Please!" nearly pleading with him. The last time she had this same discussion with Steven, he had suggested that she join the PTA, where she planned field trips and controlled raising money for those trips. And although she found that job gratifying, it still wasn't what she longed for. But by the time she had fed the family, gave the three children baths, and taken the clothes off the clothesline, Steven was asleep in his easy chair. Roxanne's spirit fell when she realized she had lost yet another opportunity.

Her insides felt the Lioness come alive, panting and growling in low tones as she circled the easy chair, where she badly wanted to jump on him and shred him to bloody pieces.

The following year, she was voted in as president of PTA organization, where she gave thanks to the influential in her acceptance speech. She duly gave acknowledgment as she introduced Quincy Blakley: the Grand Marshal and the president of our local Grange Hall!"

Quincy nodded his head, accepting his daughter-in-law's recognition before Roxanne turned her attention to the next supporter.

"Also, I would like to give thanks to all our dear friends in the Norco Fire Department!" Roxanne gave only a short moment for an applause. "Who not only donated a nice cash amount to the treasurer of the PTA …" Roxanne's luring smile was full of straight, gleaming white teeth. Long brown locks of hair fell from her slender shoulders. The crowd roared with clapping hands and whispering tones. When the crowd settled down, they automatically turned their attention toward Roxanne, waiting for another tasty morsel. "They provide demonstrations to our school children three times during the school year. Also providing a firehouse field trip, once a year!" The room filled with a roaring sound of appreciation that overpowered Roxanne. She stepped back away from the microphone with the thought of curtsying for all those who admired her.

"And to our local police department!" Roxanne continued, "our boys in blue! Whose commitment to the community is as giving as the other building blocks of our society!"

The room rumbled with approval.

"Together we should stand, to say… I am your neighbor." Together, we are building a brilliant"—Roxanne paused for just a brief moment, holding them on a thick rope—"community!" She blasted the mic with her charisma, and the audience exploded. Roxanne ended the speech on a word that left a natural smile burning in her puppet-like memory. She had practiced her speech a hundred times in front of the mirror and memorized every syllable, every pause. Therefore, she had the opportunity to watch the crowd, sitting on the edge of their seats, enthralled in her words, before bursting into applause that a politician would be envious of.

Roxanne stepped off the stage, taking her husband's hand, who was beaming with pride. "They love you!" he said, looking into his wife's warm almond eyes that smiled as she floated across the floor. Led by Steven's escorting abilities that held her by the tips of her fingers at the end of her outstretched arm. He guided her as she nodded her head to some of her biggest supporters as she slid into her seat with her head held high.

She could hear her companions applauding for the courage that had felt so natural for their Roxanne. "Wish Vanessa could see me, now!" Roxanne gloated to the companions, who needed some appeasement. Just earlier during the day, as Roxanne ignored the children while she groomed herself to perfection, her companions really did… cramp her space. And as she put mascara on her naturally long eyelashes, the Lioness was chattering to Roxy. And as Roxanne painted her lips a soft coral color, Roxy damn near bit a hole in Roxanne's ear, caused by the pent-up restlessness, over these last couple of months. She flashed back on the grand picture in the mirror's reflection. Where she had promised her companions the killing, they had longed for. "I believe there isn't a single person we can't charm!" Roxanne admitted to her companions, who anticipated many huge moments like this in their blooming posy's future.

CHAPTER 18

RESTLESS

The applaud that had been carrying Roxanne through the week had sunk into the sunset with all her other dreams as she woke early in the morning to the Santa Anna winds pelting the drenching rain on the quaint community of Norco.

Roxanne looked toward the end of the cul-de-sac where the water pooled during floods, deciding that as an organizer of the Firemen's Women's Auxiliary, it was her responsibility to call the fire department to see if there was anything the ladies could do. Roxanne turned from the window, glanced at the phone, but walked by it to begin ironing their bowling shirts.

Roxanne daydreamed while performing a task she did *twice a week!* Chastised, her hecklers with each push of the hot iron. She was contemplating Steven and how routine their lives had become with the expectations of others. She gave a faint smile with the idea that she and Steven were making a real effort out of this married relationship, which was her conclusion as she carefully hung the last shirt on a hanger. Checking it for flaws, but there were none. *Of course!* Stated Expectation.

At the age of twenty-five, Roxanne kept an impeccably clean house. Her children, spotless and untainted by the odium that she had known as a prisoner of her Mother. However, *after twenty-five years of doing the same damn thing*, the companions had been rallying, *for as long, as she can remember.*

"Shit, this is all..." drew discontent. "I know!" taunted the aggravation of the growing restlessness, Roxanne and the companion shared.

"You're just burned out!" Roxanne told herself. But the others rebutted with a question that deserved an answer.

We only wonder... if there's more, to life!

Day after day, Roxanne worked on the challenging question, as she had promised her companions she would do. She began reading the local paper, looking for the prospects of any new opportunities, while keeping her investigation under wraps, as suggested by the companions. Fearing Steven's resolution to her restlessness would be to have another baby. That thought, sent shards of ice racing through her bloodstream until the shards had grown so large, they stabbed her in the heart and froze it.

"No! No! No!" Roxanne protested with her companions as she folded the paper and neatly placed it in the proper place next to her husband's chair.

Another week passed by, the same old routine drug Roxanne through the hum drum of regrets. "You know, if I hadn't got pregnant," she counseled with both of her supportive and non-supportive companions. *Forced to marry the reluctant father of a one-night stand!* shouted Chastisement as Roxanne smoldered over the trickery played for her once-most-valuable possession. *The one thing she was saving for her knight in shining armor!* chorused her companions. Instead, she was with a man who took the honored pleasures of reminding her *The sexual duties, of a wife!* Chastised Roxanne. "While he molested her young body with his hardness!"

She had pleaded with her husband, about her fear of getting pregnant again, but Steven grunted with disregard as he penetrated her. His lack of respect set flames under the companions. *When was the last time, if ever? Did he tell her he loved her while he did his thing?* rushed her heart and stuck it with a quick jab of an arrow.

Roxanne had counseled Lisa about her fears, in which Steven did not consider. Lisa laughed with heated embarrassment. But when tears welled up in Roxanne's eyes, she suggested douching after sex.

Roxanne acted on Lisa's suggestion more than once, thinking she had cleaned herself out really well. But her darling baby boy Mark is a gentle spirit. Unlike his brother, Stevie, who refused to sleep and kept Roxanne up until the wee hours of the night.

Four months after Mark was born, Roxanne pleaded with Steven to get up with their firstborn son. Instead, he climbed on top of her and did his thing without even opening his eyes before he rolled over and went back to sleep.

"He doesn't… love you!" taunted the words.

"You're, only his whore!" Vanessa's words pounded her with his every thrust, over and over again, until he moaned and went limp. He took advantage of her nearly every night he was home. And tonight, while he did his thing, Roxanne recalled the ad in bold print:

RESPONSIBLE COUPLE NEEDED

To manage and maintain a family apartment building, in exchange for an apartment (size suitable to your needs) with moderate pay.

The ad had shot Roxanne straight up from the bellows of self-pity when she had found it. "No way!" she questioned as she had pulled the paper closer to her, folding it into the center of a five-by-seven picture, framing it in an outline of red ink while she daydreamed of the waiting opportunity.

It would give her an out! Daily interaction with other adults, other than the usual! "We could save money while living on-site! And on the days Lisa is to take the children to school, Steven could drop them off on the main street in front of the cul-de-sac, where the sun shines brighter than anywhere else in the world!"

CHAPTER 19

NEW THINGS

Uncle Spencer came over, decked out in his marine uniform, looking diabolically threatening behind those mirrored glasses that reflected his opponent's stare. He appeared to be mentally fit and firm on his choice of making a stand by defending his country in a tour of the Vietnam War.

Fear and pride washed over Roxanne as she listened to her brother's words that insisted his enlistment would prove him to be a man. And would prove to his wife and Eldon that he wasn't selfish and immature. He looked so grown up and very handsome, but mostly, he looked determined in his decisions while he considered taking responsibility for himself.

Irony laughed under Roxanne's breath. *Tough lesson for the one… who had never taken a beating for anything, he had done!* Roxanne choked back her tears as she leaned into him and kissed him just behind his ear, pausing long enough to whisper, "I am so damn proud of you!" Roxanne looked into his mirrored eyes as his lips turned with a smile that held a renewed self-confidence.

Roxanne's heart fluttered with a rush of emotions while she considered her brother's instability since the death of his second child, which eventually destroyed his marriage of two years. He may have had a bit too much to drink, but that wasn't what made him seek the comfort of another woman.

Roxanne's children were properly groomed and watching cartoons while she began preparing a hardy pile of pancakes for breakfast and listening to Spencer talk about his ambitions and his fears of this new life.

Spencer had hoped his oldest sister would provide the reassuring words that he badly needed to hear. But she only smiled at him as she came up to the dining room table and stood behind her chair with a glass of orange juice in hand. She only offered Spencer a bewitching wink before calling the children to the table.

The Lioness lay in the middle of the table, swishing her tail to the promise of a chase. Her catty green eyes squinted before she jumped from the table to the floor. She prowled toward Roxanne's children, who were watching cartoons. The Lioness squatted low to the floor. Watching as she planned her attack. If it weren't for these damn kids … The Lioness sprang up and landed on the coffee table in front of the children. She hissed, baring her long fangs. She raised her paw and swung at the scattering children. The Lioness jumped up on the kitchen table once again and made eye contact with all three of Roxanne's children, commanding them to pick up the glasses of juice that left big puddles of condensation, where they set long enough to lose their frost and to remain standing during Mama's prayer.

"Dear Lord, give us courage and strength to endure all that comes our way. Amen!" She finished with an angelic smile and a twinkle in her eyes as she thrust her glass into the commitment of her prayer. However, the clinking of the toast was delayed, as her children slid into their chairs without consideration to her sincere words. Spencer looked as though his sister's words had cleared his fears as he shook his head in agreement before turning his attention to his nephews.

Roxanne watched the expressions of highs and lows across her brother's face as he shared his story of his reason for enlisting and his experience at the recruiting office. Spencer snatched a cigarette from his sister's pack and lit it before he continued his story. "Yes, there were protesters carrying signs and marching back and forth in a rhythmic motion across the street from the recruiting office!" he answered Roxanne's question before she even asked it.

"When I came out with papers signed, contracting my life for the next two years, I was swarmed by protesters that wore peace signs—some angry, some crying. Some asked, 'Why did you sign up? Why do you want to die?'" Spencer took a shot of orange juice and exhaled the smoke from his lungs.

Roxanne sat across from her brother at the kitchen table, hanging on to Spencer's words. "Wait, what did you say!" Spencer smiled behind those dark glasses when he said, "I spoke five words!" he stated while luring his sister's anticipation as he finally lifted a clutched fist. He raised one digit for each word.

"Show them I'm a man!" He fell silent as he recalled the moment before he offered the rest of the story to his sister. "Yes, my words caused a chaos of opinions to rise and fall with the heated breath of the protesting crowd!" He finished by lifting his glasses and shot a winking eye at Roxanne.

The breakfast party was engrossed in Spencer's story while they enjoyed the short stacks dripping with fresh blueberry syrup when suddenly, the voices in the room fell silent. Only the tickling of butterfly wings, fluttering toward new exciting things, could be heard. The living room buzzed and circulated on the wings of the fluttering invaders, sweeping the crowd of enthusiasts out onto the balcony of the apartment building where Roxanne's family now lived.

"These pictures will document the beginning of bright new futures for all!" Roxanne said as she snapped a picture of her three children on the first day at the new school. Then she polarized the kids with Spencer. Then Mama with Spencer. Then Uncle Spencer in his striking authority-style uniform and his mirrored glasses reflecting his smirk of self-assuredness.

It was soon after the pictures that the alarm on Spencer's watch signaled, he had no more time for small talk and family bonding. He saluted as he spun on his heels and disappeared, with his belly full and half of his sister's gas money in the clutches of his fist. While Mama wiped the tears of jubilation from her eyes that insisted on pouring out for all she had hoped for, for so long. Her amazement that things were going the way she had planned gave her a sense of retribution for the lack of endearments received by all those who set her up to fall. Flashes of zeal stabbed at the image of her Mother as she rushed her children down the stairs. "Come on. You can't be late for your first day at your new school!" Roxanne joyously sang as she bounced up to the car with the pounce of a kangaroo, setting the high-spirited mood that led them in song as they traveled to Riverside. "B-I-N-G-O. Bingo was his name, o!" She danced with the excited butterflies in anticipation, with her expectations of a brighter future.

Roxanne had weeks of highs on the roller coaster of anticipation during the last month. But when she had found this new school, which was providing summer school to students that would be returning in the fall, she had a newfound sense of jubilation when she realized that the summer school would provide supervision for her children. *While she takes advantage of some badly needed time off!* concluded the council of her companions when Roxanne pulled into the school compound. Mama left her and Lisa's children in the middle of the school compound, where several buildings were safely hidden behind a tall chain-linked fence lined with skyscraping eucalyptuses, painting the heavens with their long, leafy branches and her promise of coming back for them at the end of the day. The school was much like any regular school. The only thing lacking was a playground, but the children put on skits that would entertain most, who didn't indulge in pushing cars through the dirt, jumping rope, playing basketball, or tetherball. Carolyn and Scarlet would perform their favorite song.

> *Joy to the world … all the boys and girls.*
> *Joy to the fishes … in the deep blue sea.*
> *Joy to you and me!*

They sang the memorized tune while they danced like the Go- Go dancers, they had seen on a popular television show. Most of their peers loved it and showed appreciation with a standing ovation while begging for an encore.

Roxanne was at the school patiently waiting when the last bell of the day released swarms of children into the courtyard. Anxiety gripped Roxanne's nerves as she conflicted with her ability to pick her children out of the sea of heads that scattered in every direction. Just as she lost all confidence and went to open the door, her boys and Brandon popped their heads in the window, scaring the snot out of her with laughter and well-adjusted smiles fixed to their faces.

On the ride home, Roxanne watched her children with consideration. Determining her view, "they had adjusted, well!" surged a shot of adrenaline into her bloodstream. *They have remained lighthearted and happy!* counseled the companions in Roxanne's influential mind. "Throughout all the big changes of moving from the only home they had ever known!" Roxanne agreed. Trading green fields for a dirt field. A front yard, for a courtyard. A backyard, for a blacktop alleyway enclosed with cement walls that acted as a parking garage and a holding area for dumpsters, where the rancid smells of fermented garbage mixed with heavy car exhaust and oily dirt that created a lingering noxious gas before the sun would set. Consenting to the cooling evening breeze to lift the stench and carry it away with the human spirits that sweltered from the scorching heat-wave temperatures. By shutting off their hardworking air-conditioners and opening their doors, allowing the rhythm of rock 'n' roll to accompany the swells of tenants into the courtyard, which had been relieved of its trapped heat, sprayed away by the manager's wife while the children took to the outdoors, in the refuge of the evening.

CHAPTER 20

TOPSY-TURVY

Mama became sick with female issues during the end of summer that required her to spend a few days in the hospital, then to recuperate for a couple of weeks at home. Steven was finishing up the last of his schooling and working twenty-four-hour shifts at the fire department. The children's summer was filled with days at the local plunge and playing in the dirt field. They saw their dearest friends only twice that summer—once when Mama was in the hospital, and the other, was the day she got out of the hospital. Mama never returned to all the things she used to do after the move and her female issues that required her to have surgery.

Steven's schedule was overwhelming, trying to balance the children's days, work, and preparing for his finals, to benefit his career. Nevertheless, he was home this morning when his children rose from their sweet slumbers, excited for another day of school.

The children never did finish summer school due to all the unexpected circumstances during the sweltering summer. But on the second day of school of the fall semester, they would attempt the new plan. "It's Lisa's turn to take all the children to school!' Roxanne informed her subject. And without further verbal directions from her. Steven knew, he was to drop his children off at Lisa's, on his way to work.

The children prepared for school while their individual anticipations continued to interrupt the orders and chastisement that the Trio thought Steven deserved. That's when the Lioness, swatted at the children. "Just, get ready, for school!" Before Mama got up from the couch and motioned Steven to follow her into the room, where Roxanne attempted to shut the door quietly, but Roxy let Annoyance kick the door shut. Roxanne turned a surprised smile into her companion's hostility as she mentally communicated with Roxy.

Thus permitting, only a few loud shouts to filter through. So, the children won't think, we are fighting!

The children had barely finished their cereal when their dad came out of the marital room and said, "Let's go!" with a strained crackle in his voice and his shaken nerves, standing at the open door of the apartment.

Happy eager butterflies hovered about the children as they took the stairs competitively, until they hit the landing, where they broke into a sprint toward the truck that waited in the stinky parking garage. Steven staggered with the weight of his burdens, reducing his pace and causing him to miss the outcome of the race. He made a mental thought, to ask the children, who had won. But when he came through the door of the parking garage Stevie was in the truck, with the doors locked. Mark and Scarlet, stood with their backs against the truck, refusing to acknowledge their contender.

Steven didn't have any nerves left, to listen to Lisa, this morning. He gripped the steering wheel even tighter, with his frustration as he turned the tuck heading north, on Temascal Street while deciding to drop the kids off on that main street and allow them to walk down into the cul-de-sac. He approached the cross road, thinking to himself; the sun didn't seem as bright here, as it used to!" punched Steven in the gut as he pulled to the side of the street, in front of the cuddle-sac, where life was good.

"The sun doesn't seem as bright anywhere, anymore!" he grumbled in low tones, hearing his wife's complaints bellowing throughout his entire existence and drowning out the boys saying "Good-bye!" before they jumped out of the truck and sprinted across the street.

Steven turned a crooked smile to his daughter as she slipped out of the truck, distracted by the race that started when they left the apartment.

"Hey, wait up!" Scarlet hollered as she ran around the tail end of the truck. Steven watched from his side mirror as his daughter darted out into the street without hesitation. "Oh, crap," slammed Steven's eyes shut.

"No, no, no, that can't have happened!" flashed behind his eyelids, the Volkswagen Beetle making contact with the outside of Scarlet's left leg, flipping her up and slammed her head into the windshield. Steven could see the surprised, unexpected grief of the young man's face as the shattered windshield fell to the hood of his car and flew into the air, along with Scarlet.

Helplessly, the onlookers could only watch the girl dance with the vehicle that spun her into the air. Without grace, she dropped like a leaden weight from the sky, concaving the vehicle's hood. If a father could feel any sense of relief during a time like that, it was when he thought he could catch her. But the antenna that was broken down to a four-inch spear pierced her arm just below the elbow and swung her body around and back into the air. She seemed to flutter forever before slamming belly first onto the hood of the car, her head slamming into the dashboard with enough force to bounce her again. Her body twisted and fell to the ground, in front of the boys and Steven. Their faces were painted with the colors of helpless horror while Scarlet bounced off the cracked blacktop before making a final impact in front of the cul-de-sac, where the sun used to shine brighter than anywhere else in the world. A surreal environment wrapped around the boys and Steven while transporting them into a time-warped atmosphere as they watched Scarlet's, entanglement with the vehicle. And now her lifeless body was lying on the ground in front of her horrified brothers, who stood in shock.

Steven, who had been frozen during the time warp, suddenly snapped into his trained rescue-instinct as he jumped out of the truck. He choked out orders, as he pressed his ear to Scarlets chest. "Run to Lisa!" He nearly vomited when he placed his lips to his daughter's lips and blew a breath into her non-responsive body. "Tell her to call an ambulance!"

CHAPTER 21

MAMA'S INSTINCT

Roxanne was at home doing domestic chores when a wave of nausea caused her absent womb to ache while a sweltering heat consumed her body and her hands grew ice-cold. "What the heck!" Roxanne complained of an agitation that caused her to pace. She rubbed her hands together, hoping the friction would warm them as she searched for the reason for the sudden instinct. She walked up to the phone and stared at it for a moment while attempting to convince herself, she was only being paranoid. Ignoring her fears, she tried to pass by the object that called for her. But the companion's pushed her away and blocked her view, encouraging her into a dance. But Mother's instinct stepped into the dance and spun Roxanne up to the phone. *One of her children… is in danger!* was the message received.

Roxanne, picked up the phone, and dialed Lisa's number while slipping into her jeans. "Busy… shit!" She slammed the receiver back into the cradle. Roxanne put on her shoes before redialing Lisa's number. Each digit seemed to take a lifetime as she pushed the rotary dial forward and waited for it to spin back before spinning another number and watching it spin back, causing Annoyance, to bite at the back of her neck. "Hello…?" Lisa's voice came as a regretful whisper and strained with a quiver. "Lisa, what's wrong with Scarlet?" caused a calculating pause before Lisa calmly said, "Nothing is wrong!" came across the line in a patronizing tone, with the power to pound Roxanne with another rush of intuition washing over her while Anxiety had taken on a boiling point in the pits of her hollow womb, brewing the persistence, that bellowed from her.

"I know something is wrong!" Roxanne insisted, into the emptiness of the phone line. "Damn it!" Her words puffed out hard. "What the hell is wrong with Scarlet?" Roxanne shouted into a line that seemed to have gone dead. "Hello … hello, Lisa?" Finally, a heavy sigh signaled, the line had not gone dead. "Lisa … just tell me!" Roxanne pleaded into her friend's ear. "Roxanne, now stay calm!" Lisa attempted to take her own advice.

"Remember, you're still, recovering from a hysterectomy!" Lisa tried to convince Roxanne, who was being led by her maternal instincts and had become fervently obstinate as waves of dread crashed into Roxanne's heart. "Damn it, Lisa, you're killing me. Just, tell me?" Roxanne demanded without the consideration that the next rush of Lisa's words would shatter her world. "Scarlet's been hit by a car!" exploded into the defenseless Roxanne.

"It doesn't look… good!" echoed through Roxanne and caused her to drop the receiver as a tidal wave of disaster crashed into her world and swept her out the door, in the direction of the community hospital.

Roxanne ran the five blocks while holding her stomach, attempting to protect her fresh incision from bursting open. Her mind screamed with static while desperate "No's" drowned in the waves of nausea that crashed through Roxanne's vivid imagination as the doors of the emergency room came into view. Roxanne's knees wobbled with exhaustion, her weak body trembled with pain as she attempted to quicken her pace. Hoping she wouldn't collapse before making it to the doors, where the ambulance should have been, with her daughter. Roxanne burst through the swinging double doors of Corona Community Hospital and ran down the corridor, screaming,

"Where is she?" Roxanne's voice echoed down the empty corridor. "Where's my daughter?" Sounded the desperate pleas of a mother.

A nurse stepped out from behind her desk with a surprised look on her face, a finger held up to her lip in a hushing motion. Roxanne grabbed the nurse as the doctor came out into the hall, and the siren of the ambulance came within earshot. Roxanne spun around and began running toward the ambulance entrance as she yelled back at the medical team, who urgently followed the frantic woman. "My daughters in that ambulance!" Roxanne informed them as she spun around and looked the doctor directly in the eyes. "You have to help her!" Roxanne sobbed just as the doors crashed open.

One EMT was relating the statistics of a nine-year-old car accident victim as he pushed and maneuvered the gurney while the other technician bagged air into the lifeless little girl. They were at a full sprint when they hit the treatment room and disappeared behind the doors that swung closed. Roxanne just stood there. She couldn't breathe. And for the first time in her life, she could not hear a sound inside or outside her mind until Steven trailed in with his eyes red and his shoulders humped over while his numbed senses poured from his tear ducts. "I have to see her!" cleared Steven's vision as a familiar voice sliced through him. The vision of Roxanne jumping up and down burned into his memory as she held her stomach and screamed, "I have to see her!" She insisted as she attempted to push past the head nurse. "Please, she's, my firstborn!" Roxanne persisted. "I promised her!" Steven reached out to hold his wife, but when Roxanne turned an expression his way, her emptiness met him. "You son of a bitch!" she condemned him.

"What did you do?" spewed Loathing's accusations, slapping him while nausea crested Roxanne; grabbing at the pit, of her stomach. Blackness turned Roxanne's eyes to coal while bells chased the static that filled the chambers of her mind as she sank to the floor.

"This can't be happening!" spilled from her abyss while Steven attempted to explain, "It, just happened!" as he picked his wife up from the floor. She formed like clay in his shaking arms as he carried her to the bench seat. Steven gently held her in his cradling arms while his shriveled heart threatened to disconnect from its lifeline, and Roxanne mumbled incoherent prayers.

A nurse approached Roxanne while slightly tapping a syringe full of a calming substance. "Roxanne, this will make you feel better," the professional assured the fretting mother as she sterilized the entry point of Roxanne's flesh.

The stick of the needle caught Roxanne's breath for a moment. It slowed the constant rumbling of prayers that earlier were broken only by sudden verbal attacks on Steven. "You, neglectful son of a bitch!" she growled at him.

"Oh God... please?" Roxanne howled while she held her absent womb. "Might as well kill me!" she rumbled with despair.

"It's not going to do your daughter any good if you make yourself sick!" chastised the nurse while she calmly blotted the blood that fought its way to the surface of Roxanne's skin.

"How can I go on?" Roxanne questioned with a lack of understanding.

"What have I done to deserve this?" she pleaded for answers as she opened her blurry eyes to shoot an arrow at the truly guilty, when her next plea forced its way out of her, instead of the poisoned arrow.

"Please ... Oh God ... please!" She sobbed for understanding until the drug slurred her words before slamming her eyes shut, sealing her in the safety of the calming drug.

# CHAPTER 22

CONTEMPT

When Roxanne was able to force her eyes open, she was laid out on the bench seat, alone in the corridor of the emergency room. Her body screamed for the substance of nicotine and caffeine as she forced her sedated body into an upright position. After several moments, her elbows felt like daggers, digging into her knees as she held her head in her hands. She could hear the waves of static being held back by her frozen senses as she allowed her eyes to drift up to the closed doors of the examining room, willing them to open.

Roxanne's breath caught in surprise when the door suddenly swung open, and the long faces of faltering hope came out of the room with Steven in tow. Steven's face was white as a ghost and riddled with Guilt as he sat next to his wife and took up her hand. Roxanne shook her hands free from Steven's hold and placed them on her ears to block the static that broke through the barriers of the sedation as her imagination ran wild.

"Oh, God … please!" shook out of Roxanne's trembling body.

"Is she … alive?" cut Roxanne's breath short, as the doctor began shaking his head in an agreeing motion, although disbelief shaped his face.

"Your daughter's condition is very grave!" His words caused Roxanne to clutch her abdomen and release a heartsick moan that sustained the sounds of pain. The doctor grasped the young mother's hand and tried to look her in the eye.

"This hospital is not equipped to treat Scarlet!" he regretfully spoke. "We are preparing to transfer her to the general hospital in Riverside as we speak!" he added reassuringly.

Roxanne lifted her hopeless, darkened eyes toward the doctor as her frowning lips turned to a sarcastic crack. Roxanne pushed herself up from the bench, with only Defiance, stabilizing her footing. She staggered while her blood pressure caught up with the wrenching of her heart. She turned and faced the assaulter with a deviant contempt while preparing to remind him of the first pain from him, which was also about Scarlet. "Damn you, Steven!" Roxanne exhaled a vast amount of disgust. "I promised her!" thumped hard at Roxanne's heart, forcing her to spin away from the bad news inflictor as tears gushed, and she began moaning uncontrollably. With her back turned to Steven, she managed to screech,

"If she dies!" cut Roxanne's throat with an unspoken but complete thought. When she turned her anguish to the doctor, she pleaded for a little more of the sedative that held back the crashing Anxiety.

The doctor's words in Corona jabbed through the transparent drug, whose job it was… to numb Roxanne's reality. While Roxy held her hand. Coaxing Roxanne… To remain calm, patiently unemotional, while the doctors in Riverside, assessed Scarlet.

Roxanne checked and rechecked the time on her wristwatch. "Come on…" she complained as the drug lost its affect and reality began gnawing on Roxanne's neck, pushing Annoyance up, into a pacing motion.

"What is taking so damn long?" Roxanne grumbled as she turned for another lap at pacing the floor when two doctors entered the waiting room.

Steven's heart nearly flatlined by the expression on the professional's faces, which caught Roxanne's breath under the lump of anxiety. Roxanne shot deadly daggers at her husband before she rushed up to the ones who held the answers to their fate. Dr. White introduced himself as the chief neurologist as he led the parents of the nine-year-old patient to a room where they could have some privacy.

It was in the doorway of the private conference room, the chubby gray-haired neurologist introduced, Dr. Rich: A young orthopedic surgeon, reached out his hand and offered a sympathetic grip. Youthfulness equals inexperience. Roxanne visualized her first impression.

The doctors attempted to ease the somber mood with half-smiles during the introduction. But their attempts sadly failed with a frustrated breath aspirating from Roxanne as her shaking hands attempted to pull a cigarette from the crushed soft pack. She knew in her gut that things weren't good. "Damn it to hell!" she cursed the unwilling soft pack before she tossed it to the floor and turned her frustration to the procrastinating doctor's. "So, is she alive… Dead… What?" Frustration labored with Roxanne.

Dr. Rich shot an understanding look that riddled Roxanne's heart with holes as he began to explain. "Scarlet's eyes are dilated and fixed!" Roxanne shook her head for laymen's terms. "Which tells us, brain damage, is apparent!" Dr. White punctuated before he stepped back to let the other doctor deliver his conclusion. "Scarlet has two breaks to her left leg."

Dr. Rich cut his words short, Stopped, by Roxanne's free hand while her other hand held a trembling cigarette to her lips. She shot a daring eye at the doctor as she lit the cigarette, Inhaling as she shifted her body language, for all to see. Exhaled and in haled the toxin that calmed the raging seas inside her.

The doctor's eyes nervously shifted to Steven when he said, "Scarlet has a laceration to her right-arm... just below the elbow!"

Annoyance exhaled Roxanne's toxins into the doctor's direction when she suggested.

"Well, sew it up!" Roxanne insisted. "And cast the leg!" came out in a demanding tone. She pulled a stabilizing hit from her cigarette; while giving the doctors a well, get to it! expression.

Dr. White came up to support his peer as he spoke the harsh reality of the little girl's condition. "Roxanne, your daughter's critically ill." His words silenced Roxanne. "The arm and leg are secondary to the head trauma!" Dr. White delivered as he offered the wobbling mother a seat.

Steven sat next to Roxanne and lit two cigarettes. He gingerly waved one of the lit cigarettes in front of his incoherent wife while offering the words. "I'm so... very sorry!" Smoldered Roxanne's contempt, as the doctors frankly continued in layman terms while waves of nausea crashed through the thawing effects of the drug that protected Roxanne from reality.

"Scarlet's arm has been severed. Nearly cut off!" Roxanne began to rock back and forth, her head cradled in her hands. A laughter of disgust rumbled inside Roxanne while the doctor continued, "Although Dr. White and I would try to repair the arm together!" The young doctor's words were slow. His diligently chosen demeanor pushed Roxanne from her chair. "It may need to be ... amputated!" rocketed Roxanne across the room until she stood in front of the doctors. Defiantly, she exhaled the toxins of her fury into them. "Well, there's no sugarcoating, that shit!" Roxanne insisted, with enough sarcasm, to slap her husband in the head. Dr. Rich was obligated to continue. But he chose the rushed manner so as not to prolong Roxanne's stressed reactions. "The left leg is broken in two spots! I will set the leg, fixing it, with a full-length cast!" He attempted to encourage the baffled Steven by looking deep into his bleeding eyes.

The orbiting Roxanne suddenly stopped. She aimed a repulsive look at her husband. Firing a shot that intended to do him harm: But a sick sense divided her concentration with the idea, the worst was yet to come. She began orbiting again, vigorously shaking the soft pack that barely survived the sweaty clenching grip of her fist. Both the doctors looked to each other before giving a preordered nod in the nurse's direction. Instantly, the nurse blasted into Roxanne's universe with a dripping syringe.

The doctors forced, patronizing smiles in the direction of the mother of their patient as the drug took effect. And with the warmth of the drug coursing through Roxanne's blood and the bad news delivered, her disposition spun like a dime. That was when suddenly, her weary look turned to a nervous smile.

"Well… that's not, so bad?" Roxanne hopefully suggested as she sat next to Steven, who dared not reflect his weary thoughts while he lit a cigarette and offered it to his wife, knowing the worst was to come.

Dr. White sat next to Roxanne and took her hand as he directed his focus into the eyes of Steven and Roxanne while he gave the final and the most crucial diagnosis. "Steven … Roxanne?" His eyes took on a look of deep concern, his smile faded as Roxanne's eyes rolled back, and she sank into Steven's shoulder.

"Your daughter is in a deep-coma!" The doctor's opinion washed over Roxanne's paling face. An audible moan tuned to a hopeful whisper when Roxanne asked. "So, she's in a deep sleep?" Came out in a drawl as Roxanne shot a poker face in the doctor's direction, anticipating his choice to call or fold.

Unfortunately, he called her hand when his head met his shoulder: In a shrug of the unknown. He provided little hope as Roxanne began to rock back and forth, clutching her hands to her ears.

Steven shot the doctor a look of despair that screamed for help, but the doctor offered little encouragement. "Talk to her!" was the doctors advise

"The longer she's in the coma, the worse the chances get!" It was his duty to prepare them. Roxanne and Steven looked at each other, searching for the answer they wanted to hear. "So, if she wakes up, then she will be all right?" Roxanne's words explored for something solid. But her search fell, vain when the doctor refused to bluff her. Instead, he laid all the cards on the table.

"If Scarlet does come out of the coma within a couple of days, there is a good chance she may remain in a vegetative state!" Their concurred words pumped adrenaline into Roxanne's bloodstream and pushed her away from the clutches of the men. "No! No! No!" Motioned a fist at the heavens.

"God wouldn't do that!" Roxanne screamed in protest before she turned to Steven with eyes that have been churned in the abyss of her agony. Bartering with her own life, for her daughter, to wake up. Black was the color of her fury that fought the waves of static: struggling to fight the message that suddenly slammed into her, hard enough to knock her into Steven with swinging arms and a premeditated thought of hurting him as much as he had hurt her.

THE LIONESS PROWLS

CHAPTER 1

IN THE BALANCES

Roxanne's attempts at remaining positive, quaked her world as she watched Helplessness, rocking back and forth in a chair, next to her daughter's bed. For hours on end, Roxanne would pace the cubicle to the rhythm of the machines that signaled her daughter's vitals. When she became weary, Roxanne would sit on the end of Scarlet's bed rocking back and forth, mumbling inaudible prayers. Bargaining with her own life for her daughter to wake up: happy and healthy. The labor of weeping and bargaining was exhausting work that would find Roxanne lying so close to Scarlet, their hair entwined. And as the days wore on, her faith wore thin from the pounding of the violent tide pools that pulled and twisted in the clamoring chambers of her mind.

On day 7, she remained at the side of her daughter's lifeless body. Roxanne was tenderly pulling long strands of Scarlet's red hair through her fingers while Roxanne made deals with God for Scarlet's life. She also questioned whether her presence was making a difference. Hopefully, Roxanne scanned her daughter's body, for any sign of life. But the only movement was on the monitors, buzzing and beeping.

Roxanne gagged attempting to swallow the acids of Disgust that boiled her heart in the abyss as she pondered an answer to the question; she dare-not say, out loud. The smoke from her boiling heart clouded any Positivity that remained as she doubted her daughter could hear her pleas.

During the wee hours of the morning, when only the spirits roamed the corridors of the intensive care unit. Those were the weakest, most vulnerable moments for Roxanne. It was then, when she was all alone, with her mind screaming for results. While she silently sobbed curses for Steven's neglect, offering anything for God to intervene. Until her sobs turned to the low, deep, painful moan of a wounded animal, she recalled, the phone call home during those loneliest hours. When she felt she would be swallowed by the gnashing Anxiety that exists with the inconsolable helplessness.

The phone had rung—two, three, four times. Each ring caused Roxanne to shudder from the thundering clap of Irony that nobody would be there to stabilize her! Slapped Roxanne in the head as she began lowering the receiver to its cradle, "Hello …" slid through the phone line just in the nick of time.

Steven's exhausted and strangled voice broke through with the sound of a leaden weight hanging heavy from his scrotum, cinching tighter each day that passed without changes in his daughter's condition. "I ache all over!" he confided into Roxanne's desperation. "Although I hadn't a relationship with God …" He paused for what seemed like an eternity. "I yearn for a miracle … in my own way!" Steven insisted. The phone line whispered with the sounds of the hospital spirits as Roxanne analyzed Steven's words. His demeanor turned up the heat on her burnt-out heart while he carried on.

"Between going back and forth to the hospital…" Steven paused for a moment. "Caring for the boys', work and going to school…" He sighed, wondering if she were still listening. Still there was no sound from the receiving side of the conversation as he exhaustively spoke. "Somewhere in between, getting his studies done and arranging babysitters for the boys!" concluded his complaints. His words swirled around her faster and faster. "You need to come home!" slammed into Roxanne and knocked her off her feet. The receiver bounced and landed under the bed where her firstborn, her only daughter, lay somewhere, unreachable. Snipped Roxanne's marionette strings. Helplessness overcame her like a wet blanket that smelled of mold. The Lioness's ears flipped up, and she flicked her tail back and forth. Harder and swifter her tail twitched.

"Blah, blah, blah!" poked at the Lioness.

"Blah, blah, blah!" prodded the Lioness from her lair.

The Lioness stretched out on the floor next to Roxanne. She sniffed the air and pulled her ears back in the direction of the receiver. "Roxanne!" The taunting sound of Steven's voice struck the Lioness again. Drawing into a crouch, eyes dilated, attempting to sever the phone line with her swishing tail.

She pawed the receiver, smelling it, sizing up the opponent of her hunt.

"Roxanne … you need to get your ass home. You still need to be a mother to your boys!" Annoyance mixed with Roxanne's motherly instinct and caused the Lioness to let out a low painful moan before she quickly slapped the receiver with her paw. Roxanne moaned from the pain that threatened to burst the seam of her patched-up heart. As Steven stated his burdens, the Lioness looked back at Roxanne, who had curled into a fetal position. "Hello?" Steven's voice came through the receiver loud enough to redraw the Lioness's attention.

"Roxanne!" Came through even louder than the previous and prodded, the Lioness to leap up into the air and pounce on the receiver. "Roxanne, when are you coming home?" Caused the Lioness to claw at the receiver, tearing into it as she reflected on how many times, she had longed to rip him apart, in the last week.

But now he's crying and whining about his own needs? The Lioness had given Roxy the notion to drive home and pound a stake through his heart. While informing Steven that if he hadn't put Scarlet into a coma, "then she … our family would be complete and at home!" However, when Steven turned the conversation to the boys.

Roxanne's heart quaked, causing her to gag and then gasp for air just before her lungs refused to take another breath, as his words churned inside of her.

"The boys aren't doing so well!" he informed her with the power to inflict guilt, which began toiling with all the other emotions, as he continued.

"Mark and Stevie are having nightmares!" cinched Roxanne's heart as she wondered whether their dreams were as desperate as hers.

"And one of them had wet the bed!" Being unable to remember which one had wet the bed caused neglect to stab at Roxanne while she continued recalling Steven's words.

"The last time they saw their sister, she lay lifeless in the street!" Recalled the static that came through the phone line, allowed a pause long enough for Steven to suck in the air that continued to push with a new force.

"Since she still hasn't come home. The boys were sure. She was dead!" Choked the phone line.

"She's still alive!" stabbed viciously back at Steven.

"Yeah … I know!" Steven spat out feebly before pausing long enough to pick up his severed heart. "We've been telling them. She just needs lots of rest in the hospital!" Stevens reflected on the boys questioning the adults, who offered transparent smiles. "We told them, 'Don't worry—the doctors will make her well!'" Attempted to resolve the inflictions that haunted their nights. Roxanne's body shuddered while sarcasm crested to the top of her tongue as Steven continued. "Nevertheless, they don't understand why they are not allowed to see her." cut the restraints of her sarcasm. Allowing it to rumble through the phone line until it severed the jugular of the culprit.

CHAPTER 2

WEE HOURS

Submerged in the quicksand of mental and physical exhaustion, Roxanne struggled to peel the blinders from her eyes that kept her bound in hell.

A voice crashed through the waves that pounded the weary shores of her mind, signaled her and the frantic companions, *Somebody's here!*

Desperately, she wanted to call out for help. But the resistance of the timid companions dubiously bit her lip. *Are they the ones chasing her in her dream?* choked Roxanne's larynx. *Or maybe, in the real world, where things have become as frantic as her dreams!* chastised Annoyance.

The unknown again called, "Roxanne, Roxanne?" Came with enough power to hold her breath as she attempted to break free from the bondage that was trapping her in a world of indecisiveness.

Roxanne broke a sweat as she tugged and tugged at the blinders until Desperation shook her soul, and screams from her companions rose from the edge of the abyss. "God" she attempted to call.

"Please, anybody, help me!" reverberated from the walls of the trapped souls and rolled to high pitches, until thunder clapped, as those in the abyss, cried for blood. "Blood for her virginity ... for his doubt, for his lust," chorused the companions at the altar.

"For him, hurting you!" slammed the gavel. "And for causing you to break your promise to Scarlet," chanted the charges throughout the abyss. The waters rocked from the turbulence of the conviction, swayed Roxanne until she could no longer hold on to the last thread of her life preserver. And as the last fragment pulled tautly and retracted from her grasp, the clouds clapped. "Roxy," rumbled from the edge and threw Roxanne a lifeline.

Roxanne's eyes popped open, and her body bolted straight up.

"Has she come out of the coma?" slurred from Roxanne's drool-blanketed lips. Her mind screamed with pain as the nurses methodically shook her head in a negative motion, as they had done many times before.

"You need to help us?" The companions chuckled over the nurse's request as Roxanne lifted her tired, aching head from her hands and lifted her eyes that were as black as the abyss, "Oh… of course!" sarcasm huffed.

The nurse inspected her patients' mother, up and down. Checking her ability to perform in this week-long ordeal; until her eyes met with Roxanne's confused stare. Roxanne's hands quivered as she brushed her tousled hair from her face so she could face the clouds of her frustrations. "What can I do?" Roxanne asked with a desperate attempt of Courage.

The nurse offered a weak smile for Roxanne's persistence. Although she had begun to lose steam, her heart was there, the nurse concluded before telling Roxanne.

"Scarlet's veins won't hold up for any more intravenous lines!" A twitch grabbed Roxanne's eye as the nurse's lips formed big red dampers on Roxanne's already cloudy day. "It's imperative she drinks electrolyte fluids so she doesn't dehydrate." Rushed at Roxanne while she wavered in consideration of the nurse's words as the steam from despair boiled her faltering faith.

Not a moment later, the pressure spouts off in an elevated voice as Roxanne choked out her confusion. "How the hell am I supposed to do that?" pulled the irritated Roxanne from the cot and forced her to take a staggering step toward the woman dressed in a blue smock dress and white shoes.

"In case you haven't noticed, my daughters in a coma!" Roxanne snapped the nurse's face with a fury that pushed the nurse away from the threatening personality that suddenly flared from a woman who before had always been patient and humble.

"You've got to be firm." The nurse stood her ground while offering a thin-lipped smile of encouragement. Roxanne's body began to tremble as she processed the nurse's advice. Her head began to rock in the rhythm of disbelief that sounded Doubt through the static of her mind. "You have to do it!" the nurse insisted as she continued to explain the situation. "Scarlet won't respond to us!" the tired and frustrated nurse said as she firmly grasped the reluctant mother's hand and pulled her toward the cubicle where her daughter lay mostly dead and swollen.

Roxanne's head swarmed with Skepticism as she stood five feet away from the full-length cast affixed to her daughter's left leg. It seemed to swallow Scarlet, along with the bandages, stained yellow with a tinge of red that bound her arm and head. Scarlet's black eyes were sunken and hollow. Monitors beeped and hummed with signs of life and death. Tubes weaved in and out of her ankles, arms, neck, and nose. Her cracked red-dry lips were cinched tight with tape around a breathing tube.

Nausea swarmed Roxanne into a stagger, causing her to reach out her hand and grasp the side of Scarlet's bed. At the same time, attempting to stabilize herself and stop the repetitive motion of the teeter-totter being ridden by her constant companions' Regret and

Hopelessness as the nurse stepped up beside her. "Remember to be firm while telling her to swallow?" the nurse rushed out her expectations into Roxanne's annoyed expression while the skeptics considered the professional's insensitivity to Roxanne who staggered for stability as she drew close and picked up her daughter's limp hand.

"Good morning, baby!" Roxanne whispered with a resolute tone of nurturing while waiting for any sign of life as she talked to her Sleeping Beauty. "It would be a glorious day if you would open your beautiful green eyes!" she encouraged her daughter while the nurse handed her a cup of fluid and nodded her head in Scarlet's, direction. Roxanne shot a weary stare at the nurse before turning her doubting fears toward her daughter.

"Scarlet, you need to swallow this juice," shrouded Roxanne with reservation as she held the cup to her daughter's lips and slowly poured some of the juice into Scarlet's nonresponsive existence.

The nurse shook her head in disapproval as the liquid ran out of Scarlets mouth and down her chin. "You have to order her to swallow!" the nurse barked as she took the cup and held it to Scarlets mouth before, shaking her head in Roxanne's direction, signaling her to perform.

"Scarlet, if you don't swallow …" Roxanne nearly choked before she grasped on to her newfound power that was tired and wanted to get on with this show. "You will be in trouble, and you will get a spanking!" Roxanne ordered with a passion she had never experienced before. To Roxanne's amazement, Scarlet swallowed three times before rejecting the fourth.

The nurse had a smile of approval plastered on her face when Roxanne looked to her for reassurance that she also had seen the light of hope.

Tears welled in the nurse's eyes as Roxanne's tears crested over the rims and gushed down her cheeks, raining down on her daughter. "I love you, baby!" Roxanne's voice trembled as she raised a hand to her daughter's bruised face and tenderly caressed her. "All of us believe, you can wake up!" encouraged Scarlet, while Roxanne and the nurse waited for another sign of life. A couple of minutes later, a reassuring smile met Roxanne's doubting hope before the nurse went to tend her other duties.

Roxanne laid her head gently amongst the tubes and wires that separated her from her daughter. "Come on, honey … Just one more sign!" Roxanne pleaded exhaustively while tears spilled down her face, forming puddles on the sheets, spreading its wetness under the tubes and wires until it pushed against Scarlet and cuddled her with Roxanne's hopes, fears and doubts until a silent numbness overcame Roxanne's body.

Hours later, Exhaustion retrieved a chair from the hall, and Roxanne sat next to the bed that held her stacks of hopes and prayers atop her daughter's lifelessness. As time ticked by, the monitors continue to beeped and hummed until they also faded while the room took on the appearance of Disney characters at play. The smell of cotton candy and caramel apples mixed in the air with sunshine and laughter as Roxanne stroked her daughter's face and hands.

The tickle of the little pigs didn't affect Scarlet but pushed Roxanne into the chorus of childhood songs and telling happy-ending stories while bubbles floated into the warm, gentle breeze. *What the hell. This isn't helping!* Smoldered the companions, aggravation, which sounded the sirens throughout Roxanne's bloodstream, in search for the life-sustaining substances for her own neglected needs, which suddenly began gnawing at her. Roxanne aspirated an explosion of frustrated sighs that had the power to spin her into pacing the small cubicle before she stopped at Scarlet's bedside.

I wonder if she still inhabiting her physical body? dared to pass over Roxanne's lips with only Cynicism as her encourager. She shuddered with consideration, heeding the advice of the encouraging voices. *Do you think she's in there?* pushed Roxanne's arm out. Her fingers grasped Scarlet's ear, squeezing with all her might before releasing her grip and watching the ear turn from red to purple on her nonresponsive daughter.

Anger shot back at the companions' failed suggestion, which only managed to daunt Roxanne's spirit as she choked back the wailing that wanted to pour out of her. The combustion of the overwhelming emotions sent her swirling about the cubicle that was closing in on her while she attempted to deal with the thrashing of her physical cravings and the unanswered questions of the taunting companion's.

Roxanne plopped down into the chair, attempting to ignore the frustration and Anxiety that pounded her. Rubbing her burning eyes… Scratching at the addiction her body craved. Uncontrollably, rocking back and forth until the convinced Roxanne, shot out of the chair.

"I need to get out of here!" flooded Roxanne with a new emotion for the day. *Your place is here!* Guilt taunted her decisions.

"Just for a moment!" Roxanne insisted as she chose to ignore the guilt and sided with the nagging addictions that caused charges of electricity to course through the consuming numbness.

The long-ignored addictions turned Roxanne's face hot as self-indulgence took priority, causing goosebumps to prickle her flesh when she leaned into her comatose daughter.

"I'll be right back!" she stated for the sake of taming the engaging vises before she gently brushed Scarlet's red locks with her fingers and placed a lasting kiss to her daughter's forehead. Suddenly, the life monitors blared warning into the corridors of the intensive care unit, causing a freight train of static to rumble through Roxanne's mind with enough power to bolt her body into a rigid stance. Nervously, she shifted her eyes to the numbers on the monitor that flashed in front of her. The incomprehensive digits seemed the same as before the alarm, signaled death.

Roxanne sucked in a breath, holding it deep in her lungs as she gazed down at her daughter. Scarlet, looked too peaceful to be lying in the hospital! Roxanne's mind concluded,

"The Lord has called her home!" violently convulsed Roxanne's entire body until the vine that suspended her heart snapped and sent her crashing to the floor, where misery tore at her hollow womb while the cries of a familiar voice of a woman rang through the sterile corridors.

"Oh God ... I pray you have taken him with you!" sounded a woman's voice with acceptance. "Praise God, he's no longer suffering!" came from the cubicle next to Scarlet's, announcing the death of her lifelong love.

Roxanne lay on the cold linoleum of her daughter's cubicle, recalling that she and the wife of the recently deceased were talking over a Pepsi and a cigarette just yesterday.

They had shared their stories and cried about their own situation and for each others anguish. An instant **bond** caught them in each other's embracing arms as they chained-smoked their daily intake. Twenty minutes later, their eyes were caught in a silent stare as they washed the scorching tar down with the caffeinated soda before they instinctively clutched hands, grasping the support they needed, as they walked down the corridor. Each of them weary and overwhelmed at the loneliest point of their lives.

They walked the final stretch in silence before turning an encouraging look toward each other as they each placed a palm on the double swinging doors of the intensive care unit when Joyce turned to Roxanne and said, "I pray ... if one of us has to lose the one we love"—Joyce squeezed Roxanne's hand with sincerity—"I hope your daughter would be spared!" Choked the lady's voice as tears poured from both Roxanne's and Joyce's eyes. They wiped the tears from their stress-creased eyes. Straight-lined smiles shaped their lips, brightening their eyes as they pressed their bodies into an embracement. Time seemed to stand still as they pulled strength from one another. They both sucked in a deep breath of air as they released their hold of each other and hung on to the tether of their faith. Uniformly, as they had done so many times before, they turned toward their adjacent cubicles. One last glance methodically found their eyes locked. And in perfect rhythm, they each signaled a thumbs- up before disappearing behind their own half-closed curtains, where they continued their prayers and their encouraging words to the lifeless bodies of their loved ones.

CHAPTER 3

A MIRACLE

Roxanne was bound, blindfolded, and gagged while riding out the destructive storm of a kidnapped hostage, in a woven basket, that had washed up on the shore of the unknown. She awoke on that beach with the buzz of attacking bees. She swatted at them defensively, but she couldn't reach far enough into her own persona to make a difference. She could hear her heart pounding the vicious rhythm of fear as she blindly ran down the beach with the wind shooting pellets of rain into her flesh.

Blood stained her tattered garment and pooled in the white sand before a powerful tornado swirled her up into the air and slammed her down into the sterile environment, where she watched the storm roll down the corridor of the intensive care unit.

Roxanne sprang up into a sitting position, wiping at the tears that leaked out as the familiar buzz accompanied her in the fountain of pain, inundating fatigue that ravished her with an anxious feeling in the pit of her stomach that couldn't be washed away.

She dropped her cascading head into her hands, attempting to recall other times she had experienced these exact feelings outside of her Mother, brother, and sister.

"When I was standing at the altar" shot out like vomit, "during the shotgun wedding, forced to say 'I do!'" She gagged out the words with a force that turned her inside out.

Roxanne attempted to dodge the noises that channeled through her fragile mind as she weaved her way across the room until she grasped the sink and braced herself on locked elbows. Facing the mirror, she raised her eyes to examine herself:

A pale face with dark circles encasing the gaunt façade stared back at her.

"Fine specimen, of stress-related issues!" she said out loud as she raised a hand to her eyes and attempted to rub the exhaustion from them.

"You need to come home!" poked her in the eye.

Yeah, time to move on! The companions broke through the bustling vibrations that had forced tenure in her mind.

"It's been, eight long days?" chewed at Roxanne until it created anger to swell in her bosom. When Roxanne finally opened her injured eye, she was staring into a reflection that had aged. *Girl, we need to think of us for a while!* Selfishness danced around the downhearted Roxanne, while Guilt continuously tripped her until her brown eyes turned black and sent the companions into a chorus: *We, we, we. Us, us, us. Me, me, me. You, you, you!* They insisted.

"God, why have you done this?" rumbled from the self-sacrificed abyss that poured tears of Doubt from deep inside her.

Roxanne spun around and began the walk down the corridor with an agitated disposition. She did not make eye contact with anyone as she approached the doors of the intensive care unit. "Please, God, let her be awake!" She groaned a prayer. "Let her be awake!" Roxanne repeated over and over again.

Yeah, this is getting boring, complained the self-oriented companions. Roxanne swatted in annoyance at the unsupportive clamor as she walked into the cubicle where Scarlet remained as lifeless as the first day this nightmare began.

Roxanne rushed up to the bed, with the intention of shaking Scarlet awake, as recommended by the companions. But when she attempted to reach out and take a hold of Scarlet, she found her arms were frozen to her chest, in a cradling position. She could only stand there, looking down upon her firstborn.

The promises she had made while she was pregnant slapped the companions, who encouraged her Failure and shook the frozen Roxanne's world, while Pessimism taunted her into the abyss of Despair. Roxanne had detested the straight faces that masqueraded the doctors, on the sixth day, told her and Steven: "Give in… pull the plug!" Their expressions didn't even shift when they offered, "Most likely, Scarlet will never have a life outside of assisted feedings and bed changes!"

Roxanne had refused to abide by their wishes that attempted to send her falling to the floor to die from the mortal wound. Instead, she stiffen her disposition with the help of Determination. "I have spoon-fed and changed her before!" Roxanne looked to Steven for reassurance. But he only stood silent, shaking his head in a negative motion. "How can you, abandon her now!" Roxanne screeched, turning her pain into the wind of her rage that sailed her up to the perpetrator. "Your neglect, is the cause of this nightmare!" She stabbed at Steven with words as her fist whaled him.

Steven danced circles in the violent storm as he thwarted Roxanne's assault. Suddenly, Roxanne broke away from the Vengeance dance and stiffened her back. Her warm almond eyes had turned black, as space. She was breathing hard. Her face contorted to a wild, daring mask.

Steven wiped at the fearful sweat that beaded his brow. A smile formed on Roxanne's lips and passed a wink of her eye—to whom, it wasn't clear—when she pounced into the air and came down on top of Steven and bit into his neck, just before, she was subjected to the poke of a calming agent that collapsed her sails and left her adrift in a clashing ocean of nightmares. Where she couldn't abandon the ship, escape, or wake up. All she could do was scream at the inflictions that caused chaos in her life until the drug permitted her release and allowed her eyes to flutter open twelve hours later.

Steven was sitting on the edge of Roxanne's hospital cot, holding his head in one hand and her hand in the other. He was whispering apologies to her while professing his love for her and their children. Roxanne silently watched him, contemplating his words and his intentions. Suddenly, she snatched her hand from his grip and came up into a sitting position. Roxanne's head swam in tidepools, hungover from the injection, as she faced the startled Steven. The expression of his red, teary eyes turned to surprise, but he would not look his adversary in the eye.

"Oh, babe?" he choked out while wiping his tear-stained face.

Roxanne grimaced as the sour substance in her stomach rose. Steven could not conceal his unconfident expression, of uncertainty, over Roxanne's temperament before he began to rush his explanation to her.

"I was just—" he began to say, but Roxanne cut him off with a sharp tongue.

"Yeah, I heard!" slashed Steven's hopes as he again swallowed the last breath he had taken when she pulled her hand from his clutches.

Steven's body went cold as he watched Roxanne drop her head into the cradle of her hands. Steven's life-supporting substance painfully oozed from his heart, pooling into a puddle around the void of his vague existence.

"Please, baby ... I ..." was severed by the snapping of her head in his direction. Her scolding eyes torched his soul as she pointed her finger like a dagger and proceeded to gut him.

"You did this!" She panted in a deep, painful moan as she held back the vomit that wanted to spew all over his attempts of appeasing her. "You son of a bitch!" Roxanne hesitated for a moment. "If she dies ..." The words were cut short by Roxanne's daggered finger, which had been stabbing her opponent. Suddenly, her hand lay flat on her mouth, blocking the passage of torment, that overflowed the suggested capacity.

That was the last time she had seen Steven, she thought, as she brushed her lips across the fading bruises on her daughter's face. Roxanne lightly placed her head on Scarlet's chest to hear her heartbeat, recalling how the only thing that she and the patronizing Steven could agree on before she had ordered him to leave, was to refuse, the outcome the doctors had predicted.

"It's up to her and her Creator," Roxanne had stated to Steven as he slipped out the door with a doubtful sigh that echoed through Roxanne's mind with choleric sarcasm.

Frustration again hit Roxanne in the stomach, with enough force to pollute her bloodstream with anxiety. She spun away from her daughter and flopped into a wooden chair. She rocked back and forth at the side of her daughter's bed.

"God, it's been eight, long, miserable days!" she pleaded in a relentless tone that was haunted by the doctor's suggestion. "She needs to live!" gripped Roxanne's abdomen. "God, please!" stabbed the already-expelled breath as tears silently fell from Roxanne's eyes.

Her body began to convulse for mercy and the replenishment of oxygen. "I'd die too!" Roxanne unwillingly sucked in the vice her system required and when she exhaled, she professed, "I got to get out of here!" pushed her from the chair and delivered her face-to-face with her Sleeping Beauty. "God, I'm useless!" she sobbed for her unsuccessful attempts. Roxanne placed a fairy-tale kiss on her daughter's lips before she whispered, "Please, wake up?" burned Roxanne's soul into a dare, forcing her to look up while in the midst of praying. Hoping to find her daughter awake and alert. Most importantly-well adjusted. "Oh ... of course not!" Her words spilled out with disappointment when she found her daughter's eyes still sealed. Roxanne fought the negativity that coursed through her senses, attempting to snip the fraying strands of hope that she dangled from.

Her compliant smile that had been frozen with anticipation began to melt while tears forced their tracks down and spilled into the crevice of her neck as she willed her daughter to miraculously open her eyes and allow everything to go back to normal.

"Please, Scarlet," she mumbled relentlessly. "I love you" fell effortlessly.

"God, open her eyes!" pulsed with the static in her mind and turned her defrosted smile into a bleeding gash when the only answer she received was from the negative companions, who suggested that she... *give up!* While they clamored and heckled Roxanne. *Brain dead!* They reminded Roxanne, who paced the small space; each time she turned to do another lap, she looked to Scarlet.

Scarlet lay lifeless while Roxanne prolonged giving in, digging deeper the groove in the linoleum with each passing.

When there was no response from Scarlet, God, or anyone, a shot of desperate loathing flooded Roxanne, agitating her innards to the point of hardening her liver and forcing her to pace away the pain in quick strides about the cubicle, where her daughter remained somewhere besides here.

Abruptly, Roxanne stopped short of her full stride and spun toward her daughter. She stood firm as she placed her hands on her hips. "Scarlet..." cut Roxanne's throat with the blades of tears until Strength, stepped on her toe and pushed out... "You better get your butt back, where you belong!" she demanded in the same firm tone she had used at the nurses' command, hoping Scarlet would respond as she had then. But after several moments of no motion and no sound, except for the humming of the monitors and the negative energy that sounded through the static in her mind, where her companions had their own opinions and selfish needs.

"God, this is driving me crazy!" Roxanne complained while wearing deeper tracks into the linoleum around her daughter's lifeless existence.

"I have to go check on the boys!" rushed out with an urgency that spun Roxanne into her daughter's direction while Anxiety completed the course and slammed into her already-screaming mind and caused her to choke over tears.

"You, continue resting!" Her voice cracked. "So, you'll get better!" pushed Roxanne out of the cubicle.

The ground quaked from the lack of the substance that had been carrying her through the last eight days.

"Faith?" she questioned. "What has it ever gotten me?" She bellowed with enough power to push her into a full sprint toward the front doors of the hospital. Her faith had spewed out in front of her. It pushed out the door before Roxanne, who had entered in a mad dash, attempting to escape all the noises that chastised her mind, where the static sided with the innuendos of the doctors.

She's not there! their flaccid smiles taunted.

Not there. Not there! The companions broke into a chorus with enough power to swirl Roxanne into disgust.

"Like, he needs her, more than I do!" Roxanne spewed defiantly, cursing God as she slid in behind the steering wheel of her car.

"So, what is it?" Roxanne cut short, calculating the cost for her daughter's life as she lit a cigarette and exhaled. "What is it, you want?" Churned Roxanne's emotions as she smoked her first cigarette of the day, still incoherent to the purpose of this nightmare. Her body ached from the overwhelming confusion. She exhaled the scorched filter from her lungs and crushed the butt into the ashtray. Anxiety stretched out her arms and gripped the steering wheel, pressing her firmly into the seat.

"I'd sacrifice, my own life!" wrenched her forward until she pressed against the steering wheel. Violently, they tug-o-warred Roxanne back and forth like a rag doll. She opened her mouth while bloodcurdling screams pushed her soul out onto the bidding table.

Without her faith and her soul, she fell across the bench seat, beaten and lifeless. Her eyes swam in the abyss of absolute emptiness. Only the Lioness danced around her, chartering their desires into Roxanne's playbook before the Lioness grabbed Roxanne and dragged her farther into the abyss. Where Roxy emerged. Roxy rose, straightened herself, and reached for a cigarette with one hand while she started the car with the other. She sucked nicotine into her lungs, allowing the substance to compete with the anxiety that clogged Roxanne's system as she calmly and mindlessly waited for an answer to Roxanne's question.

Roxy revved the engine to a warm rumble for the first time since that tragic day. Impulsively, Roxanne struck a match with her trembling hands as she fought for composure over her weaknesses. Her failed attempts at lighting her cigarette caused her to shift her attention to the third match with heightened frustration that struck the match with vigorous determination. A chunk of burning sulfur wedged under her fingernail, flooding her body with sobs to extinguish the anguish that spewed out with the loss of temperate words, some of them she had never said before. But her final words—"Damn God, for doing this!"—froze her in contempt.

She did not dare breathe God's precious air while she and Roxy shared a ride home in a cloud of despair. Roxanne's shameful guilt chastised Roxy's party, for hampering Scarlet's chances, of finding her way back.

"How can you, damn God?" bounced clearly through her mind when everything else seemed jumbled together.

"It wasn't me. It was Roxy!" pushed out in self-defense.

Mad as a hatter! chastised Regret while Roxy turned a contemplative smile to Roxanne and winked.

"Like a blind flurry!" Roxanne insisted. "I didn't mean it!" trailed off in an attempt to find a lighter subject to focus on as she searched for the day of the week.

"I wonder, if the boys are home?" her heart yearned as she pulled into her designated parking marked, MANAGER ONLY.

Well, it's been a while! chastised the companions.

Roxanne hesitated while recalling the last time she was home. "The day, I ran to the community hospital!" she breathed out with exhaustion as she finished collecting her things. She popped the handle on the door, allowing it to release its hold and swing open before extending all her effort to swinging her legs out onto the concrete.

Mindlessly, she rose into the clouds of her despondency, slowly, dragging her frail existence up the stairs to the apartment where her family (minus one) had been dwelling without her for the last eight days.

Roxanne dropped her things on the floor of the messy apartment. She would have exhaled a breath with a sigh of frustration as she kicked a path clear to the bathroom, but she wasn't breathing. She turned the water to a near-scalding temperature before closing the stopper in the tub. She sat there on the edge for a moment, feeling shipwrecked in a mindless dimension. She was welcoming the anticipation of submerging herself into the churning currents before she went to the kitchen and poured a glass of wine, which she had found, in the back of the fridge.

She stood against the counter, staring at the label on the bottle while sipping down half of the measured content. "Hmm!" Roxanne said to the companions before shooting the rest of what was in the glass in a single gulp, then returning the bottle to the back of the refrigerator.

Wonder what he was celebrating? The Lioness question as she retrieved the bottle of wine, refilling Roxanne's glass and offering a heavily aspirated sigh of disgust. *Maybe if he had killed the girl! The companion's questioned as Roxanne spun the glass in hand toward the hot tide pools of the plunging water.*

She lifted the glass to sip the impurities of the toxins, but it pushed into a wave and sloshed over the edge, splashing onto her breast bone before running down between her naked cleavage. She sank into the hot water up to her shoulders, sipping at the bitter red wine, as words thundered through the clouds of her mindless dimension.

It was in that dimension that the companions protected Roxanne from her reality, taking her far away from any cares for anybody but her and the companions.

"We got this, girl!" said Roxy, as she wet her lips on the glass of wine. *The Lioness full body caressed Roxanne. Sniffing her… Her Scent, slicked the feline's ears back, with a sneeze…*

What's that smell? The magistrate, toyed. Flicking her tail with the curiosity of Roxanne's vulnerability, she yawned… stretched… quickly, reached out and smacked Roxanne.

"If you'd just do it my way!" she hissed at Roxanne with her ears pulled back. "Why are you making this so hard, on all of us?" she batted Roxanne in the head, hard enough to knock her back into the bathtub with Roxy, who had just finished the glass of wine.

Roxy, sat on the edge of the tub with her feet in the water, smiling into Roxanne's surprised expression-unable to recollect taking her clothes off and getting into the tub. She leaned back in the tub, reflecting on the empty glass as she attempted to force herself to relax. But the longer she sat in the quiet apartment, the louder the waves crashed through the fog that clouded her mind.

She attempted to hum a song as she began to bathe, but the pounding waves had painfully traumatized her to the point of fatigue- leaving only enough sense in her brain, to pull her knees to her chest and cradle her weary head atop her knees.

Tears pooled in the gap of her pressed knees as she mustered the movements necessary to continue washing the hospital smell from her body when a sudden charge of defiance settled on a conclusion. "I cannot love a God, that would do this to my innocent child!" pulled Roxanne from the tub and spun her naked wet body out into the front room, equipped with a pad of paper and a pen, where she wrote,

Dear God,

I thank you for the privilege of loving your blessing …
If only for nine years! Although I am willing to bargain
Anything that is of fair value for my child's life.
If she is to be a vegetable, I ask that you take her.
Even though I don't think, I can live without her …
And I would not consider it fair!

Roxanne, 1971

A smile of the unfaithful shaped her lips into a crack of an untrustworthy success, feeling firm that there was no reason to address the envelope that held her demands, she thought, as she folded the letter and intended to place it in the comment box of "God Almighty!" she choked out as she let go of her written testament and watched it slip out of sight. "I need to see my boys!" Pushed Roxanne into a newfound resolution as she finished zipping up her jeans and slipping on a white button-up blouse. "Yes, I desperately need to do that!" she agreed over the escaping wheeze from her compressed heart as she rushed out, of the apartment door, in search of her needs.

The hours slipped by as she spent time with her boys, just enjoying their time together as if nothing was wrong! The substance of their smiles spun the merry-go-round, faster and faster, pacifying Roxanne's anguish. A sudden rush of adrenaline lifted her onto the spinning disc, forcing her into a position, she could maintain on the whirling object while laughing… laughing with her boys until their tears of laughter, washed away the repressed feelings of abandonment, the boys had repressed… until it hurt. As the disk slowed, Roxanne considered staying in this place and time, where her remaining children, were overjoyed by her presence. Only their smiles, lit her dismal world and eased the overwhelming pain that cinched tighter every ticking moment of the clocks in the corridors of the ICU.

When the family, minus one, sat down to eat at one of the local diners, Roxanne laid each hand out on the table, palm up, while considering, "Anything would help!" She mumbled in her mind before she raised her eyes to her curious and fidgeting male family members. She saw a sparkle of light in their eyes while they hoped, it was positive news that brought her home.

Roxanne cautiously, cut them a smidgen of a nervous smile. Serving humble pie as she spread her arms out further. Encouraging the remaining participants of her family to grasp her hand and embrace the power of God's intervention. But fate stabbed Roxanne in the eye as she met Steven's hesitation with a daring glare that pulled his hand into hers with a grip that promised, never to let go.

Roxanne lay with her back to her guilt-ridden husband. He had found it easy to fall into a sound sleep, leaving Roxanne alone to toss and turn with the indecisiveness of being at her daughter's bedside or living life with her boys. "Who has been patiently waiting for their needs to be met."

Roxanne defended their case in a whisper. "At least, the boys and Steven know I am here," she concluded as she teetered toward pretending all the bad stuff with Scarlet never happened.

Starting from Scarlet's conception! Sarcasm slapped at Roxanne.

Roxanne and the boys were swept into the lightheartedness of childhood songs as they drove to the school in Riverside when Mark suddenly, fell silent. His teeth clenched and ground in hesitation. His bottom lip began to quiver as tears began to spill from his eyes. "Mama …" He paused for a moment, long enough to collect the undivided attention that he needed.

"How long, has Scarlet been resting in the hospital?" shot an arrow into Roxanne's unsuspecting heart. "Nine days" pulled the arrow from her heart, defiantly as Roxanne fought back her own tears. "Is Scarlet, ever gonna get enough rest?" Mark asked with the voice of a doubting Thomas. Roxanne flashed an uneasy look into her youngest son's question while she fought for the answers that remained aloft as she pulled into the driveway of the school, where Roxanne hugged her boys long and tight, assuring them that she loved them.

"We love you too, Mama!" they repeated a few times before wiggling loose from her relentless hold and shooting off toward their classrooms without an answer to Mark's question. Roxanne's forced smile faded as she slid back into the car, and tears pushed over the rim of her eyes. "So, God, what am I to tell her brothers?"

CHAPTER 4
ELUSIVE STATE

Scarlet danced in the harmony of the green meadows where the lions lay with the lambs, amongst an array of vivid-colored wildflowers that blended into a warm, caressing scent. The stream flourished by the cascading waterfall of the majestic purple mountain that shimmered with emerald, sapphire, gold, and silver.

That was where Scarlet's heart joyously fluttered while she remained elusive and unaware of any other life, except for the unity found in the promised comforts of her Creator. He came to walk with her on that ninth day of bliss, gently taking her hand as he spoke the words that shook heaven and earth.

"I love you!" he said with conviction. Scarlet's heart pounded with pride and deep admiration to have such an honor bestowed upon her, to know nothing but His love. "I always promise to love and protect you!" He assured her as his grip, slowly released the hold on Scarlet, when he promised her, "Always, I am with you," while guiding her back into her body. "Be strong," thundered through the sky.

"Hold your ground!" Quaked the universe when he, let go of her hand and commanded, "Open your eyes, child!"

Instantly, the seal was released, and Scarlet's eyelids fluttered open into the blinding brilliance of her deity. Only to find the room had faded to a dull white, with the next shutter of her unsealed eyes.

Scarlet's nearly-naked and uncovered body was blanketed with goosebumps of the unknown. Her eyes blurred and then focused on the sterile environment where the hum of the fluorescent lights and the sound of beeping machines filled the air.

Suddenly, a sheet of cold sweat replaced the blanket of goosebumps with her inability to draw a memory, and confusion flooded her existence.

Scarlet bolted into a sitting position. Her eyes shifted through the room of white linen curtains that created walls and enclosed her search for hidden information. The only thing that became transparent was that she was all alone, and only God knows where.

A white plaster contraption devoured her entire left leg, weighing her down. Feeling weak didn't discourage her from understanding the things that bound her arm and head. She traveled the miles of tubes that were laid about her and in her. But she landed on a dead-end of memories that left her baffled as she searched her mind for any recollection. Again, her eyes followed the never-ending tubes connected to her as she vainly searched the empty chambers of her soul. To find only the promises of God inspiring her.

Fear slapped the panic button, igniting Scarlet's fuse. Frantically, she began untwining the bondage that held her in place behind the fabric walls.

"What have you done to me?" echoed throughout the corridors of the intensive care unit. "Where am I?" Scarlet insisted as she began pulling at the tubes.

Unexpectedly, a woman dressed in white appeared from the other side of the curtain. Her lips moved, but Scarlet could not understand the words that were muffled by the bandages that held Scarlet's body in trepidation.

"Who are you?" demanded Scarlet. "Why, have you done this to me?" she cried as a man with a surprised look on his creased face appeared from the other side of the makeshift wall. He also was dressed in white, with a funny thing hanging around his neck.

His lips moved in the woman's direction with the power to replace her look of disbelief to urgency before she disappeared behind the curtain.

The man with the funny instrument about his neck smiled into Scarlet's anxiety while talking softly as he shined a light into her eyes. He then put the black end of the funny instrument in his ears and raised the smooth part to her chest, then to her back. The lady in white returned to the bedside as a question shot out of Scarlet's existence.

"Where am I ... who are you ... what are you doing?" the miracle patient insisted on knowing as the lady leaned over her with a smile. Before poking her with an object that caused a pinching sensation on the surface of her flesh but burned underneath.

"It's so good to see your beautiful green eyes!" Faded with Scarlet as she floated into the land of lullabies.

Scarlet's eyelids fluttered, allowing the cries of a hopeful woman to filter through the fog. "Oh, God!" The woman's cries quivered at the first sign of movement.

And when Scarlet's eyes opened, the woman's cries became sobs of praises.

"Oh, thank you, sweet Jesus!" Roxanne sang as she pulled away from the arms attempting to comfort her. She rushed up to the bed with Steven in tow.

Roxanne stroked the red curls from her daughter's bewildered expression. She tenderly left long kisses on Scarlet's forehead and her cheek while leaving wet tracks from her tears of joy, staining the young girl's flesh. Their elation shook Scarlet's confusion as she searched her mind. "Who are... these people?" But the elusive answers played with her as the woman leaned over and said, "Scarlet ..." The lady choked with consideration. "Your dad and I love you so very much!" the lady said as her body visibly convulsed with relief.

"Thank you for coming back!" the woman cried with huge crocodile tears as the man stepped up next to her. "Hey, sis, welcome back!" His voice sounded firm with relief, although Scarlet looked at them as if they were strangers while she continued her secret search for answers. *Welcome back*, Scarlet's mind taunted. "Where did I go?" Without a memory of them or anything, she searched. "What's a ... Scarlet?" She searched through the empty memory banks as she toiled in the confusion that swept her into the abyss of uncertainty before she, drifted into a slumber of dreams. In a restless sleep of chasing what, she wasn't sure! But she ran desperately toward an object she couldn't quite make out. She had come close several times.

But every time she would reach out to grab it, a huge wall would rise from the ground and slam against heaven.

Scarlet opened her eyes, for the third time in this world, to find her bed had transformed into a cage. Her consternation assured her they had intended to trap her in a space that enclosed her with the confusion.

Her flesh prickled with anxiety before widening her eyes with a fear that affixed her hands to the bars. Scarlet's mind beseeched with silent screams while the couple who claimed to be her mama and daddy stood outside of the cage, their hands embracing the bars as eager smiles plastered their faces. "We have a big surprise for you!" they claimed, as they reached into the cage and blindfolded Scarlet in the darkness of elusiveness. Uncertainty dug deep into Scarlet's soul as the cage shimmered and shook through the swinging double doors of the ICU, where Joyce had offered her husband's life.

"Okay, are you ready?" the lady screeched with anticipation that startled Scarlet. Too nervous to nod her head, Scarlet sat in the forced, darkness for what seemed like an eternity, in a space that fell dead silent. Panic hit Scarlet in the stomach, signaling the only defense she had. She pushed out a bloodcurdling scream that caused Roxanne, to pull the blindfold from her daughter's eyes.

Two young boys, clung to the one, who called himself Daddy. Their eyes staked wide open with the bewilderment of disbelief as the man gave them an encouraging push forward. The tall, blond-haired boy's expression changed from that of a cynic to an exuberant believer. The younger boy with red hair and freckles blinked his eyes with the enchantment of make-believe as they delayed their step toward their sister. Afraid if they moved too fast, she would disappear again.

"Go ahead!" the mama and the daddy encouraged the reluctant boys as they reached through the bars and touched their sister.

"You rested a long time!" Mark breathed out softly, the disbelief that had ensnared them for those nine days.

An amused smile crossed Scarlet's lips, but there was only fog mixed with the ambiguity of her elusiveness while she searched her empty mind for tangible answers. "What do they mean, finally, see me?" She tripped over that statement during her search as the man, and the woman walked up behind the boys.

"Your brothers have waited a long time to see you!" the mama and the daddy claimed. The taller towhead boy said, "Yeah ... we thought you were dead!" caused a nervous laugh to reverberate through the hall and create a whirlwind that pushed the mama, the daddy, and the brothers down the hall and out of sight.

Scarlet considered the words her visitors chose: *mama, daddy, brothers, love,* and *dead*. But she found that they made no sense as the people in white pushed her and the cage into a metal box. Curiously, Scarlet watched as one of the people in white pushed a button with a dark inscription on it that seemed to trigger the doors to close. Sealing inside it, Scarlet's fear, tickled her stomach as the box lifted.

She questioned the meaning of the rising metal box and the lit-up button with the symbol *3* on it. When the moving box came to a sudden stop, a bell rang, and the doors slid open. The people in white pushed the cage down the corridor. Scarlet locked eyes with the girl by the window, who watched the commotion with amusement as the people in white opened the cage and placed Scarlet in a bed without bars.

Scarlet spent many days in confusion, which she hid behind a fixed smile while visiting strangers talked to her and kissed her on the forehead as if they knew her. However, at night, Scarlet would cringe from the unknown shadows that danced on the ceiling and walls while cries from children filtered down the long, empty corridor. As the days wore on, so did the crowd of unbelievers thin out. Scarlet sat in the dayroom, being informed by a picture book called *What's That?* It named faces, places, animals, people, buildings, airplanes, cars, and the symbol *3*, among other characters called numbers. Scarlet devoured the material from front to back several times, attempting to retain what felt necessary. She was completely mesmerized, tracing each object with her finger as she whispered the titles, only asking relentlessly to anyone who passed by, "What's this?"

Scarlet laid claim to that book and had reviewed it for the millionth time as she sat in her bed, in deep thought, of all the things she had taken in.

She closed the book and inspected the grains of the burlap cover with her finger. "Are you ready to go home?" Startled Scarlet. She shot the suspects with a surprised expression as they shot back with rushed words.

They moved about the room, collecting Scarlet's things and placing them in a box. Then the mama and the daddy approached the bed with smiles, revealing their nicotine-stained teeth, making them yellow as the clown's smile in the book.

The mama had a dress, according to the book, that she slipped on her daughter while rushing sentences of unknown subjects at Scarlet and using words that were not in the book. A lady in white came up to the bed with a wheelchair and swept Scarlet from the only place she had ever known.

Scarlet contemplated the title of the place she came forth; as the chariot rushed toward the doors, a big light in the sky blinded her. According to the descriptions in the book, Scarlet looked straight up toward the sun that sat high in the sky above the young girl. Scarlet raised a hand to block the blinding warm rays, to find the man that she came to know as dad, she recalled seeing in that picture-book- Hospital and the lady in white, a nurse, Scarlet recalled, desperately holding on to the only things she did know.

"Let your dad have the pleasure!" the man said as he picked Scarlet up. He held her to His chest for a moment before lowering her into a cream-colored car. Although the one in the book was blue, Scarlet, thought as she scooted across the back seat and put the heavy white thing that encased her leg on the seat before turning her attention to the mysterious acts of the daddy and the mama, thanking "Sweet Jesus!" she heard them say it before they climbed into the front seat and began moving the car and Scarlet toward a place they called home.

Scarlet's heart pounded with the pursuit of the unknown as they sped past other cars, buildings, houses, trees, stores, stoplights. She recalled from the pictures in the book that she had to leave at the only place she remembered being. "What did the book call it?" Scarlet stumbled in her mind for the word. "Hos-pit-al," she broke the word down into syllables as the car pulled up into a dwelling where homes were stacked on top of each other.

Scarlet searched for the information list for such a dwelling. But as she recalled, she hadn't seen anything like that in the picture book, she concluded while Steven opened the back door with a smile of satisfaction, beaming from his eyes.

He reached inside the car and scooped Scarlet into his big, strong arms as a surge of emotions rushed him and hit him in his gut.

He took in her scent. *Damn, it feels so good*—he squeezed her a little tighter—*to hold her!* Steven thought without a change in his stature. Only in his heart could it be seen—the joy he felt, to have his family back together, again.

Scarlet's heart shook with spasms of disorientation while she floated like a prized package, gingerly over the doorway of the apartment, and was placed down the hallway in a room that portrayed a soft lavender of fresh paint. The bed was accented with a lavender spread with pink floral print, matching the pink and bellflower-blue pillowcases. White nylon curtains fluttering in the gentle breeze.

The calming colors gave her a vague memory that brushed her softly with the whims of lost information. She seemed to know something about this place—just what, she wasn't sure. But she was sure that lavender was the color of the flowers in the meadow where she recently belonged! This caused tears to flow down her cheeks as anxiety seeped into her bloodstream. It took only a fleeting moment for the anxiety to catch up with her racing mind and pollute the fading tranquility. While the wave of a perplexed heart rhythm returned, she began to doubt her place with these strangers.

"Wouldn't I remember them?" Caused her heart to flip-flop indecisively. "This?" She investigated all the treasures that adorned the room. "Anything?" her mind screamed with doubt.

CHAPTER 5

NORMAL

Roxanne glowed with the light of an expectant mother as she heeded her present opportunity. She was picking up where things had left off when she was an attentive, loving mother and a supportive wife. She paid constant attention to the ever-mounting, short-tempered, and obstinate Scarlet. Whom considered herself, jaded… while her brothers went to school. Roxanne listened to her daughter's constant complaints for the long seven days of the week.

Each day Scarlet's growing resistance toward Roxanne dashed her loving efforts and began to fray her self-esteem.

"She won't interact with the tutor!"

"And she doesn't play!" Muttered through Roxanne's dry and quivering lips. "Not like she once did!" Pushed tears over the rims of Roxanne's eyes and plopped into the sink full of dishwater.

"She's distant!" argued Roxanne's instincts. "And disconnect- ed!" thrust a powerful blow into Roxanne's gut while the Lioness stole a glance in Scarlet's direction, fixing her sight on the target of her agitation until Scarlet caught her mama's eyes. Like a deer's eyes in the headlights of an oncoming car. Surprise washed the look of resentment from Roxanne's face and turned it into a nervous smile.

Steven pondered while running up and down the aisles of the grocery store. Checking the list that his beautiful, strong, and committed wife had dictated to him over the phone. He reflected on the spotless house and the well-balanced meals she had been sweating over. "All for our family!" Steven announced proudly to the world as he drove toward his family.

"Roxanne seems to be content!" Steven's head bobbed to the rhythm of his happy heart that buoyed him up to the top of the stairs.

"I want to go to school!" rocked the foundation of the apartment building and the pressure of the explosion rattled the windows as Steven reached out to open the door.

A frazzled Roxanne sat on the couch, with her head in one hand and a cigarette clutched in her other trembling hand. She looked exhausted, with her greasy, dirt-stained shirt tucked into her hip-hugging blue jeans. Her hair was pulled back and tied up with a red handkerchief. "Why can't I go to school?" Scarlet insisted with the fury of determined persistence that spun toward the man who was called dad.

The reality that Roxanne had been reporting rippled and quaked with the rhythm of the room. He could only stand there attempting to hold his ground with his mouth spread wide open, like a famished carnivore waiting to feed on the thick state of affairs.

It didn't take long for Steven to slam his mouth shut in his disgust. He was attempting to quickly, digest a fix all solution. But when he opened his mouth, he could not talk over his gag reflex. His eyes only shifted in the temperament of the quaking room, swaying from Scarlet to Roxanne, back to Scarlet and back to Roxanne, whose head was still in her hand. His defiant daughter stood red in the face, her hands on her hips and a questioning glare in her eyes. Suddenly Roxanne exhaled the breath she had been holding. Inhaled a refreshing breath, exhaled hard, with a voice tuned relentlessly.

"Honey … please!" pushed through a cloud of cigarette smoke until the words found their way to her daughter. Roxanne raised her head during the quick, short pants of exhaustion, pushing her bloodshot eyes open to find Steven riddled with dashed hopes.

Annoyance struck a flame to Roxanne's smoldering agitation, providing the ignition to blast her from the couch. She began orbiting around the room, shooting daggers of helplessness at Steven with her smoldering almond eyes, which had begun to darken. Steven shot a watchful eye on the comet Roxanne, who was puffing away on a cigarette, creating a trail of smoke. He calculated the gyrating, Roxanne. And when she passed by him, he invaded her airspace long enough to place the groceries on the table and exited her orbit with no close calls.

Steven took his daughter's hand as he sat in his chair. Scarlet shimmied her way into the dad's lap as the comet Roxanne sored by. Steven and Scarlet allowed Roxanne full range to orbit.

"Dad? I just wanna go to school!" Steven smiled into his daughter's pleas as he began to explain to her tenderly.

"The school staff and the doctors thought you need to take it slow!"

Caused Roxanne's orbit to screech to a halt. "I told her that!" charred Steven's soul with the abyss of her dark eyes.

"I'm fine!" Scarlet bellowed. "Except for this stupid cast on my leg!" Scarlet complained as she tugged and pulled on the heavy plaster appendage that nearly had the bottom walked off.

Scarlet began pounding on the nagging itch that would not be satisfied.

Roxanne thrust a stretched-out coat hanger to Scarlet while considering her daughter's words. *She's probably right. She might be fine?* slanted Roxanne's eyes as she analyzed her daughter, who was digging the coat hanger throughout the full-length cast. *But she is different!* Roxanne concluded her thought as she watched her daughter conquer that nagging itch. *Something's definitely different about that girl!* Pounded the gavel of those in council, over the edge, with enough force to tremble Roxanne's heart as she offered a faint smile to her irritated daughter. "Let's call the doctor!" Anxiety shot out as Roxanne picked up the phone, dialing the doctors number; cutting the tension in the room and permitting Steven to side with his wife.

"If he says you're ready, then you can go back to school!" Assured Steven's restless daughter.

CHAPTER 6

BONDING

Jubilation shook Scarlet's world into a wiggle dance of sovereignty as she watched the doctor prepare to write orders to have the cast removed. She listened to his encouraging words, which sounded with the warmth of a bonded relationship.

"I think you deserve to go back to school!" he stated with a smile as he scrawled a release for school on his prescription pad.

"You have been so very patient while letting your body heal." He rubbed Scarlet's head, which was nodding in agreement. Her smile froze in place as she limped out of the doctor's office with Roxanne in tow, beckoning Scarlet, to use her crutches. But Scarlet only waved her mama off as her satisfied smile crutched her weak leg and delivered the determined girl to the car.

Scarlet slid across the seat of the Cadillac with images of running and playing with her brothers at school and at home, made her heart leap with joy. As the scenarios of happy TV children playing in laughter coursed through Scarlet's mind and stretched her frozen smile even further.

Mama drove with an expression of contemplation, distancing her from Scarlet, who was lightly rubbing the long-darkened hair on her new and improved leg. Suddenly, a sharp turn bounced the car and its occupants into a parking spot at one of the new malls.

Roxanne shut the engine down as she rocked back and forth, anticipating her compulsive whims.

"In celebration of your leg …" Mama turned in Scarlet's direction, her wild eyes smiled as animation quickly moved her lips; In a fashion, Scarlet had never seen.

This character was self-motivated and confident as she talked with her hands and blew smoke from her mouth before turning a pointed finger out the front windshield. "We're going into this huge store!"

The actor smiled, turning her wide eyes into Scarlet's astounded expression. "In there, is a bunch of smaller stores!" She reached over and squeezed her daughter's arm. "Let's go shopping!" Exhilaration, swung Mama's door open. "You can pick anything you want!" She insisted, into Scarlet's overwhelmed expression, before she slipped out the door. Scarlet kept an eye on the culprit that transforms Mama from time to time.

The transmuted closed the door with a solid push of her hip and slid down the slender body of the Cadillac. She stopped at the rear end of the car and leaned her butt against the bumper. Scarlet watched the lady blow on her nails, like they were wet. Taking that as a cue, to exhale the breath, she had been holding. She sucked in a lung full of courage and met the Mama at the rear of the car.

Scarlet roamed the isles, stopping at the Tonka trucks and the cars. She look long and hard at the hot wheel race tracks, trying to pick something, she could share with her brothers.

"Get something, just for you!" the Mama personality insisted as though she could read Scarlet's mind. The imposter, snatched up

Scarlet's hand and pulled her down the isles until they reached the new doll that had just been released.

The invader's eyes smoldered without contemplation to the price tag as she continued to admire the doll. She demonstrated how the hair would grow longer or become shorter by pushing a button on the doll's back. "Cutest thing, I ever did see!" the imposter testified, while stroking the doll's hair before she batted an eyelash at Roxanne's daughter. She spun on her heels and nearly walked on clouds that led up to the register. Scarlet followed just behind the lady, called Mama, as she pulled the doll from the box and cradled it in her arms. Cooing to the doll as she paid cash, for her new baby. Scarlet scampered to catch up with the imposter as she rushed out the door, cooing the doll. Scarlet was out of breath when she reached the car, where Mama sat with the doll, stroking her long hair.

"Scarlet, you've always wanted a sister," the imposter informed Roxanne's daughter. "I've decided this is your sister, Princess!" Roxanne's eyes smoldered. "It is your job, to take care of her!" stated the very strange-acting lady. "If anything happens to her, your mama will be very upset!" Roxy blew smoke into Scarlet's face, then kissed the doll's face and cooed to it.

"Princess, this is your big sister, Scarlet." She again stroked the doll's face before she put her ear to the doll's mouth, listening to its silent words. "Don't worry, Scarlet will take care, of your every need!" And on that promise, Roxy gingerly offered Scarlet her first responsibility. Scarlet wasn't sure if that was her cue. She remained still, her hands in her lap. She was breathing deep with exhaustion and with her leg hurting.

"Well, girl"—Roxy stroked the doll's face—"you think, you can handle this?" Roxy's eyes shot arrows of a dare into Roxanne's daughter's direction.

Scarlet reached out for the doll, but the lady pulled the doll back. "Can you keep your mama from getting mad?" Roxy's, question Raised Scarlet's eyebrows, before she reluctantly snatched the doll from the person behind the steering wheel and laid it face-down on her lap. Roxy winked during a chuckle, at Scarlet's rebellion. The imposter put Scarlet's name atop of Steven's, on the destroy list, then exhaled in Scarlet's face before she straightened her back behind the stirring-wheel.

Stevie and Mark were waiting on the stairs when their mama came around the corner of the parking garage. She was smiling and talking to their cast-less, crutching sister, who had a new toy clutched between her arm and the crutch.

"Huh ... what are yah boys doing here?" Their mama cackled as she walked by, patting each of them on the head. "The door's locked!" Wrung Stevie's words out in a hurtful tone while attempting to express irritation for their Mama's constant attention for Scarlet. And for making them feel left out, more than once.

Mark said nothing; he only noticed the annoyed look on his mama's face while a nonnurturing motion waved the boys off as she began to climb the stairs.

"I'm sorry, but your sister," the unfamiliar personality said.

"Blah, blah, blah!" Stevie muttered as he followed her up the stairs.

"The conversation is always all about her!" Stevie continued his grumbling up the stairs. One stair behind her, Stevie mimicked his mama's walk. At the halfway point of the tall case of stairs, Mark caught his brother's scowl over his shoulder. Beaming down at Scarlet, his heart pinging for half of the attention, Mama gave to his sister.

A week later, a particular act of neglect had caused the kidnapping of the doll that Mama had picked out. Nevertheless, the ransom was never delivered. And the missing doll had been gone for three days before Mama needed to know what had happened to it. She needed to know so badly, she cried while tearing the apartment apart and yelling at the boys. "Mama… Mama, please," the boys pleaded through her judgment. "We didn't take the doll!" they testified.

The defiant Scarlet wanted to step in for her brothers and take credit where credit was due.

But she didn't, because the doll was stupid, and she did not like being singled out! She settled on that mindset while watching the chaos of the frantic commotions of the lady who called herself Mama. Scarlet finalized her determination with reasoning.

"Most of all, she didn't like Stevie and Mark being mad at her!" she mumbled under the loud and angry Mama. Scarlet's eyes smiled deviously. "So, I sacrificed the doll!" she admitted, her guilt, under her breath while recalling bandaging her latest wounds. The ones she had received while attempting to help build dirt roads.

"To drive the boys' cars on!" came out in the whisper of a memory.

"Chased off with an artillery of dirt clods!" And the pounding of Stevie's hurtful words.

"Pansies that can't go to school are too fragile to build roads!" Those words sent Scarlet's blood into a rapid boil. The steam blew through her nostrils. It was charging her toward the only other alternative, which was to retreat to the top of the stairs. "The boys, never want to play with me!" she protested before turning to lick her wounds. She watched her brothers continue to laugh at her cost as they planned to excavate the mounds of dirt into nice, smooth roads.

Scarlet concocted a plan of her own just as the boys were close "to having, some of the best roads in America!" They gloated just as Scarlet rushed into the apartment to prepare for her retaliation. "I want to go to school!" she insisted to her parents as she blurred by them on the way to the kitchen. "You have to wait until the other doctor releases you!" the mama and the dad chorused in a repetitive tone.

"I need to go to the doctor today!" Scarlet called back from the kitchen, where she began filling a pitcher with water. "I will call him, on Monday." Roxanne's voice shook from the front room.

Scarlet calculated the days as she struggled to lift the full pitcher of water from the sink. "Today's Thursday … Call him, today!" she demanded with a heavy voice as she walked back across the apartment.

Roxanne watched her daughter with a queer expression as Scarlet carried her determination out the door before she rushed to the phone to call Dr. White's office. She related to the nurse, "Scarlet's becoming agitated … and was making demands!"

The nurse chuckled with experience when she said, "Sounds like she's feeling better?"

Roxanne repressed the explosive expressions that boiled in the acidic secretions that belonged to, Anxiety. "No, I think something is terribly wrong?" she said firmly, with enough power to change the nurse's disposition to serious. Roxanne insisted, "Scarlet was not the same, let alone okay!" her voice quivered into the nurse's ear.

"Bring her in tomorrow morning. We'll take a look!" Said the nurse, calming the waves that threatened to swallow Roxanne.

Silently, Scarlet balanced the pitcher on the railing just above her brothers. While calculating her aim, the butterflies tickled her stomach as they picked up the broken pieces of her heart, gingerly placing them back where they belonged.

When the butterflies had nearly finished gluing her life support together, her shrewd smile turned conniving as a slight giggle released with the butterfly's lead.

Slowly, Scarlet began to tilt the pitcher when she received orders, dump the container upside down-explode those, soft dirt roads. Mud splashed everywhere and left the boys dripping with a soupy mess of dirt road artifacts.

"Hey, what the heck?" they shouted as they jumped up to find the culprit.

Suddenly, heroic laughter echoed off the cement walls that enclosed their world, which now had the remains of mud-splattered roads all over the place.

Scarlet's laughter echoed throughout the courtyard with a job well done. But when the boys looked up in her direction with their muddy faces, her laughter began to rumble thunderously, clapping loudly and rolling over the tainted destruction. Scarlet's index finger extended and pointed in their direction as she convulsed with laughter. She was doubling over in an attempt to stop the pain that burned in her gut.

She fought to regain control over "the funniest thing, I'd ever seen!" she stated out loud. Scarlet slapped her leg before wiping at the tears that clouded her vision and choked back the last of her giggles. When her vision cleared, she found she was "the only one there!" She choked on her breath as anger flooded her bloodstream.

She used the rail of the staircase to crutch her weak leg down the stairs and did a half skip-run out toward the street, where her brothers were riding bikes and howling in laughter.

Scarlet walked right in front of the oncoming bicycles with a defiant disposition that dared them to hit her. Stevie came barreling down on Scarlet, playing chicken with his sister, who was quickly becoming an adversary. He swerved only inches from her as he stuck up his middle finger and blared his pretend horn. "Get out of the road, stupid, before I run you over!" His finger missed stabbing her in the eye, but his words pierced her heart.

Scarlet's entire body began to shake from the heat that boiled her blood. Making her want to cry and scream out with frustration. Instead, Scarlet spun on her heels, refusing the opponent's the satisfaction of publicly impaling her and watching her die.

She retreated to the top of the stairs, sulking in solitude and licking her wounds in isolation, her heart pounding, perspiration from every pour. The tension in her shoulders pinched hard enough to roll her body onto the cold concrete.

Her body, lay lifeless. Not one thing went through her mind. Just an absence of everything. Her pain continued to throb and absorb her life's ambitions.

"Be strong!" caressed the spirit of the young girl. "Remember, I love you!" voiced her soul. Then it reminded her. "You don't belong here. Anyways!" encouraged her as she attended her remaining wounds. Sparking a conclusion: "People can hurt me; only, if I let them!" Numbed Scarlet's existence a little more when she accepted the condolences of the comforting words as a resolution.

Scarlet walked through the apartment and passed by her mama on the way to her lavender-accented bedroom. She saw Mama's doll lying on the matrimonial bed of the mama and the dad. Outside of how the doll found its way back, she gave it no real consideration. She could only sit on the end of her own bed, allowing the promises of her deity to soothe her. Suddenly, an arrow pierced the lower tender spot of her back. Spinning her into the direction of the doll, who was staring her down with x-ray vision. She was attempting to burn Scarlet's soul from across the hall. Scarlet sprung up, stealth maneuvers, delivered her unnoticed into mama and dad's room. Scarlet gave the doll a smile full of bad intent as she snatched the doll by its hair and silently glided back to her room.

Scarlet stood on her bed, struggling in her attempts to open the window when Persistence showed up and offered to help. Scarlet laughed along with Persistence's hardy chuckle as she dropped to her knees with puffs of success heaving her chest. Exhaustion from the day secreted Scarlet's mind, but that didn't stop her from giving the doll an angelic smile before she threw it, as hard as she could, down onto the blacktop of the rancid-smelling parking garage.

Roxy was watching Scarlet out of the corner of Roxanne's eye. The girl had pushed her dinner across the plate throughout nearly the entire dinner hour.

Roxy considered, for the fourth time, to reach out and stop Scarlet dead in her tracks.

But Roxanne abruptly pushed her chair out, gravitating toward the cigarette pack that sat on the counter behind her daughter. Roxy first struck a match to Roxanne's cigarette, then spun Roxanne in the direction of her daughter. Scarlet hadn't even noticed the deviant eye that aimed at her. *We know, it was the girl!* Roxy insisted, to Roxanne's disbelief, with enough power to expel the smoke from Roxanne and pollute Scarlet's personal space.

"What's up, Scarlet!" lingered over the dinner table, long enough to draw the entire family's attention. Scarlet only shrugged her shoulders and ignored the staring eyes by not engaging their inquiring minds. Weeks of frustration had hit its non-compassionate point- Causing Roxanne, to exhale bellows of toxin from her cigarette into her daughter's face. "Young lady, you can go to bed!" spun Scarlet's look of defiance through the smoke and attempted to shoot her Mama. But the imposter stepped in front of Roxanne and fired back at Scarlet with a pointed finger. She was demanding that she follow the orders of her Mama, or die. Scarlet intentionally dropped her fork to her plate. The clanking continued to reverberate throughout the apartment as Scarlet spun away from the table and disappeared.

Damn her defiance! insisted the chastising companions as Roxanne snuffed out her cigarette and lit another. Her eyes darkened as the companions suggested, *she needs a good spanking!*

Scarlet lay on her bed with her legs extended up the wall and her head hanging off the bed. Her eyes burned, and her cheeks felt flush with anger and resentment. "They can only hurt me, if I allow it!" She insisted to the only deity in the room. "I won't cry, and I will be strong!" she assured the one who placed her into this situation, just as the door opened.

Dad stood at the door, with the brooding Mama behind him with her dark eyes.

Spank her! dared the companions. Roxanne's eye twitched as she considered the suggestion.

"Hey, bubble butt!" the dad said into the distance between him and his daughter.

Scarlet's eyebrows knitted for the meaning of his words as the parental units attempted to cross that distance between them and their firstborn, with doubt painted on their faces. Scarlet pulled back from the mama and the dad's intents as they leaned in to kiss her, good night.

"Can I go to school with the boys in the morning?" Searching relentlessly for an answer she wanted to hear while the parents insisted their kisses onto her forehead.

"No. Tomorrow, you have an appointment with Dr. White!" Roxanne offered in a rushed fashion.

"Then next Monday, you can go to school!" the dad said with a hopeful smile- but doubt, echoed his words.

Scarlet considered their lack of optimism with her own challenging smile of persistence, which refused to be hindered.

"The doctor will say, it's all right!" was all she offered as she rolled over, listening for her parents to leave her alone in the dark. It was there she contemplated all she had learned in the past two months. And with a fresh covering of sleepy dust coating Scarlet's eyelids, they grew heavy and began to shutter. "Things are not so bad!" she whispered to the fairy that dumped more sleepy dust on her eyes. "I wish my brothers... would let me play..."—Scarlet yawned, and her eyelids slammed shut—"with them!" She mumbled a whisper to the fairy as her body took flight into slumberland and began the trajectory of her questioning subconscious.

"What exactly is school?" Her words trailed her as she spun into the astral plane, like a shooting star. "Maybe there, my brothers, will play with me?" She could see herself mumbling in council with the overworked fairy, who insisted, "Next stop, deep sleep!" the fairy announced, as she dumped another load of dust on Scarlet's eyes.

"What's the difference, between home and school?" Scarlet asked before she curled into the fetal position. "Mama, won't be there!" delivered her safely in lullaby-land.

Scarlet rose with the sun to find her brothers eating cereal at the coffee table and watching cartoons. She stood almost in front of the television while waiting for their recognition. After a few minutes of being invisible, Scarlet climbed over the arm of the couch and squeezed in between her already-annoyed brothers. "I want to go to school with you guys?" Rushed at them before Stevie shoved her into the cartoon-enthralled Mark.

"Stop it!" Mark protested as he slammed all his might into his sister and smashed her into Stevie.

"Move!" Stevie demanded as he pushed into Scarlet, toppling over her. He scooped her up and threw her onto the floor before returning his attention to the animated characters on television. Scarlet was lying crumpled on the floor like an unwanted piece of trash, heated by frustration that threatened to push tears over the rims of her eyes. Her hopes for their morning interaction weren't going as planned. But she found the strength to stand her ground.

"If the doctor says it's OK, I will be starting school, on Monday!"

Scarlet attempted to enlighten her brothers, who were practicing ignoring her without the slightest bit of interest, enthusiasm, emotion, or any reaction at all.

Scarlet's hopeful smile, which had beamed from her eyes and poured out onto the path she walked this morning, had now turned to a dark, somber frown by the time Dad came out of the room. "Ready, boys?" Created a ruckus as the boys jumped up, hugged Mama, and ran out the door. Steven traded smiles with Roxanne as he leaned down and kissed his daughter without noticing the look of dissatisfaction spread across her face.

"Good luck, at the doctors!" Steven encouraged-as he peered into his daughter's eyes for the first time this morning.

Scarlet, defiantly wiped the kiss from her face. "I will be, starting school on Monday!" She underscored a daring tone. "Just you, wait and see!" Bruised both of her parents into thought.

The Mama and the dad turned a spontaneous look toward one another while concern painted their faces before they spun and walked out the front door. They paused long enough to talk about her. But Scarlet, didn't care. She felt resolved in her steadfast decision as she pronounced each word with conviction.

"I won't, accept no for an answer!" she barked in a tone for everyone to hear. "If anyone... is listening!" Sprang her from the floor and delivered her behind her bedroom door.

CHAPTER 7

LACKING

"Funny thing—not being able to remember, ever dressing yourself!" Scarlet challenged her memory as she put on her last shoe, mama opened the door.

"You dressed yourself?" surged Roxanne's voice with the sound of amazement as she advanced toward her daughter's irritated demeanor and sat next to her on the bed. "You look, beautiful!" Roxanne offered as she reached out and pushed back the long red locks from her daughter's face.

Scarlet turned a watchful eye to the constantly meddling woman. *Everything I do, is such, a big deal?* Scarlet thought as she turned with a courteous smile to the doting lady, who continued chattering away.

Why is it I have no feelings for this woman? Not good or bad—just nothing! Scarlet continued searching her mind while a blanket of goosebumps covered her flesh.

Anxiety wooed Roxanne's heart while waiting for her daughter to reply.

But Scarlet only sat staring back at her. Deep consideration shaped her face while shards of ice ripped through Roxanne's veins.

"Well, let's brush your hair," She attempted to encourage her daughter's speechless mood. "Then we'll go see Dr. White!" Roxanne came to a stance while she finished her sentence, reaching out to take her daughter's hand.

"I, can do it!" Scarlet insisted before she shot out of the room and left Roxanne isolated in shock from the cosmic distance between her and Scarlet.

"What the hell … we used to be inseparable!" shook Roxanne's soul.

"Why is it, she never smiles or plays?" Roxanne questioned.

"Why does she act so defiant when all I'm trying to do is, love her?" Roxanne's body shuddered from the shards of ice that stuck her in the heart, causing her to choke back her tears before she was able to paste a fake smile to her lips and go to find Scarlet.

Scarlet was sitting on the couch looking at a book when Roxanne walked into the front room. She paused to watch her daughter for a short moment, to reconsider her questions concerning her daughter. Suddenly, Scarlet looked up at her and then turned to inspect herself for flaws.

"What?" Caught Roxanne in the act of consideration.

Maybe, this really isn't your daughter? signaled Anxiety to expel the next group of scorched words from her throat.

"Are you ready, to go?" rushed from Roxanne's parched throat.

Scarlet sprang up from the couch, sprinting out the door and down the thirty-six stairs. Taking them two at a time as she had watched her brothers do many times from that stupid wheelchair. Images flooded through Scarlet's mind as she approached the bottom of the stairs. She was moving briskly enough that her hair bounced on each step.

The momentum sprang Scarlet from the third step, landing at the bottom of the stairs. She spun and made a mad dash to the car.

Roxanne opened the driver's door and slipped in behind the steering wheel, turning to smile at her daughter. "I saw you take those stairs—that was great!" Roxanne watched her daughter adjust herself in the seat so she could see out the window. But still, no words. "You must be, really excited?" Roxanne said to her fidgeting daughter.

"Yeah, I can't wait, for school on Monday!" Scarlet agreed as she wiggled in her seat with anticipation before reining her excitement and turning her attention to the view out the window.

Scarlet curiously turned an inspecting eye toward Mama. She drove with one hand while drinking a Pepsi and smoking a cigarette with the other. She sang, out of tune with the radio. A beautiful, well-groomed woman with thin features.

Her dark-auburn hair bore a streak of gray that she pinned back from her pale face. She had long fingers, perfected by strong nails that grew long.

Softness caressed her face, but pain and concern darkened the flesh around her eyes. Unexpectedly, those haunted eyes turned to Scarlet with a needful smile that silently gravitated their hands to the center of the seat until their fingers intertwined. Roxanne's smile widened as she exhaled a breath she had been holding since her run to the hospital. While a funny feeling pulsed through Scarlet's body and caused her heart to beat a little faster.

CHAPTER 8

NEVER THE SAME

Roxanne couldn't get the keys out of the ignition before Scarlet was standing at the door of the doctor's office. "Come on, mama," she called impatiently before sailing into the building and docking in a chair. Scarlet sat looking at a magazine while mama talked to the people behind the desk, but before she turned the page, the nurse had called her back to the examination room. Eagerly, Scarlet leaped up onto the table and sat quietly with confidence, knowing she would get what she came for, as Scarlet turned her attention to the fancy documents that were sealed in black frames with spotless glass. Suddenly, the spotless glass caught the reflection of the opening door as an older plump man came into the room.

Scarlet felt a warm respect for this jolly individual who wore gold-wired spectacles that hung on the edge of his nose as he reviewed a five-inch-thick chart that contained information about the young girl's progress.

Scarlet's heart skipped beats with anticipation when Dr. White sat on his doctor's stool and sailed across the room, docking in front of her. He took her hand and gently squeezed it. Scarlet wrenched his hand with all her might. Demonstrating her ability to remember and follow directions with determination and strength.

"Oww ... mercy!" he cried in play before smiling into her dull but eager eyes, noting the right-side, somewhat droopy. The doctor smiled as he patted the young girl's leg. He stood up and walked across the room, picking up one of his sterile instruments. He turned back to the table where Scarlet was wiggling with expectations.

The doctor shined a light into her eyes and stared into them. Scarlet became impatient with the well-known routine and suddenly jumped down from the table.

"I'm fine!" she insisted into the surprised and laughing face of the doctor.

The companions chuckled with embarrassment as Roxanne slapped the doctor on the leg and gave him an "I told you!" kind of look. But the doctor ignored Roxanne's reaction as he patted the examining table, insisting he finish his exam.

Dr. White took an instrument with a rubber end, tapping her knees and her ankles, then did the same to her elbows. He looked up into Scarlet's eyes. "Can you close your eyes? Hold out your arms and touch your nose with your fingertip." She eagerly completed his examination and passed his test with flying colors.

"Scarlet, how're your brothers?" Turned Scarlet's smile to a frown. The doctor didn't wait for a reply. "How're things at home?" Scarlet's eyebrows rose at the mention of the word *home*. The doctor, smiled at his patient and patted her on the knee. "How do you feel, Scarlet?"

Caused the girl head to react like a turtle, retracting into its shell, when she shrugged into his question. "I feel fine!" She hesitated. "I ... I want to go to school. So, I can play with my brothers!"

The doctor nodded his head as if he knew what her silent words meant while he rolled away from Scarlet into the center of the room.

Scarlet's nervous giggling plastered her face with a forced smile while she watched him silently scribble notes into a file that had her name on it. A minute later, he sat back on his stool and kicked his legs out in front of him as he looked into Roxanne's worried eyes. "She looks great!" Turned Roxanne's watchful eye over to Skepticism.

"So, what's the problem?" he questioned. Roxanne's eyes shifted from the doctor to Scarlet, whose eyes were also locked on her mama. The ground quaked from holding back her opinion. Her inability to speak frankly in front of the child irritated the hostile companions and set off the alarms that caused waves of static to pollute Roxanne's bloodstream. "She's acting, defiant and impatient ... maybe even detached!" The Lioness bit while Roxanne shot the doctor a daring look. Trying to signal him, that she may have brought the wrong girl home from the hospital without letting Scarlet know.

"She doesn't play, and she doesn't smile!" Roxanne searched her mind for other evidence. "She's just ... not the same!" Roxanne labored her one-sided explanation in a shaky voice.

Dr. White turned and looked at Scarlet. "How do you feel?" Caused the young girl's shoulders to shrug with the consideration—she had nothing, to compare to. "When can I go to school?" Remained her top priority, to conquer.

The doctor smiled at his patient, who defied all odds—a miracle, he might say.

"So, you want to go to school?" He enticed the girl into a smiling wiggle dance. "On Monday?"

Scarlet shrieked with an overwhelming excitement while vigorously nodding her head in agreement. "Please!" she begged into folded hands.

The pleased professional smiled at Scarlet's enthusiasm while he finished writing notes in her file. "Your daughter, is physically fine!" He turned to his released patient's worrisome mother.

"Yeah, but—" Roxanne tried to protest.

"You're fortunate to have her, at all!" cut Roxanne's words short as she related; Scarlet, really was not Scarlet. The doctor confirmed as he reached out and grasped Roxanne's hand, "You just need to be patient." Caused Roxanne, to shoot him an offended expression. "Scarlet has been through a lot!" the doctor stated as he turned his eyes to Scarlet before continuing to write in her chart. "She may never be who she was before!" he added as he tore a paper from his pad and handed it to Roxanne. The note released the physically and mentally strong girl, back to school. "It is good to see you doing so well!" he said, as he stood up in front of Scarlet with a sincere smile painting his rosy cheeks.

"You look great!" caused Scarlet to begin another wiggle dance as she bobbed her head in agreement. "I think, you are ready, to go to school!" sent the young girl sailing off the table and into the arms of the pleased doctor. She broke loose when she began a victory dance that landed her out in the waiting room.

Roxanne shot the doctor an inquisitive look while her gut instinct challenged his judgment. "Are you sure?" Defiled his qualifications. But Dr. White smiled into her doubt, placing his hand gently on Roxanne's shoulder as he guided her out into the waiting room while speaking in a whisper.

Roxanne felt some relief as they left the building, with her daughter leading the way when she heard that Scarlet was physically fine. Although Roxanne wasn't sure she would ever have her daughter back, slammed into Roxanne's solar plexus hard enough to activate her gag reflex. "God, please!" rushed from her soul, chorusing from every fiber of her being. Her hollow womb burned with pain. While the doubting Thomas and Roxanne's companions taunted her.

She might as well, wear black! heckled Irony.

Scarlet, will never be the same! puked out onto the floorboard of the car. Roxanne shot an inquiring eye in Scarlet's direction, who was staring out the window, where everything appeared new to her: The lights, buildings, cars, and the people on the streets fascinated her! Roxanne concluded privately with the companions, who insisted on chain-smoking. Suddenly, Scarlet's head abruptly snapped around to find suspicion glazing from Mama's eyes.

Mama's suspicion shifted to guilt before she shifted her eyes from the alien and turned them back to the road. Roxanne's body trembled from the waves of anxiety, fueled by Scarlet's pensive stare. *What is she thinking?* burned Roxanne.

Ask… her! The compassionate companions challenged. *Who really gives a rat's ass?* insisted the callous companions. Roxanne stole a glimpse of Scarlet, who sat staring at her with a blank expression on her face. *Who is that?"* set the companions on edge while sparking Roxanne's blood to a boil and scorching her heart.

"Where's my daughter?" forced tears to the rims of Roxanne's eyes.

"When's Monday?" broke the private inquest and sprung Roxanne into a quivering motion with enough power to shake a nervous laugh from her that caught in a cough.

Roxanne cleared her throat and her mind as she indulged in conversation with this stranger. "Today's Friday … Saturday, Sunday, then Monday!" Mama offered before looking into the girl's direction. Scarlet was quiet for a few minutes as she looked out the window.

"How many days?" the puzzled Scarlet asked.

"Three days!" Mama assured Scarlet into contemplation.

"That's a long time," Ended Scarlet's interrogation.

Roxanne laughed as she pulled into the school driveway. "Not really!" she offered as Scarlet spun in her seat until she spotted her brothers sitting on the grass. "Stop … stop!" Scarlet insisted. "There they are!" she said, holding the doorhandle in anticipation of the car stopping. But the door popped open before the car had come to a complete stop. Roxanne's heart stopped as flashbacks of dreaded moments threw Mama across the bench seat to protect the child, but Scarlet's body sprang into the air like a bomb that exploded on top of her brothers.

"I get to go to school, on Monday!" sang the sister of the annoyed brothers, who only rolled her off them and scampered to their feet without giving their sister any recognition at all. "Monday, I'm going to school!" she attempted again to the backs of her brothers as she rushed up behind them. Stevie continued to usher his little brother into the back seat before he slid in. But when Scarlet attempted to go through the door, Stevie blocked it with his foot.

"Girls, sit in the front!" he demanded before pushing her back and slamming the door. Roxanne shot a disappointed eye at her boys before she called through the open window and patted the front seat. "I want you to sit with me, anyways!" she said, in hopes of consoling her daughter's hurt feelings. But all she managed to do was to wedge the siblings further apart as the boys shot glaring looks in Scarlet's direction and stuck their tongues out into the pleading expressions of her wanting eyes.

Mama drank Pepsi and smoked cigarettes while the brothers wrestled in the back seat. Scarlet's heart ached with confused emotions that turned her to stare out the window as she recalled her mama's words that left her wondering, *What, did she mean, when she told the doctor—she was not the same?* This deepened the crevasses of her confusion.

"How could I be different?" flooded Scarlet as she searched for the meaning of *different*. But the answers remained elusive. And no matter how hard she tried, she could not remember anything before the bright light dimmed. Trying to remember the time before she was told these boys were her brothers. And this woman, her mother.

Scarlet turned an eye to the reflection in the mirror to find her brothers smiling in a united bond. Scarlet was somewhat amused by their connection. While searching for the reasons why her brothers disliked her. Or why her dad, rarely paid attention to her?

But, most of all, she didn't understand why everyone marveled at her, as if she were a miracle.

CHAPTER 9

INTANGIBLE

Elation shook the butterflies into a freedom flutter as Scarlet quickly groomed herself while daydreaming of new and exciting things. The dancing butterflies tickled Scarlet into laughter as they waltzed her toward the kitchen, where mama was preparing breakfast. "It's Monday!" Scarlet sang as she jumped into the chair and landed on her knees. "It's Monday, Monday, Monday!" filled the room with her chorusing excitement as she wiggled down into her chair. "I can't wait, to go to school!" she harmonized with the butterfly's rhythm.

Roxanne watched her daughter sway to the tune that she sang softly while straightening the hem of her dress and sweating out the last minutes of her imprisonment. "Is it time to go to school?" voiced an anxious Scarlet with high expectations as mama placed glasses of juice on the dining table.

"Honey, you must be excited," Roxanne offered with a quirky smile.

"You got ready, really fast!" Mama said into Scarlet's nodding motion as the boys came from their room, half-dresses and plopped down at the table.

Scarlet watched them rub sleepy dirt from their eyes as she pulled her knees up under her, straightened her beautiful dress before she leaned across the table and whispered into her brother's direction. "I get to go to school and play!" Created a budding song to ring into a shrill pitch from Scarlet. The boys covered their ears in protest as they shot their sister an outlandish look before popping her bubble.

"You, don't go to school to play!" Stevie chastised Scarlet.

"Yeah, you go to school to learn!" her youngest sibling cast his stones into his sister's pond of hope.

Collapsing into her chair, Scarlet turned a pale white, baffled by the news that nearly knocked her out. Their words danced in her head with pitchforks stabbing at her efforts. She silently watched the boys finish their breakfast in a brotherly bond before they left the table, giggling and leaving their sister baffled in isolation.

Scarlet pushed her food around on the plate while her mind interrogated her brother's words. "What do they mean you don't go to school to play"—Twisted her eyebrows with confusion—"but to learn!" Slapped the button of the unknown of another intangible notion going unanswered. "How am I going to earn my brother's respect?" closed the doors on her anticipations. "What is learning!" pushed the muck of confusion around in her head while fear of the unknown bubbled in her stomach.

"Now that it is clear school is not going to provide me with that opportunity!" Choked out her hopes and replaced them with her only other option. "I will work hard at that school, learning things!" stirred the pot of the unknown. "Prove to them all, I can do anything I put my mind to!" Again, her mumbled thoughts stirred the pot of the unknown. But the last thought silenced her for a long moment when she could not recall putting her mind to anything before.

Roxanne came out of the kitchen to find her daughter sitting in a pout of somber deliberation. She frowned from the nagging temptation that urged her to ask what was wrong. But Dread silenced her as she recalled the doctor's words. "She may never be ..." Scorched Roxanne's heart. "You're lucky!" Trembled Roxanne's world, causing tears to pool and almost gush over the rims of her eyes, as she forced a smile to curve her lips while she dabbed the tears from her eyes. "So, you're ready to go?" Roxanne asked the alien that invaded her daughter. Who prohibited Scarlet from noticing another presence in the room?

Roxy, wanted to reach out to touch that girl, for a good week now. She began urging Roxanne, *Smack her!* Mama entertained that thought with reservation when she reached out and touched the girl's shoulder. She wanted to beckon the alien's attention so she could ask a question. Just when she was about to touch her, Scarlet's head snapped up. Her sorrowful eyes shot a look of oblivion into the woman's eyes for a long moment. When Scarlet shrugged her shoulders and sighed a hesitant reply. "Yeah!" was all she said, but it was enough to make Roxanne's heart quiver with disturbing emotions. What has stolen her daughter's zeal? Created a strong urge in Roxanne's bosom to grab a hold of the invader who had possessed her daughter and vigorously shake the body snatcher out of her. However, when she took a step toward the invader, "You're lucky, to have her at all!" spun Roxanne in her tracks and carried her back into the kitchen, where the remaining dirty dishes waited.

Scarlet was sulking in frustration when her brothers came out of their bedroom laughing and pushing each other onto the couch, where they rolled in play. Scarlet couldn't help laughing, as the competition remained on an even ground. But when Stevie had dominated his younger brother by sitting on his head and slapping his belly until it turned pink, Scarlet instinctively jumped out of her chair and tackled the rascal, slamming him hard into the ground and pinning him under her.

"Get off me!" Stevie moaned as he attempted to struggle out from under his sister's champion wrestler's hold. Mark howled with laughter when Scarlet began grinding her knees into Stevie's arms and making him squeal out his next words of warning. "You little twit—I'm gonna kill you!" Clenched Roxanne's bowels and pulled her into the living room, with her mouth open and her legs in quick stride.

However, when she found her daughter sitting on Stevie's chest, administering the Chinese torture to him, Roxanne froze in her tracks as her eyebrows untwisted and an unfamiliar emotion bubbled up. Roxy busted a gut, and laughter exploded out of Roxanne. She laughed so hard she slapped her knee before she held her aching gut and wiped tears from her eyes.

Stevie's face turned a deep red, pushing the veins in his forehead to the surface and igniting a demonic anger that threw his sister into the wall. He levitated from the floor. "What's, so damn funny?" Stevie screamed into mama's face, cutting the giggling sound from her throat. "That animal, attacked me!" he spat out as he pointed a daggered finger at his suspect with enough power to cut Roxanne's breath as her eyes shot from her hostile son to her daughter, who lay crumpled on the floor.

Static blared over the whispers of her companions, who attempted to push through the muddled mess and advise her. Instead, the voices were washed away in the churning agitation of fretfulness. "Are you ready, to go?" quivered through Roxanne's body and spilled from her mouth, hastening the disarray, by moving past it. Without recognition for his emotions, Stevie's eyes widened as his mouth fell open. A million questions bombarded him in a heated barrage while searching for the skills to cope with this situation. But when his search came up unfruitful, he realized he had only one option.

Instead of talking and giving his emotions life, he spun away from Mama and ran out the door.

Roxanne sucked in long drags of nicotine and released billows of smoke into the car while nonchalantly peering into the rearview mirror. Her boys were goofing around in the back seat with content smiles, disguising their scabbed emotions.

The view created a sense of satisfaction to envelope Roxanne and pull another drag from her cigarette with pleasure. On the exhale, she began singing.

I got the house, I got the car, but I ain't got Jack!

Turn my back on Jack. He says he ain't coming back.

Vague sensations numbed Scarlet into a daydream of reruns as pensive questions probed her for answers that remained mysteriously aloft.

What led me, to defend the youngest sibling? she pondered.

Did I attack, or was I playing? Shrugged her shoulders.

Why, did Mama laugh? only made her head hurt with confusion.

Why, won't my brothers play with me? swirled her emotions.

How can they act, as if nothing happened? Scarlet's eyes ached from the uneventful search in the fields of the fluttering butterflies that no longer tickled.

On the contrary, it hurt and made her nauseous, to swarm in the unknown.

Mama pulled into the first parking space behind the tall fences guarded by skyscraping trees and turned the engine off. "Okay, boys!" she said, stretching her long, thin arm to the back seat. "I will see you after school!" Mama assured them just before she pulled back her ignored hand. "Have a good day. Remember, I love you!" she called after them, watching her boys in the rearview mirror. But neither of the irritated boys made eye contact or communicated with her in any way before they ran off.

Roxanne felt her heart ache with the notion of a mother before turning to her next challenge, who had a look of disgruntled confusion painted on her pale face.

"Are you sure, you're up to this?" Fell into Scarlet's lap and forced her to raise a doubtful look in Mama's direction while nodding in an agreeing motion and offering a reassuring smile. "Well then, let's go!" Mama said, with a crack of an enthusiastic whip.

Roxanne proudly paraded her daughter into the front building for songs of elation that were harmonized to great heights from the people who were happy to have the opportunity to see this young girl, again. Intangible sensations coursed through Scarlet as she searched her mind with the determination to cut down any old cobwebs that may be hiding the answers.

Nevertheless, she found her mind spotless. Except for the confusion, nothing else was found. "Scarlet?" bellowed an older, overweight woman with graying hair piled on top of her head as she waddled from the direction of the back office. She reached out to touch the miracle. "Praise God!" Her face creased with a sincere smile.

"Hello, Scarlet!" the woman patiently said into Scarlet's timid expression. "I was wondering if you were going to make it back before the end of the school year!" the woman said like a long-lost comrade. She leaned over and kissed Scarlet on the forehead and took up the hand, Mama wasn't holding. Roxanne could see insecurity in her daughter's eyes as they nervously shot a look of hesitation around her environment.

"You remember Mrs. Roslyn?" Mama insisted, as she dropped her daughter's hand, releasing her in the capable hands of the school principal.

Roxanne leaned over and told her daughter, "I love you, and I will be back after school!" She brushed her lips across Scarlet's forehead, then disappeared out the door, leaving Scarlet alone and frightened in this strange place.

CHAPTER 10

BUTTERFLIES

Mrs. Roslyn squeezed the young girl's hand and smiled, attempting to reassure Scarlet, "You will be... just fine!" She smiled into Scarlet's uncertainty.

"Now, young lady, let's find your classroom!" A nervous smile shapes Scarlet's face as they began to walk across the school compound.

"What's a classroom?" Scarlet considered while she walked with the woman and listened to her paint a picture of the compound, which contained nine separate buildings in the midst of fruit-bearing trees and dusty dirt roads.

"Only the front of the school, where the administrative building sat, had grass shaded by trees!" Mrs. Roslyn stated before she pointed to a dorm-house.

"Some of the children attending the school, reside there!"

Scarlet decided all the buildings looked like houses except for the dorm building, a long rectangular shape. The kitchen house was crowded with five cafeteria tables in the front and a banquet table separating the kitchen in the back.

"Here, children, learn to pray before they eat the meals they are provided!" Mrs. Roslyn explained as she guided Scarlet to the other side of the dining hall and up to the building that housed fifth graders. "And this, is your classroom!" Mrs. Roslyn said gleefully as she opened the door and encouraged Scarlet into the homespun atmosphere.

In that classroom were walnut-stained walls with pictures scattered on them, melting into a lighter tone of a brown wood floor padded with big woven rugs.

Past the rugs were sixteen desks in the center of the room, rows of four, where children sat with their mouths open in amazement. A big calendar with markers, made by children, separated the two windows on the south side of the building. A chalkboard covered the entire wall at the other end of the classroom. In the right-hand corner of the chalkboard hung a flag with the Stars and Stripes on it. And underneath the flag, a thin middle-aged lady sat at a desk with a smile that made her eyes shine.

The woman stood up as Mrs. Roslyn guided Scarlet through the curious eyes that peered at her as she passed to the front of the room.

"Scarlet, you remember Mrs. Chapman?" insisted Mrs. Roslyn.

Scarlet smirked a queer expression. "How could I remember her?" Mocked Scarlet's memory. "I've never been here before!" She searched through her spotless mind as Mrs. Chapman took her hand. "Oh, Scarlet, it's so good to see you!" pressed her smiling red lips into a thin line as she spun the young girl around to face the class.

"Boys and girls, remember all the letters you wrote and all the prayers you said for Scarlet?" caused a commotion of agreement to rush out with an explosive exhilaration.

"Well, here is your proof: God answers prayer!"

The class rumbled with stomping feet, cheering for the honorable verification of their beliefs. "Scarlet's now well enough to finish out the school year with us!" signaled a handful of children to jump up from their chairs and begin singing in chorus, a cheer that sounded rehearsed as they spelled out,

C-E-L-E-B-R-A-T-E. Don't hesitate in your walk with destiny!

C-E-L-E-B-R-A-T-E. Yeah, celebrate!

The performance was almost unbearable for Scarlet, whose embarrassment burned the oxygen from her lungs as Mrs. Chapman escorted her by the hand to her chair. While the children applauded God's phenomenal power. Until Mrs. Chapman finally stopped at an empty desk and ushered Scarlet with the swipe of her hand.

Scarlet briskly slid down into her chair and hid her face in the cradle of her folded arms, attempting to discourage the attention. Only when the room fell silent did Scarlet find the courage to lift her head discovering that most of her peers were smiling and the others were staring at her as if she were a ghost. Scarlet turned to search for security in the teacher, but Mrs. Chapman was sitting in her chair with a blank look on her face as she too gazed at the young girl.

Scarlet's heart burned with annoyance as she wondered where her brothers were. She considered running out the door to find them. She smiled past all the watchful eyes that sat between her and the door when suddenly, she found comfort in a picture of butterflies.

Their hues of color fluttered in a caressing breeze in a luscious green meadow that grew tall with sweet green grass and vividly colored wildflowers, wet with dew. First, the picture gave her a refreshing sensation. It was calming the frustration and anxiety she had been experiencing. The second wave of sensation lavished a warmness upon her. That only belonged to a sense of familiarity and well-being. Something she hadn't experienced since the brilliant light faded with any memories she should have contained.

CHAPTER 11

WARNING SIGNALS

Cruising the scenic route through the miles of dried grassy fields that had begun to rejuvenate life in the early spring waved in the warmth of the south winds. Roxanne was thankful to have time to breathe for the first time since that car had hit her daughter. *Damn near, killed her!* Pessimism reminded Roxanne while she popped open a Pepsi and lit a cigarette before leaning forward and turning up the radio, allowing the screaming disc jockey to announce the selected choice that would compete with the static, muffling the words of the companions; That lived… to taunt Roxanne's mind, with their opinions.

A rush of annoyance crushed the cigarette butt into the ashtray as Roxanne began singing at the top of her lungs. Desperation shook her with foiled attempts of drowning out the constant invaders when the static grew louder than the radio and her own crackling voice. "What the hell?" forced the volume knob until it would give no more, to calm the turbulence that had accompanied her since that day: Her downheartedness, denounced her faith.

On that day, the two sounds collided like tidal waves slamming into the defenseless beach of Roxanne's subconscious were her companions existed. *Over the edge, we go!* Free Will sang where the churning waters destructively exploded. Fracturing Roxanne's already-unstable foundation, threatening to plummet the crumbling debris into the tide pool of emotions.

She gripped the steering wheel and fought to turn down the radio while yearning for the ability to turn down the noise that seared her mind with pain.

Dripping its excess into her bloodstream while she fumbled through the contents of her purse. Roxanne pulled out a picture of her family and clutched the photo to her heart as she prayed for strength. She opened her burning eyes and found big, happy smiles beaming from the Kodak memory. Once again, Roxanne dodged the voices that bounced off the static and reverberated in the abyss of her being, in search for her soul. The companions hoped to find what kept her from the edge that desired to consume her existence.

Roxanne traced the faces of the photo with her finger until an infectious smile creased her own face. Tears began to well up in her eyes as she flipped the picture over. It was dated exactly one month before Scarlet was plowed down in the street. "Where the sun used to shine brighter than anywhere else in the world!" Roxanne whispered over the sobbing tears that coursed down her cheeks and into the nape of her neck.

With every ticking moment, the foghorn of static blared increasingly louder. Signaling danger and forcing her to pull the car over.

Roxanne's head pounded, and her stomach churned in the distress of a violent sea of nausea. Simultaneously, she opened the car door and shoved the engine into park, nearly rolling out onto the ground before finding her feet. Grasping the long, solid body of the Cadillac, she stumbled around the front of the car. Being driven and pushed by those who didn't have the best interest of Roxanne's family. She couldn't control her eyes from bobbing up and down in the furious storm. Or over her trudging legs that carried her out into the field of tall grass until she reached the outstretching shadows of an old oak tree.

Several hundred feet from the road, sweat beads singed her eyes, causing her last steps to go blind and stumbling. She fell helplessly, into the shade of the old oak, with the span of time weighing its tired arms down. The sturdy, twisted body shook its branches, welcoming her company in the lonesome field. Its serenading leaves waved tranquility into the breeze as Roxanne rocked back and forth. Distant darkness had swallowed her eyes as she bobbed in the abyss. She mindlessly tied dry grass into knots. Her mouth muttered the melody of a familiar but unnamable tune while numbness consumed her instead, of answers to her questions.

Your own personal Jesus! Hummed methodically

Someone to hear your prayers! Attempted to drown out Roxanne's questions. "Will Scarlet ever be normal again?" squeezed her heart to a bloody death as she competed to be heard.

All alone, flesh and bone! the companions sang over Roxanne's first attempt. Roxanne's second attempt scorched her throat with the flames of persistence. "Would things ever be like they used to be?" muttered her pleas through the thick darkness of the abyss.

Unconsciously, Roxanne crushed the handful of leaves the old oak had given to her as a gift. *Put you to the test!* seared a path to the crushed, dry leaves that Roxanne continued to hold while the companions attempted to coax her into submission.

Instead, Roxanne released the smoldering leaves into the wind with determination. And as she and the companions watched the embers take flight, they each pondered her final and most crucial question. "Will I ever, forgive my husband?" escaped from the abyss where her soul exists.

CHAPTER 12

DISTURBED

Mayhem increasingly cracked the foundations of Roxanne's world when she found herself sunk on the bottom of the tub with her lungs pleading.

"Breathe … PLEASE BREATHE!" secreted her mind as she opened her eyes and let the water distort her vision, to the same stratum of her mind. Only to heed the clamoring in her head, that just won't stop!

Roxanne tried to think back. Exactly how long had her head been buzzing? Propelled her toward the defiant decision after the snapshots of a lifetime rushed from the recollection of her memory. Although it was more prevalent at times than others? Roxanne contemplated the irritants that provoked the static to sound with an alarming frequency. She compared the times it was only a constant chatter—so distant she could not make out the words. Other times, it was blaring so loud. And if not for the static frequently blocking the frequency of the damnation, the words would push her over the edge.

Bubbles escaped from her nose. Her eye sockets began to bulge. Her heart rate dropped to a putter as she shifted her thoughts to recall how she had gotten into the tub. And wondered exactly how long she had been despondent on the bottom of the tub.

"Please breathe!" shot Roxanne out of the water, gasping for air to find she was not alone. "Oh, shit!" escaped through her pasty, dried mouth as she sprang up into a defensive position without thought to her vulnerability. For a brief moment, she only stood there with a look of confusion that washed over her, fixing her eyes on the oncoming headlights.

Suddenly, Panic signaled warning. Frantically, waving her arms in front of Roxanne's nakedness. The ground quaked and shook instability, in her muscle control, submerging back into the restless waters; Along with Steven's lustful expression and dragging the debris into the sea of madness.

"What's wrong, babe?" ridiculed Roxanne's attempts to disguise the confusion that seeped from her frail mind as things came into view.

She could hear the radio blaring in the background as Steven leaned over her and lifted her out of the tub. With Roxanne cradled in his arms, Steven draped a towel over his wife's thin, shivering nakedness before he carried her to the bedroom and placed her on the neatly made bed.

"Why are you crying?" Steven watched a glimpse of light spark in her dark eyes as a mask of suspicion covered her face.

"You scared me, to death!" Roxanne insisted as she turned to look at the clock. Relieved, to find, it was only one o'clock in the afternoon. "Why, are you here?" shot Steven with an arrow of dubious contempt. "You're supposed, to be at work!" stabbed him with her inquiry of Cynicism that slit Steven's airway, leaving him gasping for his next words. "I … I … I've been trying … to call all day!" Gurgled his words.

Roxanne aimed a perplexed expression, prepared to shoot daggers at him, as she pulled her defiance up from the bed. "When I couldn't get an answer," Steven offered as he watched Roxanne waver in her step before she decided to sit back down, "I thought, I better come home!" came out, in a heroic tone of an egotistical man.

Sit down before you get, knocked down! The companions' suggestion passed by Steven's rushed petition for an explanation.

Roxanne held her head in the makeshift pressurized bandage of her hands. Attempting to restrain that damned noise to just one spot in her clambering mind. Suddenly, she began shaking her head as she whispered.

"No...!" caught her thoughts in hesitation for a brief moment.

"Things are not... okay!" Roxanne squeezed out before a smile curled her lips into the desperation of Irony, huge tears fell from her eyes, looking to her husband for answers.

It was in his baby-blue eyes, she found the silence, that defeated their world. Steven swallowed hard, attempting to choke down the pain that quickly capacitated his chest cavity and caused those baby blues to crack with red streaks.

Water rushed to the rims of his eyelids, his heart ached, to grab her and hold on.

"Do you think, things will ever turn back to normal?" Roxanne's voice quivered as she shot a haunted look into his eyes with enough force to toss the waters. "You know like it used to be?" she sobbed with scattered emotions, striking fire in the abyss. The flames shot up, threatening to scorch anyone... who got to close. While the companion's named for each emotion violently thrashed her in the churning tide pools of Steven's unspoken words swirled her faster inside the burning ring of fire that had charred Steven's innards.

He coughed with an attempt to speak but only managed to pollute their atmosphere. Making it impossible for him, or anyone, to see through the darkness of the unknown.

Helplessly, Steven bobbed in and out of the depths of the churning current, signaling for hope as he occasionally broke the surface of the cresting waters.

"To escape, with his family intact!" He fought with every ounce of his efforts to gurgle and cough those words out. "Happy and content!" pounded against the tide that attempted to drown him under the abandoned and sunken merry-go-round of obstacles. Where his children were trapped. But when he looked over the edge of his life preserver, his entire family's well-being reflected in a murky mirage, blurred in the dense water under his bobbing body. Suddenly the violent storm ripped open the bottom of his efforts, spewing persuasive gas from the cooling molten in the abyss. Obscuring their future even more. Steven became lightheaded, swaying in the motion of the storm until his sea legs finally gave out, and he fell into his wife's lips. Where he locked on, kissing her desperately hard, without any answers or promises.

Roxanne's mind screamed with the chatter of her resistant companions, which broke through the static attempting to repress their hostess's opinion that would rebuke the question. "Can I… forgive him?" came out repetitively. But after a long moment of indecisiveness, those chanting voices haunted her. Dancing with her. Swinging her and dipping her until she sank completely into the conflict of vulnerability, and her personal desire to hold on, was wounded. Her attempts, at standing firm, as a drafted soldier standing against the commands of the non-concurring governors. Which chastened and began molding her with the idea, *it's like sleeping with the enemy … being a traitor!* echoed into a vibration that flooded Roxanne's entire existence as Steven released his hold on her lips and straightened his stance.

He stood there silent in front of Roxanne's nonreciprocating existence.

His body trembled with uncertainty, searching for her. Begging, with his baby blues. That she, would comfort him, when he needed her the most.

Roxanne suddenly sprang up from the bed, allowing the towel to fall to the points of her breasts. The terry cloth attempted to clutch at her skin as it slid to her hips and down her long legs. A devious expression passed over her face, and for the first time ever Roxanne stood naked before him. Absent of any childish innocents.

Intentionally and seductively, she pressed her moist-naked body against her husband, allowing her vulnerability to be exposed. As she tightly closed her eyes, attempting to prevent the tears from flowing, as she raised her trembling hands to Steven's face. *Traitor! Traitor! Traitor!* broke through the static, which caused the rebellious Roxanne to abruptly push into her husband with a lack of passion and dry lips. She enticed Steven's anticipating needs, and for the first time since Scarlet's accident, they tried to find comfort in each other.

Whistles and green flags signaled Steven to dive in and ravish her, lick her and touch every inch of her sweet softness. His entire body shook with desire. His heart pounded passionately as he calculated his moves. He dared his first caress to her flat abdomen; just barely, touching the hairline.

"Just, hold me ..." Roxanne shivered. "Hold on to me!" Roxanne pleaded as she curled into a fetal position in Steven's arms. "Don't let go!" she begged in relentless sobs that soaked his chest. "Hold me ... tight!" pleaded the mother of his children. "God, please!" she beckoned over and over in a whisper.

Afraid to disturb Roxanne's peacefulness; Steven continued to hold her, in his protective clutches. Listening to his wife's breath blow-dry the tears that had stained him with her desperation. Thoughts rushed him. But he could not conceive what made her so vulnerable at one moment and strong and convicted the next. His body shrugged with the confusion that had taken residence in his mind, leaving his optimism baffled when he attempted to reassure her. "Everything, would turn back to the way it was!" Steven coaxed with what little hope he could find. "That's good, baby." He stroked the damp hair from her face. "You have been running on empty, for some time now!" His heart throbbed for her. "Sleep is what the doctor, Steven, ordered!" mused to his wife's dead consciousness as he slid a blanket over her naked body.

He sat on the edge of the marital bed, watching over Roxanne, long enough for his self-consciousness to frolic with him, stabbing at him again and again.

Something's, terribly wrong! Forced Steven to suck in a breath. Contemplation held that breath while Steven searched within himself for the proof of such discernment. His head rocked in a digging motion, aiming for denial, sinking him into the depths of codependency.

His head continued swaying in a disagreeing fashion when he leaned over and gently kissed Roxanne's forehead. "She just needs—" He stopped, to ponder for just a moment. He then rose and stretched the tight muscles in his neck.

"Some rest!" he announced firmly to the doubting Thomas in the room before spinning on his heels and making his way to the bedroom door.

Quietly, he exited and closed the door. Leaving only a whisper of air to be heard over the ongoing debate with the pessimistic doubting Thomas that the majority of the room was trying to ignore.

Steven pushed any recall, of the dispute, he had just endured with his gut feeling into the trash heap of unwanted emotions as he drifted into the front room. His target was aimed at retrieving the pen he had left on the coffee table this morning. But the table had been polished to a high glossy shine and cleared of any items except a clean ashtray. Steven straightened his stance, glanced around the small apartment that looked as though it had been hit by a tornado just this morning.

"Spotless!" washed over him in the sparkle of immaculate that gleamed all around him. A smile creased Steven's face as a chuckle crept up from his groin.

"She never ceases to amaze me!" Steven chuckled as he searched for a pen and paper to leave a simple note:

Babe, I went to pick up the kids ...
The place, looks great!

Love ya,
Steven

Steven left the note with a full pack of cigarettes on the coffee table before spinning toward the door. Where his consciences greeted him with a head butt to the right eyebrow. Steven wiped a tear from his eye while guilt climbed onto his back and rode out the door with the ramification of that horrible day, playing over and over. "If only, I had escorted my children, across the street?" pounded at his livelihood, tormenting his soul. "None of this, would have happened." A foamy froth of burning acid secreted into his respiratory system as he drove toward Riverside.

When Steven rolled down the window, to spit the assault of a greasy froth, his face soured, his stomach heaved a steaming spray of that which was eating him from the inside out. He choked and gagged, tears scorching trails down his cheeks. While Roxanne's questions speared him-Angst rode him, like a wild mustang. Cinching him tight about the scrotum with the constant mood swings that Roxanne had been reviling. "Can't blame, just her!" Helplessness mimicked Steven's conscience. While spreading a blanket of denial that had been woven from his unresolved fret that he tried to ignore. Thick enough to blind him from everything but the obvious conclusion. *I will, continue to love her!* he contemplated. No matter what, is to come!" He had sworn his oath, the day, he put a ring on her finger. "Forever indebted, for her virginity!" Pulled him into the driveway of the children's school.

He parked in a partially shaded space and rolled down the window as he contemplated the day Roxanne had drawn him out here. Steven checked his watch, trying to ignore the advisories of his memories. Impatiently, he sighed when the watch reflected seven minutes to go. Damn seven-minute boxing match, Steven nervously chuckled as his thoughts pulled him back into the ring with the promise of a date that sunny afternoon when she drove them toward the secret venue. Steven sucked hard on the vise his body screamed for, exhaled, and drew another long hit. As he recalled, Roxanne was vastly charged with an electrifying energy as she drove the conversation train into a wide range of topics. Stumbling over a few words but, she retrieved them nicely as she began digging through her purse. While calculating her maneuvers during that brief moment of silence when she pretended to stumble over her words. But she had neglected the school topic until they were sitting in the parking lot of the secluded Christian school in Riverside.

Steven's masked sentiment remained hidden along with his confusion as he watched his wife turn the engine off. She turned her attention to the rearview mirror, checked herself for any flaws while her husband dangled on the line.

"We have an appointment with the principal!" she informed him while pressing a fresh line of lipstick onto her lips. "At one o'clock!" She finished in the mirror before she turned her roasting almond eyes to him.

"This is the perfect school, for my children!" The selection of her words seared Steven's already-gutted carcass as she concluded the need-to-know information. Pausing for a moment to make eye contact with Steven for the first time before stepping into the office. And now, she waved him in. For a guarantor's signature, on the contract and to make a hefty payment via credit card.

After the meeting, Steven drove Roxanne to her choice of destination as she chattered sweetness into his raw wounds. The ones she had just trodden through, with her heels of self-assuredness. It was that day, over lunch, when Steven offered a wry smile as he considered stating his case. About the kids going to school so far away from home. And what's more troubling? He wasn't happy about paying the private school tuition for three children. He considered all they had saved while living in the apartment. And how that was now going to the hospital, in installment payments, for Scarlet's care.

Regret, reached out and sucker-punched Steven in the head with a reminder that he was still paying for Roxanne's surgery. While Roxanne's conversation became adamant about *her* children, having a good education. How she, wanted only the best for them! It was enough for Steven to disregard his trepidations, as his heart throbbed to be bathed in the bubbles of her steadfastness. And how he adored his wife more than life.

No matter what! Or how he felt! Or whom she opposed! He would give in to her. "Especially, in these days, when it's easier to appease her!" he concluded out loud as he snuffed his cigarette butt and slid out of the car.

CHAPTER 13

QUEEN'S WAVE

Steven's inquiry had been cut short by a woman who stood up with a big smile on her face as she reached out both of her chubby hands in a praying motion.

Deep impressions of, until recently, a long-worn wedding ring scarred her wedding finger. "So, you're the lucky father, of Scarlet?" she bluntly gave recognition as she stuck her hand out in a greeting fashion. "We are so pleased God, spared your daughter's life!" Insisting that Steven take her hand. Steven nervously smiled, giving the woman little notice as he went through the expected motions. His eyes, fixed above her hairline.

He, faked a smile. Disguised his regret, of engaging with this stranger, about a subject he would rather not discuss. Steven, released the grip of their greeting. But, the woman's hold lingered, as her orange lips continued to move. Steven, was no longer hearing her. His skin began to crawl, making him twitch in a matter that aggressively pulled his hand from the woman's grip as a familiar face appeared from the half-closed door of the principal's office.

"Mrs. Roslyn?" Steven said with recognition.

"Oh good, I'm glad to see you!" she said, as she checked Scarlet's name from her to-do list. Steven began to speak, but Mrs. Roslyn held a hand up with urgency.

Not too distracted from the reason for Steven's appearance, but staying steadily focused; getting one job done before starting another; Had always been what you might call, a compulsive disorder. She chuckled, then continued saying, "One persistent quality, that has kept her in a principal position, for seven years!" She smiled into Steven's self-assured smile for, her quirkiness.

"Now," Mrs. Roslyn said, as she pushed back her pair of Benjamin Franklin–style glasses, higher up the bridge of her nose. "It's a tradition of the school to celebrate, May Day!" Mrs. Roslyn shot Steven a deliberate and determined look before continuing.

"Since Scarlet had received the miracle of the year, we thought it appropriate that she be the May Queen!" With that said, the principal turned her blushing face to meet Steven's eyes, with a clever smile. Steven returned her smile with a hint of relief, that he hadn't missed a payment.

"Well, Mrs. Roslyn, I don't see any reason why she couldn't!" almost secured the nomination. "I will, have to discuss it with her mother. And she'll, let the school know!"

Pleased with Steven's response, Mrs. Roslyn, offered her hand in agreement, as the final bell rang for the day.

"Mrs. Roslyn, can you tell me, where I can find my children?" Steven beseeched the robust woman for the reason, he had come into the office.

Mrs. Roslyn smiled as she graciously walked him to the door and pointed to the back of the school compound. "Thanks!" Steven said, as he passed through the door with his hand trailing behind in a waving gesture.

The boys howled with the courage of well-bred warriors as they charged their dad, head-on. Suddenly, the duo split; each came in from a different side. Ambushing him and latching on to separate body parts. The boys groaned, with their efforts, while they imagined themselves to be thousand-pound weights while Steven dragged his cumbersome appendages to the truck. He raised, one leg at a time, lifting each boy into the truck. He wrestled them to the bench seat of his pickup until they were wrenched without power.

The boys laughed and giggled from the stimulation of a bonding moment when Steven turned the key into the ignition and started up the truck. Only, when he looked over his shoulder to back out, did he see Scarlet. She stood in the reflection of the driver's side mirror. Her arms down at her side, her eyes searching to understand the interaction between the boys and the dad. The fly on her lip, considered entering Scarlet's gapped mouth while Steven blushed, as his heart fell into the pit of neglect. He recalled, Scarlet was not home, when he had gone to check on Roxanne.

Today, was Scarlet's first day back to school! Sucker-punched Steven in the solar plexus and pushed words out in a harsh grunt, meant only for Scarlet. "Other side!" came out in a bark that spun Scarlet and sent her running a wide turn around the truck and nearly colliding into the school van. The horn honked. The tires neglected to grab the dirt road and came to a sliding stop only inches from Scarlet. Steven grabbed his daughter by the shoulder and spun her to face him. "You need, to watch for cars!"

He began to march her to the passenger side of the truck. "Most people, don't live through being run down in the street!" he chastised her. "Only cats, have nine lives!" Scarlet didn't know if he was trying to be funny or serious. "And you, young lady, have just used two lives!" he finished his speech as he opened the door. Steven turned to meet Scarlet's wide-eyed expression, searching for the meaning of his words. "Get, in!" was all he had left, to say to her.

The occupants in the cab of the truck sat in silence, biting their tongues. Every bump the truck hit, Stevie made sure the jarring, caused him, to dig his elbow into his sister. Scarlet couldn't move any farther without opening the door and stepping out. It was on the long journey home when Mark's face was puzzled with irregularity. "Where's Mama?" The question broke the silence in the cab of the truck. Steven offered his son a ponderous look before altering a reassuring smile on the mask that hid the harsh reality.

"Mom's, at home, sleeping!" Steven's answer began ironing out the creases in the young boy's face.

"She badly, needs her rest!" Steven looked to his children for approval, but when he got nothing back, he continued, "So, we are going to surprise her!" Which aroused the children's attention? "We will bring her dinner, flowers, and our well-adjusted attitudes!" Steven shot a cautious eye in Stevie's direction. "We are going to treat her, like the queen that she is!" Signaled the high-pitched squeal of the children's delight.

"Yeah, that's a great idea!" the boys agreed.

"She'll, love that!" was the conclusion that sent Roxanne's husband and children to prepare for the queen's festival.

Steven stopped the children at the top of the stairs. Arms full of dinner, flowers, and a six-pack of Pepsi. "Shh," he whispered. "Quiet as mice!" he ordered, while leading the festivalgoers. He would surrender himself as the sacrificial scapegoat, if necessary, to protect the children from Roxanne's swinging disposition, he decided, as he slowly turned the doorknob, while hoping, this was a good ideal.

The radiance of mama's smile made their whole world shine. Dad levitated up to her and took her into his arms. Slowly, he kissed the gap of her neck and whispered something into her ear that made her giggle. Steven slid his hand down her long arm and took a step back. Then with an abracadabra gesture, the flowers magically appeared from behind his back. Mama's eyes lit up with surprise. "For me?" she cooed into the bouquet cradled in her arms. She pushed the petals around with her nose as she allowed the aroma to deepen the tranquility of this moment. She was differentiating the distinct smell of each of the four different colors before she lifted her face with delight spilling from her eyes.

"How sweet!" she assured her captive audience with a smile that enlightened Steven's heart, compelling him to pull her close and gaze deep into her eyes with admiration. "My soul, aches with commitment!" he confessed. "I love you, babe. Today and forever!" he assured her. "I want you, always to be happy!" Encouraged an enthusiastic giggle to flutter onto Steven's arm when he offered to escort his love to the dining table.

The queen stood at the head of the table, bowing her head in approval for the boy's presentation of a well-prepared table, including a Pepsi with lots of ice, just the way the queen, liked it. While Scarlet finished arranging the flowers in a vase of fresh water and gingerly placed them in the center of the table.

Pleased with her creation, Scarlet turned her smile, in the direction of Mama. But the queen, had stopped smiling. Instead, she sat in judgment of the young female peasant. Who sat in anguish, as the queen reached out and hastily swooped up the vase, with the power to create a funny feeling that scorch Scarlet's heart? Turning it to a pulp that left her feeling, wanting, for something much more than what she had been left with.

Scarlet's funny feeling shook the reeds of insecurity, setting the butterflies in motion. Where they danced and fluttered in anticipation until Scarlet reached down and rubbed her belly, trying to calm the reeds as mama examined the vase for flaws. The queen placed the vase back down on the table in front of her before she turned a scornful wink in Scarlet's direction. The queen hastily, pulled flowers from the vase. Rearranging the colors and the lengths until she was satisfied. Only then did the queen look up at her subject with unspoken words that said, *Next time, this is how it's to be done!*

The judgment, shook Scarlet as funny, but she didn't dare laugh. As she thought, *Isn't that exactly, how I had arranged them?* Her self-esteem was questioned. Scarlet's confusion was dancing with the fretting butterflies until she felt that she had to puke, forcing her to cover her mouth instead of protesting the applause the queen was receiving for the well-arranged flowers.

Scarlet's smile, had spiraled downward at the corners and sucked in her cheeks, as if she had eaten something sour. While the queen raised her arms and spread them out over the table, giving thanks for being able to sit down and eat, as a happy family, once again.

Once again? mumbled Scarlet's mind. *This, is the first time, I can remember!* Blew wind into her mindset sails, in search, of calmer seas. But all she could see, through her viewing-glass; was a threat of a storm. The eye of the storm suddenly, incased all about her. The sun shone, so bright in a tranquil blue sky, Warming Scarlet's heart with the harmony, of God's creation. It's there, Scarlet, could find the peace she badly needed.

Scarlet, reached out her arms, giving glory for the beauty of tranquility. When the boat began to rock. The eye of the storm, grew smaller. The wind, caught the sails of her curiosity when she was greeted with a curious wall of silence. Scarlet's eyes popped open, expecting to catch someone off guard-in the investigation, of the sudden deafness, of the room.

Dad's face, was mad red. His hand wavered at his belt, like a gunslinger's steady hand, twitching a split second before the right moment. The look on his face dared Scarlet to breathe another word. As a wet spit wad, suddenly hit Scarlet in the cheek, as she realized she had spoken her thoughts out loud.

The queen remained confident and self-assured as she continued standing with her eyes closed in prayer. "Help us to be considerate and grateful!" she finished. "Let's eat!" the queen commanded, as she slid into her seat, without giving recognition to the matter of her daughter's words.

Scarlet fought back the tears while she sat quietly, pushed food across the plate that was in front of her. The boys were telling stories to the parents, who giggled with delight. Scarlet, excused herself from the table, without disrupting Stevie's illustration of his school day.

She quickly, shuffled to the bathroom and closed the door. Finding herself, standing in front of the toilet, anticipating the bile of sickness to come rushing out. Instead, she just stood there salivating and spitting into the toilet while she tried to examine herself. Deciding, except, for the sickness in her stomach ... Scarlet considered, as she spun around and sat down on the toilet. "I feel nothing. Just, kind of numb and disconnected!"

Steven checked his watch, anticipating Scarlet's return to the table before telling the family about Mrs. Roslyn's Request. He tried to recollect when she had left the table as he remained attentive and mindful of the playful conversation between Roxanne and the boys. He rechecked his watch. Seven minutes had passed since Steven had last checked the time on his wristwatch. Made him consider, maybe she had gone to bed?

A rush of laughter rang out from the young male peasants as the queen told them stories of how they would win all the land as spoils for her with their Trojan horses. Eleven minutes had gone by when Steven stood and walked toward the back of the apartment.

"We'd wave our queen's flag high!" stated her loyal male servants.

Steven turned back to etch a mental Kodak memory of the boys sitting at the table with their mother, pledging to defend her honor.

Steven had found Scarlet behind the closed door of the bathroom, where she had been for nearly fifteen minutes, as far as he knew.

"Well ..." He hesitated. "What are you doing?" he inquired. A little longer than a brief moment later, he heard her say. "Just sitting here!" Her voice was steady and calm but a little drawn out. "Scarlet, come out and join the family!" Steven's hesitation caused Scarlet to gag, but the butterflies were able to hang on. "Okay, in a minute!" Scarlet pleaded. "Well, hurry up. I want to share a story!" "Steven said before, he lightly tapped on the door with enough vibration to startle Scarlet and scatter the butterflies into flight.

Scarlet began wishing she had asked for more time as she straightened herself in the mirror while the butterflies began to settle and sleep as Scarlet patted her damp skin dry. She attempted a smile into the mirror before she spun toward the door and grabbed the doorknob. Just as an intrusion of pounding scattered the butterflies from their slumber.

"Scarlet, I got to pee!" Mark insisted. A combination of resounding intrusions from outside influences rattled Scarlet further into the soothsayers, disastrous-prediction; Swarming about her with the fury of the butterflies; Trapping her in the hidden intentions of those who want to destroy her.

"Hidden ... right!" Scarlet crowed with sarcasm. Her intuition zoned in on their intentions. But she refused to accept it. She was firmly deciding to stand and fight. Her endurance sparked a fire under her conviction. Insisting, they love and accept her unconditionally was the only emotion that pounded her heart when she swung open the bathroom door and flew past Mark.

Unsure of her place at the table, Scarlet flopped down on the couch and began licking the wounds that would eventually heal over with titanium. A soaked spit wad pulled Scarlet from the depths of isolation when it stung her just below the eye. Only then did she notice Dad motioning Scarlet to present herself to the queen.

Scarlet's blossom-pink-lips quickly moved, speaking to Mama without clarity of the subject. She spoke in short sentences. Stumbling and searching for words until the queen's nontransparent smile cracked with thunderous laughter. Roxanne reached out and touched the top of Scarlet's head with the pride of a leader after winning the spoils of war.

"Yes, of course!" came out with a wink of her eye. "You may be only the May Queen!" she announced. "After all, you are my prodigy!" She and the companions gloated in the fat of the spoils.

Stevie's aggression blasted him back in his chair. Much like a plank of wood, Stevie's body became ridged and stiff, his hands gripped the table. Muscles contracting, bellows of labored breathing, smoldered the ambers of Stevie's resentment.

Once again, his sister, was receiving all the attention. Overloaded the firebox of the steam engine, setting the ambers ablaze, and swelled the smokestack that bulged the veins in his neck. "That's not fair!" Stevie shouted, signaling Mark to pick up on his older brother's objection.

"Yeah ... Scarlet gets everything!" Mark said, sticking his tongue out at his sister. He then slid deep into the chair until his flesh felt the indentation of the woven backrest when he crossed his arms and a pout scarred his lips.

Scarlet stood baffled between following orders and fulfilling the queen's expectations at the risk of alienating herself even farther from her brothers. Scarlet didn't even know what Mama was talking about. May Day or May Queen, whatever that was—she couldn't have cared less. ""What I care about... is my brothers being mad at me!" Scarlet whispered into her own pout.

Mama sat with a content smile at the majesty's end of the family's dining table; Smoking a cigarette and sipping from her glass of Pepsi that sat in a puddle of condensation. While Steven firmly discouraged any more outbursts from the boys by pointing a finger at them. Like a gunslinger, he pulled back the trigger and shot.

Slowly and deliberately, he blew the chamber clean before he placed it back to the beltline around his waist. Replacing his son's willfulness with guarded resistance as they slumped down further in their chairs, saying not another word for the rest of what was to be a pleasant family dinner in the queen's honor.

The queen's desire for this evening's entertainment was for Steven to escort her to the Lake Elsinore card room for her first night out since her reality had become "so damn serious!" puckered her lips in the mirror of flashing images, then smacked the stain of lipstick into her lips with a sense of confidence. She studied the outlines of her work in the mirror, crowded with Roxanne's companions. Where the Lioness tore through the fabric of the static and devoured the flesh as Roxy's shrieking laughter clashed with Roxanne's soul.

Earlier in the day, the companions assured Roxanne, *It would be okay, to leave the children with the only babysitter available at such late notice!* They insisted as Roxanne wrote the number of the card room down on a crisp piece of paper and stuffed it into the pocket of her sweater.

It was behind the safety of a locked door and the watchful entertainment of the television that Steven and Roxanne would leave their children. With the phone number that had been scripted earlier, witnessed by the companions, now a crumpled piece of paper left by the phone. "Call if there is an emergency!" Mama said, attempting to kiss her oldest son, who brushed her off like she had brushed him off at dinner.

Roxanne nervously wrung her hands, considering her son's actions. The hesitation of her confirmed actions caused thunder to roll across Roxanne's atmosphere and create so much static that lightning crackled and seared Roxanne's backbone. *Would you stop coddling the brat!* the most prominent companion insisted.

Tonight, is our night! The Lioness nipped.

Roxanne's hand fluttered gracefully into a queen's wave. Free of concern as she waved goodbye with a smug expression smearing a coolness into the discouraged barrage of children before she sailed out the door. Steven was shocked by the audacious mood that suddenly appeared and escorted Roxanne out the door. He shot a nervous eye at his children, feeling reluctant about leaving them alone. But the children really gave no mind to the situation that had just cleared the room, Steven decided as he turned his concern away from the boys, who had returned to watching television. But Scarlet sat on the floor, her chin resting on her knee, deep in thought. Steven watched Scarlet as she pulled at the toenail she had split while attempting to kick Stevie. Instead, she missed and made contact with the frame of the bunk bed.

Steven felt the tug of the challenge in his mind and his heart, the indecisiveness. *Torn to follow his queen… Or stay with the children?*

His mind decisively stated, *His place is … with his queen!* his conscience demanded a voice. "Without her, none of this would be possible!" pumped his impulses and made him instinctively bite his tongue. Attempting to keep the confusion from ruining the ride out to the club while Roxanne wiggled in her seat like an eager schoolgirl. Roxanne's eyes, darned a web of anticipations.

"I think Scarlet is doing much better since returning to school," she exhaled and crushed a cigarette butt into the ashtray while she waited for a reply from the man, she had been married to for nearly ten years. Steven only nodded his head, offering no verbal reply. Instead, he threw exhilarants on the fire that roasted Roxanne's soul—melting and forming her into the creation the Lioness desired.

"I've been thinking … I would take on a job?" She waited only a brief second for his disproval. "You know… to help out!" Roxanne added just before turning toward him to find his expression tight-lipped and puzzled.

"I could help with the children's tuition and other financial matters?" she insisted while neglecting to tell him, or admit to herself, that it wasn't only Scarlet who had changed. But she was afraid that something was very different in herself. "Very different!" her own voice reverberated throughout her domain. Creating a laughter that built between the vulnerable Roxanne and her companions.

We're not going to let his tight-lipped disposition hamper our mood; Or ruin our first night out!" the Lioness insisted with a flick of her tail that enticed Roxanne.

CHAPTER 14

OPPORTUNITY KNOCKS

Roxanne recklessly decided just the other day when she could no longer be heard over the companions, constant opposition; Toward her, present, rebellious fortitude. "Getting a job... would be an escape!" Her thoughts cut short on the trailing words as she searched for assurance she hadn't said "escape" out loud.

Silently, Roxanne stole a glance of Steven; finding him, pale in the moonlight. his jaw locked painfully tight, according to the visual sign of a pulsing vein throbbing at his temple. And behind closed doors, where secrets are kept, Roxanne felt some empathy pang at her heart for her husband. When she considered his thoughts, to be fretful. While she resisted touching him. Although her stomach did wrench with the guilt only a submissive wife could feel.

Struggling with the reason, she had made the decision to distract the hostile feelings. Roxanne kept many secrets. This one, she would also keep, became a law as she stole another glance of the man she had given her everything too. The recall of those memories stabbed Roxanne in the eye, blurring her vision and projecting her thoughts to how the companions loathed Steven.

From the beginning of their visits, when it was only occasional periods, the companions showed up at random moments to crowd and complicated every space of Roxanne's existence. But now that the curtain of static had been shredded, the voices blew through the opening that now rustled in the triumph of her companions.

Desperation began bobbing Roxanne's hand in the effort of convincing her to reach out to Steven. But the waiting period for her to become responsive had suddenly expired. Encouragement pulled Roxanne's hand into Steven's direction. In hopes of saving the ideal family, she had been diligently working on for years.

But the Lioness batted down any hope of that happening as her feline curiosity turned to killing Steven and leaving his carcass for Roxanne.

Assiduous backed up what little fortitude could be found, fighting alongside Roxanne's tattered soul. Diligently attempting to protect Roxanne from swinging so far out that she would slip over the edge. What was left of Roxanne's rebellious fortitude wiped the sweat from the brow as they realized, like the battle for Roxanne's sanity, they were also losing the battle of explanation. Unable to rationalize, the gaps of time she couldn't recollect. Or about the feelings of overwhelming Fretfulness and aggression that seemed harder to control every passing day! All of these scenarios pushed into Roxanne with tremendous pressure.

A vise squeezed Steven's manliness as he fought for control over his personal emotions, wants, and needs. He sensed her stare burning into him, yet he could not make contact with her wanting expression. Instead, he fought for words that she might want to hear. "Babe, if that is, what you want?" Steven said as he turned a hesitant but watchful eye toward Roxanne's physical features.

Her beauty burned him like a familiar memory he longed for. But when their eyes locked, he could see her warm almond eyes had roasted to the color of charred remains. Steven had realized more than once that Roxanne's personality was that of someone totally different at times. Steven had been studying Roxanne's mood swings, memorizing the telltale signs of when he should attempt to appease the one that seemed calculating and self-indulgent. The one that dared Steven to trespass in the territory of an entity that wasn't looking for permission.

The Lioness paid little attention to Steven as she again traced Roxanne's lips painted with blood-red lipstick remained in the light of the visor until she was pleased with the perfect curves that would meet her destiny. The Lioness forced Roxanne's lips into a smile in the reflection of the mirror before she flipped the visor back to a fixed position as Steven silently pulled into the parking lot of the Elsinore Card room.

"Oh, this is so cool!" Roxanne giggled with a heated passion. "I've needed to get out for a long time!" she confirmed with an accelerated rush that tickled her fancy.

A really long time! agreed her companions, projecting their verbal firmness with a bat of an eyelid aimed at their opponent.

Steven ducked the shot intended to spear him and came up waving a white flag. "Well, babe, tonight is your night!" Encouraged her into a bounce that sprung the exhilarated Roxanne into Steven's lap. She pressed her body into him like never before. She planted a long wet kiss on his mouth before she bit his bottom lip, pulling until he moaned. She turned and popped the release on the door and swung her legs out onto the blacktop, waiting for her entourage.

Steven held his arm out to his queen, receiving her whimsical disposition. His world seemed complete when Roxanne smiled, and with his family intact, he too had reason to smile. Roxanne turned her smile toward her escort and batted an eyelash, accelerating Steven's heart and giving him the go-ahead to blast off. Lifting Steven and his queen ten-feet off the ground, sailing them to the doors of the card room. Crossing the threshold of the night's adventure, Roxanne wiggled her caboose.

Steven laughed as he observed months of suffering roll off Roxanne's shoulders and present a whole new persona for all that desired to meet her. She floated on that ten-foot cloud, waving and smiling to all that looked her way.

Steven let go of her hand to pull out a chair at one of the poker tables, ushering his queen with a swooping motion of his arm. Seductively Roxanne smiled, tenderly stroking Steven's face with an attentiveness he had never received from her before. Steven's face lit up with a pleased smile as he watched her slide into the chair. Only when his beautiful lady was settled did he lookup. To find every man at the table engaged by her smoldering eyes and her aroma of tantalizing disposition that danced around her and with everyone she came in contact with.

Steven studied Roxanne, and even folded a couple of times for her will. While she set the room on fire with her charming lady luck. Surely, not the almond brown, Steven reflected. But not quite black, as he had seen in the car, and several times… in the last two months. *Who is this intruder?* Steven questioned while throwing back the last of his drink, attempting to wash down a ball of jealousy that tried to choke him as Roxanne and her good-time companions danced the men into a fascinating good time with her nonsense talk, laughter, and flirting.

Not that she would have noticed, but Steven smiled as Roxanne pawed a pile of poker chips from the center of the table, teasing and cooing the men for their misfortune.

Her laughter rose to a giddy climax that encouraged her to stand on her chair and do the "good-fortune jig." Steven set with changing expressions plastering his face as he watched his young queen, spellbound in her luxury time. Occasionally, his eye would twitch when the sweat from his heated embarrassment dripped with a stinging effect. And about the time, his emotions had become bruised by her disregard for her husband being in the room. Steven became further unnerved by an annoying itch that had set sail on the flowing sweat behind the mask that covered his true feelings with a smile.

Never before had he seen this side of Roxanne! he contemplated until the blindfold of denial cinched tighter. Easing his growing emotions that wanted to pull his wife off the chair, she continued to dance on and drag her out of the room. But now that he was bound in darkness, he came to a conclusion: "This day couldn't have gone any better!" he told himself before he winked into the attentive smile Roxanne suddenly gave, just to him. "She just needs a little time to get herself together!" he confirmed in a murmur spoken loud enough for him to hear.

A little pampering, a little something to break up the humdrum of being a full-time doting mother and housewife." His conscience agreed as his head bobbed in Roxanne's direction. "Maybe this night out would put to rest any preposterous thoughts of her going to work?" He shrugged his shoulders and patronized his own judgment. "Then she'd stay home, be an attentive, loving mother and wife!"

He counseled himself with a straight poker face, which kept him even in his stakes as far as the poker game went.

Roxanne was laughing and joking with everybody while Lady Luck held her hand and helped her scoop piles of winnings into her space. Steven hadn't seen her laugh like that in a long time. "If ever?" suggested his memory, looking for conformation, while Roxanne was on fire. Bubbling with excitement, captivating the attention at their table. Some of the onlookers gathered around. Others stole glances of her from across the room.

Observing Roxanne's lifted spirit caused Steven's heart to flutter, shifting his poker face into a smirk with his next thought. God, how he had grown to love, cherish, and respect her! His heart throbbed with recognition.

Although I hadn't had those feelings when I married her! Guilt rode on the reflection, coursing the shot-gun wedding. She was now, his only desire! He concurred into those guilt feelings as Roxanne leaned into Steven. Softly she whispered something into her husband's ear before she excused herself and walked away from the table, her head held high and a skip in her step as she coursed her way through the room, as she owned it. Roxanne batted her eyelashes and nodded recognition to the men who turned to catch a glimpse of this stunningly confident, beautiful woman.

Giddiness floated Roxanne into a full dance by the time she reached the bar, wiggling her caboose into a barstool before locking eyes with the bartender. He offered a curious smile with a nod of his head. She wore her inexperience like a brooch pinned to her chest as she explained. "I'm not a regular drinker!" She blushed into the bartender's patient eyes. "But tonight would be a good night to have a drink!" She rocked her head decisively into the glimmer of the bartender's brilliantly white teeth.

Roxanne leaned into that moment to acknowledge the fact that, for the first time in months, did an indecisive thought come out firmly. Her heart began pounding out a hunter's rhythm that ushered her into a giddy giggle that pushed her up onto her knees on the barstool. She allowed Roxy and the Lioness to spin her around—once, twice, three times. Before she came to a stop in front of the amused tender, her head spun in the dizzy motion as the Lioness laid her lean young body across the bar.

"I don't know what to order!" she mouthed heavily.

The bartender gave her a special smile that was reserved for only the inexperienced. But the wink of his eye was meant especially for her when he turned on a promise to come back.

The Lioness panted, mouth wide open, taking in the scent of the prey as Roxanne tapped her long nails on the bar. Roxy spanned the room with a wider-viewed telescope with the intent of taking the spoils. She refocused the viewfinder until she had set her sights on the gent sitting to her left.

Roxanne nodded her head in recognition at a balding older man wearing gold-rimmed glasses. She smiled when he raised his glass in Roxanne's direction and nodded.

A stunning one-carat diamond adorns his right pinky finger! Roxy told the Lioness. *An expensive gold watch fancies his left wrist and presents well-manicured fingernails!"* Enticed the Lioness to circle this appetizer. His olive skin led Roxanne to assume he was of Italian descent. A bit overweight, but he looked to behold great importance.

The lens fogged up and distorted Roxanne's judgment when the man's eye caught Roxanne peering through her telescope. She was grabbing for the life preserver when he leaned into Roxanne's inquisitive expression. "You're ordering drinks?" Caught Roxanne in an unskilled embarrassment. She shook her hair, damp from a nervous sweat while glancing at the life preserver, floating away, crested a wave large enough to shake her head in agreement. "Bartender seems to be busy?" Roxanne smiled patiently into the man's briefly raised hand. Quietly demanding attention from the bartender.

In a split second, the bartender asked the lady what she would like to drink. Roxanne smiled at the man who had freely offered his influential service and ordered with confidence, "Two tequila sunrises, please!"

The bartender smiled. "Seems the lady, all along, knew what she wanted!" Caused the Trio to giggle in the tender's direction before returning their own intoxicating concoction to the intriguing man next to her.

"Dixon." He offered a hand with a smile. "Dixon Stallino," he said, exposing signs of weakness to be captivated by this beautiful woman.

The companions gently took his offered hand while the Lioness purred lusciousness all over him.

"I'm Roxy!" panted the Lioness in a captivating tone as she rose and slipped one leg under her. "This looks, like a fun place to work!" Rushed from her, the sound of suggested consideration. Spontaneously, she kicked the barstool into a spin, spanning the room from a higher perspective.

Dixon was smiling when the stool stopped directly, bringing her in eye contact with him. He noticed her smoldering eyes were dancing with life. "Are you looking for a job?" he finished into the affirmative motion of Roxanne's eagerly nodding head.

"I was considering it?" Sounded like a "Yes" to Mr. Stallino as the bartender came back with the drinks and placed them on top of the waiting napkins. "Anything else, Mr. Stallino?" the bartender asked.

Roxanne dipped and swirled her cherry in the sunrise as the bartender slipped away. Deep in calculating thought, she raised her cherry to her lips and sucked the sunrise from it. "If you decide you want a job"—he looked up to her as he finished scrawling a number on the cocktail napkin, and she softly rolled the cherry across her bottom lip, enticing Dixon into a chuckle—"you should come see this man!" Mr. Stallino said as he handed her a napkin with a man's name and phone number.

The Lioness punctured the cherry, and its juice trickled down Roxanne's lip. The Lioness licked her clean as Roxanne whispered the man's name that was written on the napkin.

"Mr. Angelino?" Roxanne stated before she walked across the burning coals that set her smoldering eyes on fire. "Thank you so very much!" She pushed her sweetness into his hand and squeezed her fingers firmly around his hand.

Dixon squeezed her hand back, thinking at that moment, *He never would let go!* Was a decision, he would quickly act on.

"Call me Dix!" he insisted before he kissed her hand. The signature of his kiss branded Roxanne's hand, leaving her breathlessly hot.

The Lioness sniffed Roxanne's hand before spraying atop of Dixon's remaining imprint while the Trio watched this new attraction, walk away. Irony's chuckle rolled up from the abyss and slapped the queen of the kingdom on the back, into laughter... Laughing... Laughing, spilled the excitement that swelled in Roxanne's bosom and jiggled the drinks she retrieved from the bar.

Steven's concerned look washed away when he spotted his wife approaching with her hands full of the drinks *that took her close to twenty minutes to retrieve!* Steven secretly observed.

When he raised his eyes from his watch and refocused his admiration on his stunning love, he noticed the effervescent poise that carried her without disturbing the lip-level cocktails. Her eyes burned with the hidden enigma that locked Steven in her powers to bewitch him. Her smile was that of the Cheshire cat as she drew closer.

"God, how I love her and that smile!" The sentiments consumed Steven until Roxanne greeted him with a wet kiss firmly planted on his lips.

When she pulled back from his lips and Steven opened his eyes, he could see that her self-confidence had pulled her shoulders back and held her head high as she offered Steven his drink.

Steven returned her smile with a wink as he accepted the drink from his intoxicating wife, who had already wooed him into a trance. The Lioness tolerated Roxanne sitting in his lap, cultivating him. Steven bit his tongue, not wanting to second guess the one he couldn't change no matter how he tried. When she was sure that he was under her spell, her smile faded, and seriousness carved her demeanor as giddiness carried her voice.

"You're not going to believe what just happened!" Lifted Roxanne out of his lap and onto her toes. She did a victory dance that spun her back into her husband's lap.

Steven bit his tongue, not wanting to second-guess the one he could not cage no matter how many times he tried. The Lioness sensed intimidation polluting the air when seriousness replaced the fixed smile of admiration on Steven's face.

He dared look into her demeanor to find her dark eyes burning with a wild passion, her chest panting powerfully, while this daring personality stalked her prey into position. The Lioness lapped her tongue from his neck to his ear, then bit down. Paralyzing Steven with her dominance, leaving him unable to defend himself. She rubbed her scent all over him before she cuddled her nose into the curve of his neck and bit down firmly.

Not enough to wound him! thought the Lioness.

Steven's eyes were closed while he was submissive to her powers. It was then he realized he was her prey ... toy—whichever pleased her!

"What happened?" seemed forced from miles away. But now, past the point of no return, it was too late to retract the hesitation that coated his words.

Instead, he presented an awkward smile.

"I got a job!" Firmly pressed her lips over his.

Meow! Shook Roxanne's butt into a wiggle dance of arrogance while the Lioness sized up Steven. "Send the lady to get a drink, and she comes back with a life-changing opportunity!" Choked Steven's fortitude with sarcasm, during his rebuke.

Steven's brow sweated during his attempt to make her happy. While his true feelings sat repressed deep in his bowels. Although he acted pleased about the slap in the head. Instantly, regretting the night... cinched the blinders tighter; Wrapping his arms, around his desire.

She rubbed him with her entire body, purring like a perfectly satisfied domesticated feline. "How did you manage that?" Steven deep-massaged her heated pride. Her back arched, and she stretched from his touch.

When she turned around, she was waving a napkin like a winner's banner, coming close enough to smack Steven in the face. But he dodged and swayed with Roxanne's mood and that tad bit of script that caused his heart to plummet from a shot of revelation. "This would change every aspect of our lives!" He whispered just above the rumble of his indigestion that painted his candid clown face with a smile. Which allowed him to deny the warning signs as long as he played along and remained in character.

CRACKING FOUNDATIONS

CHAPTER 1

WITHOUT LOOKING BACK

"**G**ood morning, sunshine!" Steven sang as Roxanne smiled and stretched in his firm hold.

"Morning!" nuzzled into his chest.

Steven cradled the back of her head with his hand, tenderly massaging her. "Are you feeling better today?" Steven whispered softly.

Roxanne rose on an elbow and gave him a queer look before she flashed a nervous smile. "I feel great!" squeezed out before she sucked in and trapped a breath under the fear that she may have experienced another episode.

"Why do you ask?" snuck out from under the breath she held.

"No reason, just thought. You may have had too much fun last night?"

Relieved of her budding anxiety, she almost needed to wipe her brow in relief. Instead, she wiggled out of Steven's hold and came to a sitting position on the edge of the bed.

Flashes of last evening's events caused a rush of adrenaline to flush through Roxanne's system, recalling last night's hunt. "I had a great time, last night!" Roxanne purred, stretching out across Steven and began smothering him with soft kisses, each lasting longer than the first. Suddenly, Roxanne rose and looked into Steven's eyes with conviction. "I think having a job will be good for me—I mean, for all of us!" Her reverie made Steven shake his head in agreement. But trepidation consumed him, signaling a warning. "Bite your tongue!" was the Morse code given by the commander at arms.

Steven held his breath until he had decisively chosen the path of a man who would question his queen, even though it might cost him his head. "My biggest concern is the kids being home alone. Getting them back and forth to school!"

She bit a kiss into Steven's lip, slowly luring him into submissiveness. "Don't worry!" The Lioness assured him, playfully. "I will take care of everything!" She pushed into him, purring loudly. Maliciously whipping the Lioness's toy with a flick of her tail for longer than a moment. "Including the kids!" She licked his jugular, long and hard, contemplating her next words. She bit in and pulled him almost to tears. "Maybe we could ride out to the club together, and after I get the promised job, the family could go to the park for a picnic?" Put him into a submissive hold.

He stumbled over his gut instinct and rolled for words. "Yeah, let's do that!"

Roxanne road the coat-tails of Steven's submissive disposition out of the bedroom with a smile for the queens, gain.

When the queen rounded the corner to enter the front room, her strong-willed cohorts crowded around her with their pet in tow. They found the children watching cartoons and giggling. Steven and Roxanne looked at each other with their own opinions. Steven noted, "A good start to a beautiful, loving day!" Before he offered a wink to his lady. But the impersonator took Roxanne's stance and winked a bold eye at Steven, and said, *This is going to be... a cinch!* Promised the Lioness before pulling a hit from Roxanne's cigarette.

Her disposition sharp... contemplating those fixed in her headlights when she exhaled into the direction of the children with collective intent.

The entourage spun on their heels and headed to encourage and counsel Roxanne during her grooming. Steven could hear a faint chatter coming from the marital chambers while he fed and readied the children for the day. An hour later, he was doing the dishes and making the children's beds; Wondering... how things, would ever return, to normal. "Especially with her going to work?" Stretched his growing list of grievances.

Steven sat behind the steering wheel, tapping his fingers and smiling. The children laughed and songs filled the car while Mama chained-smoked and re-checked her reflection in the rearview mirror with deep contemplation. When they hit the mile-marker, announcing "almost there!" The Trio interrupted the nonsense in the back seat.

To reveal the changes that were soon to come in the kingdom of Queen Roxanne.

"I got a job!" Sliced the atmosphere, which grew thick with surprise and confusion. Knitting the children's eyebrows in webs of abandonment while Mama continued delivering her news. "On the days, your dad and I have to work." She rushed her words, pronouncing them like ordinances and laws. "You will spend those days at Aunt Tina's!" The Lioness, anticipating protesting to break out, added. *She's looking forward to spending more time with all of you!*

The children looked to one another for comprehension as the queen finished delivering her new orders to Roxanne's children. Guilt painted Roxanne's face red, with the realization... The Trio's lies, came so easy. Making the efforts of tainting the children, simple, with a fake smile that smothered them with deception. There, *that's done!* The Lioness assured Roxanne, who sat fidgeting with her attire when the Lioness brushed up against her, on the way back to her lair.

It's only castles burning...
You will find...
They will come around!

Roxanne sang her companion's request without thought of the children's confusion until the children's lengthy, silent grilling shook the nerve of the Lioness.

She sprang from her lair and crowded into the back seat with Roxanne's children. The majestic animal laid across the laps of the children, contemplating, which to eat first.

You know... they have an opinion? Roxanne pleaded for consideration. But the companion's rallied together with the power to persuade. Daring, any one of Roxanne's family to deviate. *Their opinions don't Matter!* The queen's determined reinforcement was taking, no hostages this time. *Just ignore them!* Became the new dogma that would soon be signed into law books, everywhere.

"Sounds like fun!" Stevie broke the silence with an apathetic tone, iced over with sarcasm. He kicked the back of the front seat, nearly hitting his target. Mama flinched with concern. But the companions pulled her back, insisting she couldn't fold.

Roxanne's hands shook with the instability of her decision as she lit another cigarette. The entourage kept their scope in the rearview mirror, studying the children's reactions. Scarlet's face washed pale from the unknown that secreted her senses and made her nauseous with fear of the unfamiliar.

"Mamas stays home and take care of their children while daddies work!" Mark complained in a hostile whine, which shook Roxanne's existence and caused the Lioness to set out for prowling.

Her ears pulled back. Her mouth opened as she smelled the scent of the one, she should devour first. Her huge fangs glistened in the reflection of the sunlight that beamed into the car. She shot a wild eye across the back seat, daring them with a slash from her strong tail, a warning. *Do not cause any conflicts in Roxanne's mind!*

Steven silently observed the hostility brooding next to him intending to defend the young lad if this dominant impersonator, chose to attack. But if not, he decided to decline, starting a war on the peaceful day in the kingdom of Roxanne. "No, indeed! He chuckled in his discernment before he announced to the quivering emotions that taunted him. *I would let her, take the reign!* He decided before concluding out loud.

"Go ahead, babe!" Steven nodded his head in the direction of the club while his eyes remained locked in the burning pits of her fiery eyes. "If this is what you want?" He encouraged her to shoot a look of, *No account,* toward her children.

"We'll wait here!" Steven assured Roxanne's look of disregard. Before she turned a nervous sneer into the direction of her opportunity. Steven could see the dare in her eyes that refused to consider the children. "If you're sure …" Steven's words were cut short when Roxanne opened the door and swung her legs out, steadfast in her decision. She lay back and kissed her husband. "For luck!" she insisted before she slid out of the car, and without looking back, she strutted across the parking lot.

Roxanne could feel the pounding of her heart, beating viciously.

Willfully calling for the majestic prowl of the Lioness as she reached out for the handle of the card-room door. She pulled back the door and let the atmosphere of the club blow into her. Enticing her into the warmth of temptation. A devious smile replaced the look of hesitation as Roxanne stepped into the club and approached the bar and docked in front of the bartender, who had served her the trailblazers, several hours ago.

"So beautiful—what can I get you?" An aplomb shape curved Roxanne's lips as she slid the folded napkin across the bar. "I'm here, to see Mr. Angelino!" Roxanne pronounced, with a confidence bigger than her experience. "May I tell him, whose calling?" the man said with suspicion. Automatically, Roxanne's hand glided out toward the bartender. Instinctively, he allowed her to seductively squeeze his hand, with a firm conviction that shook the experienced bartender's soul. "My name, is Roxanne!" she panted with the pride of the Lioness, who licked the hunt from her puffy red lips.

"Dixon Stallino, sent me!" the huntress batted her eyelashes.

The bartender's sudden recollection gave a sly smile, of satisfaction, to the beautiful feline. Recalling Dixon, at the bar, with this young beauty last night.

"Ms. Roxanne!" His teeth reflected a brilliant white against his deep-dark complexion. "My name, is Charlie!"

The Lioness shook her head with expectation as she met his hand with a rush of recognition.

"Mr. Angelino, has been expecting you!" he continued as he picked up the house phone. While Charlie was on the phone announcing her arrival, Roxanne heeded the Lioness's relentless prowl that nipped at her heels. Alerting her to pay attention, to all the new things, coming her way.

"Mr. Angelino will be out in a moment!" Charlie assured her before turning his attentiveness toward her every need, as the boss had ordered when he offered her the drink of her choice. A sense of notability blew through Roxanne and caused her to skip on her usual drink of choice when "Chardonnay!" passed through her lips. Charlie's straight white teeth illuminated broadly across his handsome black complexion. "Ah … not only is the lady beautiful, she also has good taste!" Chuckled Charlie in a baritone laughter that had him nodding his head in approval as he descended the length of the bar. Roxanne attempted to fret with uncertainty. Wanting to check herself as her hand fluttered to her throat. She squeezed her throat, trying to loosen the lump that had lodged there last night. Thoughts of the children sitting in the car with Steven attempted to enter Roxanne's heart, but the Lioness batted it out of the park.

Her enchanted smile was still visible when Charlie returned with her glass of wine and a logo-baring napkin. "Club Elsinore," she whispered, tracing the logo with an index finger from her left hand. With her right hand, she picked up the waiting potion disguised as wine. Raising the glass to her nose, breathing in the promised intoxication. Mm… enticed the Trio. Placing the glass to her lips, letting the trance of tantalizing expectations begin fermenting her soul.

She found herself tracing and retracing the club logo, whispering in a muffled tone the plan her companions had instructed her when Charlie suddenly directed his attention past Roxanne to greet his approaching boss with a genuine admiration.

Nodding a smile to Mr. Angelino before beginning an introduction. "Ms. Roxanne!" Spun her barstool, to find an older man, also of Italian descent.

It was apparent that although Mr. Angelino was physically short in stature with narrow shoulders, he confidently stood the ground of a giant, the companions thought as Roxanne's heart quivered with excitement. She slid off the barstool and offered her hand to the influential man that would soon be her boss.

"Mr. Angelino!" the Lioness panted his name in the aroma of Dentine and Chardonnay. Luring her opportunist to take Roxanne's hand and stretch her out, as he admired what he saw. His fascination muted the static in Roxanne's world as he groaned with satisfaction.

"Lady, you are as beautiful and charismatic as Dixon said!"

Roxanne blushed, in her well-rehearsed curtsy. "I haven't worked in a long time!" Her disposition showed her inexperience for a brief moment when she apologetically humbled herself to his greatness, but that didn't unnerve her enthusiasm any. He was sizing her up and calculating, "No concern about that!" he told her.

"I'm sure, you will be an asset to the club!" Roxanne's heart did a giddy gallop of a schoolgirl as she struggled to find the control that kept her from pushing the Lioness from his lap and springing into his arms.

"Does that mean, I get the job?" she managed to push through the bouquet of budding giggles that clogged her chest.

Mr. Angelino winked into her smile with a sense of satisfaction that Dixon had picked the prime choice of the crop. "Oh yeah … yes, yes, indeed!" Mr. Angelino spoke with an alluring tone that pushed the Lioness from his lap. Mr. Angelino sucked a long drag from his fat Cuban cigar with consideration. "You will come to be our number one, girl!" his words knocked her off her seat and pushed her into his arms. Hugging him with a saving-grace zeal that spilled out all over the place as the Lioness caressed their union. Roxanne pulled back, seizing his hand, shaking it vigorously. "You got a deal!" sealed the agreement.

Meow! the Lioness concurred before she turned to groom herself and her composure. *Meow!* Stretched out the mollified Lioness, filling the atmosphere with the purring of contentment.

Roxanne sat at the bar with her new boss, sipping glasses of Chardonnay as she attentively listened and obediently answered his questions.

"This job, can be demanding in time and commitment!" He studied her body language, which presented her convictions, remaining stable.

"You may find, other things being neglected; in order, for you to perform your job!" Without hesitation, Roxanne shrugged her shoulders with a lack of concern. Unable to consider anything, or anyone, that could keep her from getting what she wanted.

"Your job title will be, chip girl!" He smiled into her absorbing reflection. "You will be serving drinks, exchanging cash currency for poker chips … and encouraging the customers to spend their money!" Roxanne shot him a look of skepticism that was thriving on her lack of experience. Mr. Angelino laughed as he reached out and patted her hand.

"Don't worry, Roxy. Men love to impress beautiful ladies!" He winked into her tempest eyes that set ablaze when he called her Roxy. "It will be easier than you think!" He smiled warmly at her. Turning his attention to his gold watch, he swallowed the last of his wine. Encouraging Roxanne to do the same, he stood up. "Roxy, be here Friday, at five o'clock in the evening!" Roxanne nearly floated off the floor, rocking back and forth, giggling. "We'll get this party started!" blasted her off into …

The promises of the good-time land-gleefully swung her hips into a small victory dance. Giggling, she grasped his hand, insisting he spin her into a new place and time, where the number one rule was, no looking back!

Full-heartedly, she grabbed the inviting lure, curtsying to him, for the second time since their brief meeting. The first, out of nervous respect. But the last, symbolized loyalty and sincerity. Promised one to another, without any more words, as she rose into a wink that showed approval from Mr. Angelino's smiling face. She giggled before winking back at him and spun toward the door. The Trio, turned back toward, their enticer when she had taken her eighth step. He was still watching her, studying her. "Friday, at five!" She assured him before she swung her hips back toward the door and with her head high; dignity and grander, sashayed toward the exit. Roxanne could feel Mr. Angelino's eyes piercing her soul before she turned and faced him with a self-assured smile.

Meow! shaped her lips as her new boss signaled, a thumbs-up.

Got yeah! the Lioness chattered as Roxy pushed Roxanne's butt against the swinging door and spun out. *Transformation complete!* cooed the Lioness into Roxy's ear.

CHAPTER 2

CHANGE OF PACE

The Lioness noticed Anxiety budding atop of the guilt that supported the foundation of failure as Roxanne recalled putting off the trip to the park with the family. *What, with having only five days to prepare for our first job!* the companions defended. While techno-colored displays of her last job visited Roxanne and viewed with her the last days in Reno.

Annoyed and unnerved by such contempt in the Castle of Roxanne, the Lioness padded from her lair, silently followed the crevices of Roxanne's mind. In search of the marauders who have plundered too long. When the Lioness slid on her belly around the corner and into a common space where Reluctance hewed Roxanne's self-esteem. And where Mark's words of protest blared for recognition. "Mama's are suppose to stay home!" Emphasized the tearing of her soul, the burning of her ears. Roxanne's body was screaming for mercy when the Lioness beckoned the horse of Independence. The dominant feline assertively persuaded the council; her prey, be place on this mighty beast, Independence. And the culpable, be rode far away, banned from the kingdom of Roxanne. The companion raved for Roxanne to slap

Independence's ass! Let it carry your unwanted conspirators away! Pulled Roxanne's soul back and forth, ripping her soul slowly, back and forth. Tearing and pulling until finally, she swatted that Independence in the ass while screaming, EMANCIPATION!

Roxanne's command, launched Independence into a full run. The long mane of the magnificent horse began to shed colors until it glistened a cold blood against the white muscles that beaded with sweat. The hair of the unwilling riders blew in the hurricane-force winds that tore at the entities—that had been molding Roxanne, for so damn long. Smacked Independence in the ass again, causing him to dig his front legs in with robust power. The back legs pushed combusted energy, blasting the horse of Independence into a change of pace.

Indecisively, Roxanne and the dominating companions searched through the closet. At first, Roxanne considered dressing conservatively out of respect for Steven. The Lioness coughed with disgust as she began clawing and shredding anything that had to do with pleasing Steven. Roxy lit a cigarette and held it to Roxanne's lips. She kept smoking while watching Roxy pull from the closet items she couldn't remember owning. Suddenly, there were outfits laid out that Roxanne would be allowed to choose from. The new artifacts glistened in her eyes, causing her to seek sunglasses before she could finish admiring her bright new future. Her stomach fluttered with excitement as she quickly slipped the glasses on. Grander would have been dancing on the bed, but out of fear of wrinkling the nice new things, he swept Roxanne up and spun her into his web.

Roxy and Grander danced around Roxanne with matching outfits—shoes to nylons—and accessories of gold and silver to enhance her attire while surges of energy pulsed through the host's body. Wiggling, shaking, spinning, and chatting out loud to the others when Rod Stewart came to an end on the turntable.

The host of the companions emerged from the bedroom, prancing butt-naked through the house. Suddenly, and without expectation, she rushed forward with a squeal while kicking her legs up in a victory dance. She landed in a squat, and without thought, she rolled a complete somersault with enough power to spring back onto her feet. Surprised by her hidden acrobatic talent, Roxanne giggled with the sound of revelation. "Damn, girl, you may be going into the wrong business?" she stated before strutting toward the turntable, gleefully clothed in her egocentricity.

Roxanne giggled into the fun she was having at her transformation party while she made another selection from her growing record collection. Considering nothing else except herself. Until she leaned over to retrieve the album from the turntable, abruptly, her thoughts reflected on the images of her disappointed children's faces that reflected in the high-glossed vinyl record. Mirroring, that early-morning courtship of Steven and the children, trying to convince her to go fishing off the Newport pier. "I wish, I could go …" She awkwardly pulled lint balls from her sweater so she wouldn't have to make eye contact. "But now that I'm a working Mama…" She sounded on the verge of annoyance.

"I have many things to take care of…" came out slowly and methodically. Persistence forced the words out—"Before I start work on Friday!"—Rushed out at Roxanne's family and swarmed around them. Shrugged the shoulders of her peasants without comprehension of the new things that prioritized Mama's new life. While uncertainty creased the faces in the crowd, Mama began to explain. "Everything will be great—just you wait and see!" Roxanne insisted into the faces that went blank.

Roxanne slipped on the silky smoking jacket she had found in the closet. Surprised to find it was a perfect fit and in one of her favorite colors. A deep chocolate brown she admired as she slid her hand down the slippery slope of her breast. Smelling the collar, she wondered where it came from.

Suspicion reared its horns. *Do you think Steven has another girl?* A twinge of Jealousy stabbed Roxanne in the heart before she opened the Pepsi that was waiting on the coffee table. She lit a cigarette while the companions howled with doubtful laughter. *He admires only our girl!* They chuckled louder as Roxanne dialed her sister-in-law's phone number.

On the third ring, Roxanne snuffed her cigarette out in the ashtray. On the fourth ring, Tina answered the phone. "Hey, Tina?" Roxanne exhaled the cloud of smoke she had been holding in her lungs into the receiver. "Roxanne, how's it going?" Tina's voice rang with sincerity for her Sister-in-law.

"I got a job!" Enthusiasm crackled before the phone line went dead for a long moment. "Hello … hello?" ruffled the queen's feathers before Tina's question came across the phone line. "What about the children?" Lisa attempted to dash Roxanne's spirit.

"That's why I called"—caught Tina's attention—"I thought of you, the most qualified, to care for my children." She tried to smooth a coating of praise over Tina. But all Roxanne heard was a sigh of disdain.

Roxanne considered asking if they were talking on a bad phone line. Because again, there was a long pause. Tina's heart panged with sorrow as she looked around the room at the five other children of working mothers. That she also was the most qualified to watch. "Roxanne, don't take this the wrong way," Tina begged her brother's wife with experience shaking her voice. "Every mother who goes to work loses the intuition for her family's best interest!" echoed through the phone line, causing static to build in Roxanne's abyss, with Tina's expressed opinion stirring the pot. While the tension of Doubt, wobbled Roxanne's backbone—when she could find no clarity, on the phone line.

The Lioness pawed her weight onto Roxy's back. Pushing her on cue to suck the tar from Roxanne's cigarette, a substance that might calm their queen's, stress level.

Abruptly, Roxy exhaled the toxin into the mouthpiece of the phone as a cold disposition gripped their host and took control. "Tina, I admire you and your ability in rearing children!" The phone line crackled as the words froze inside the lines. "However, in your thirty-three years of life, that is the only thing you have experienced!" Roxy bit at what threatened to be a hangnail as she listened to her words finish crackling through the iced-over phone lines. Chards of ice cut a trail in Tina's direction, nearly cutting her throat, leaving the line of communication severed. Only an occasional drip of Hope attempted the sound of a defrost while Tina pondered over Roxanne's words.

Ringing true the reality of her bad marriage, with a man who was an alcoholic. Whom lusted for the worst type of infidelity. Images of past fights with him, after waiting for him till wee hours in the morning. But not until the cock crowed did, he usually arrive home, drunk and heavily coated with that horrific aftershave he wore.

Emotions swarmed around Tina until she could only find fault in herself. "It must be something wrong with me!" tainted her passion, for everything around her. Attempting to suffocate her before she could run away from the heartbreaking issues of her own and fought her way back to the conversation at hand.

"Roxanne, I love your family. I would take care of your children, anytime, any day!" Lisa's promise echoed into Roxanne's anticipation. "But … blah blah blah blah!" Building static in the phone line, clashing with the queen's expectations, the Lioness diligently padding with expectations. Panting and flicking her tail with annoyance on the offbeat of Tina's words. "My house is full of children … of working mothers!" Tina pleaded. "All the material objects … or babysitters, can't give them, what they truly need!"

Tina waited for a brief moment, saying a silent prayer when she found the phone line close to death. Praying her words would encourage her sister-in-law.

Still, the only sound she could hear over the phone line was the padding of the feet of what she thought to be some animal. She could hear a brushing of some sort, swiftly cutting the air, when the Lioness's tail brushed Tina's words aside. *Well then, the children will be dropped off on Friday and stay until Sunday evening!* the Lioness demanded Tina's obedience. "Girl, did you hear anything I said?" Tina pronounced her words in such a manner of ingraining her opinion on Queen Roxanne.

Defiant minion… dare to object!" Stated *the Trio.* The wild instinct of the Lioness lashed out at Tina, tearing her with irritating words and bites of guilt. Roxy sucked the last puff of carbon from the cigarette butt before she crushed it into the ashtray. The Lioness severed Tina's aorta artery on the exhale. *"Yeah, I think…"* she paused not with prejudiced thoughts, really! But the Lioness was chattering a *Heads off!* sentence for treason against the kingdom of Roxanne!

"I will call someone else!" Tore into a nerve, causing Tina to shudder at the image of mistakes that couldn't be undone. And doing more damage than good! Just before she uttered the words, Roxanne wanted to hear.

With the threat of a pounding headache coming on, Roxanne rummaged through her purse. And after a successful search, she tossed three pain relievers into her mouth and washed them down with the last of her Pepsi. Checking her written agenda, she smiled as she crossed off Tina's name. Doodling a smiley face before dropping down the list and moving to her next task without looking back.

Roxanne traced Lisa's name, dotting the pin hard into the paper, swirling circles all over Lisa… considering, if she would still be mad.

To this day, I haven't a clue... pondered, the locked crevices of her mind. "What set her off? Blurted out with disdain that insisted, they discontinue any contact, at all!" Blew through the holes of Roxanne's cobwebbed mind. Riddled with 'blackout moments; of minutes, hours, days?' began pulling Roxanne away from her priorities, causing the foghorns to signal a blast of static, to adjust her attitude, as the Lioness bit at her heels. Roxy shoved her index finger into the rotary phone and deliberately spun Lisa's phone number.

"Hello?" The voice of her long-missed friend caused Roxanne to choke up with tears. "Hey, Lisa." Shook her confidence. "How've you been?" came over the line in a whisper. The line went silent, just like before a storm. Alerting the companions, that the front defense had been breached.

Roxy stroked the long, lean body of the Lioness as she brushed up against Roxanne and softly bit the back of her knee. "Look, I'm sorry." Rushed, void of empathy, over the phone line. The Lioness flicked her tail, threatening to chew the ear of the reluctant participant before a low belly moan echoed through the room when no reply came back.

Anxiety rushed more words from the host to fill the void. "I still don't know why, you are mad." Roxy lit a cigarette for Roxanne as she continued to confess. "I don't want to lose your friendship!" Roxy coached Roxanne's weaker side.

The Lioness hissed with intolerance, on the prowl for her prey. She manipulated and played with them until they were in a perfect position and with the imminent apology delivered. The Trio sat in satisfaction as Lisa giggled into the phone with a breath of relief. The Lioness sat up and stretched her back, letting the hunt roll off her shoulders. "I've been hanging on suspense, for this call!" The phone line began bubbling with glee, snickering into the phone. Roxy turned from the Lioness, who was cleaning herself and batted an eyelash at Roxanne.

"God, Lisa, I have missed you!" Roxanne spoke with her hidden intentions.

"I missed you, too!" Lisa cried into the phone. "I felt, I needed to prove a point!" The phone line became void again, this time from Roxanne's end. The Lioness crouched down, and her ears pulled back. Her wild eyes dilated, back on the hunt. "Really ..." She bit. "And what is that supposed to mean?" Roxanne exhaled her words over the loud static that shot from her stomach and crashed through the walls of her mind as Lisa courageously spoke.

"I thought, if I put some distance between us ..." The Trio drew a hit from the cigarette, sucking it in deep while she listened and calculated a sentence for the insubordinate. "You would realize, how inconsiderate you have been to almost everyone you know!" Roxanne sucked in the last of the smoke and crushed it into the ashtray. Letting the phone line go void as she watched the butt smolder a smoke signal from a rose-colored Tiffany glass ashtray. The Trio pushed their frustrations back, in an attempt, to safeguard their original motive. Roxy chuckled as she forced the next words from her mouth in a submissive pattern.

You're right ... I am sorry. Please accept my apology? the Lioness coached Roxy into trapping the prey.

Therefore, there was no sincerity on Roxanne's part. The Lioness chewed with conspiracy. *How can you be sorry for something you can't remember!* Tore the Lioness.

Elation, coated with an unforeseen state of affairs, rocked Lisa's end of the phone line. *Maybe, she has learned something?* Lisa thought to herself.

"That's okay ... I forgive you!" introduced Lisa's conversation, of the significant happenings in Lisa's life.

Roxy's mounting annoyance brandished her efforts with sharp tones and lack of consideration. Roxanne firmly stroked the Lioness's patients in long stride while the friends rushed topics and exchanged small bits of information about Lisa's current events. Suddenly, the Lioness batted at the audacious questions and watched it roll into the phone line with enough power to sever Lisa's words.

"Would you"—silenced the jabbering—"pick up my kids on Fridays and take them to the fire station, for the rest of the school year?" said the Trio, with personal expectations, that seemed to freeze the lines of communication.

Roxanne's words sent Lisa searching for stable ground. With her back pushed up against the wall, she felt set up and falsely courted. "Why do you need me to do that?" Her voice thundered suspiciously. The Trio didn't notice their mentors' scornful disposition. Instead, they let Roxy elaborate. "*I got a job!*" she wiggled into the dismayed expression that had molded her insubordinates face.

At the Elsinore, card room starting on Friday! Roxy blurted into the phone with enough power to assault Lisa's ear.

The pause on the phone line was long enough for Roxy to get a hold of her excitement but too long for comfort. Roxanne fretted while conjuring up more of the essential nerve to continue the conversation. Instead, of slamming the phone back into its cradle. The Lioness followed Roxy step-by-step in a pace of provocation, slashing the air with her tail. She panted with heated determination while the Trio recalled the same dead sound that came from Tina's phone line. They knew, Lisa was forming her own opinion. *Which we may have listened!* stated Roxy into the Lioness's irritated disposition. Who had already began alerting the entourage to fortify their position?

"Roxanne, I think you should reconsider taking that job?"

Shook the Lioness from the pedestal, enticing her into a routine of further contemplation. Lisa's complete lack of support knocked Roxanne off balance. "You don't understand," she pleaded into the phone. "I need to work!" she aspirated heavily into Lisa's ear.

Why, would she care? chewed the Lioness.

"She came from a stable family!" Roxanne attempted to defend her friend.

The epitome of stay-at-home mothers! growled the heiress.

Thanks to her mother, who never beat her or ridiculed her! And to her natural father, who never left her! Stomped Roxy's feet, in protest.

The static grew to great heights in Roxanne's entire body as the companions joined in course. *Give her tools of self-worth and tangible purpose!* Conflicted with Roxanne's normalcy. That had been installed by the one person who was supposed to love her unconditionally. Wreaked havoc with Roxanne's heart as she stormed back and forth in a pacing motion. *Therefore, she can't understand why Roxanne's needs are more important than her family's well-being!* The companions counseled in an attempt to waylay the waves that crashed on the vulnerable beaches of Roxanne's mind, where she harbored the need for someone to back her with some positive support.

The Lioness bit at Roxy's heels, insisting Roxanne collect, some humility. *Thank Lisa and end the call!* rocked Roxanne in the storm. Where the tug-o-war between Roxy, the Lioness, and herself competed in opinions. Roxanne contemplated how she had no choice but had been shoved into a relationship with her many companions with whom she had learned to live with, no matter what's sacrificed of herself. But the suggestion of the Lioness left Roxanne feeling destitute of satisfaction. Causing her to shove back with the longing for Lisa's understanding.

Suddenly, the intense static lowered to a hum. Roxanne wiped the sweat from her brow and then cleared her throat. While noticing a mental echo, ringing through the crevices of her mind, breaking down the closed doors and allowing reality to flood her existence. Roxanne found herself trapped and distracted from the subject at hand as she investigated the echo.

This job, is a good thing! suddenly broke through the phone line. Unfalteringly, Roxy insisted, *I need to, focus on myself just for a little while!* reverberated through the phone line, attempting to convince Lisa. More like, inform her. *Roxanne needs to be, the number one priority, for the first time in her life!*

Many seconds went by with no response. Causing the companions to imagine Lisa shaking her head with no regard, for Roxanne's words or feelings. Agitating the echo into a high-pitched static in Roxanne's mind. Roxanne sat down and clutched her head into the pressurized bandage of her hands.

Just how, *to manipulate Lisa,* was at hand. Suddenly, the phone line crackled with life when Lisa reluctantly agreed. "I just have a bad feeling about this job thing!" Lisa said daringly, expecting Roxanne to explode. Instead, a cool breeze blew through the phone line. "Everything, is going to be fine … just, don't you worry!" Roxy assured her reluctant jury. But the unconvinced Lisa, choked back her next words of contention before she wished Roxanne luck.

Now that, Lisa's taken care of! the Lioness nipped at Roxy, signaling her.

Roxy smiled at the importance of her job as she inhaled a huge breath. And on the exhale, she blew that breath into Roxanne's lungs. Who was allowing the darkness of her blackout to brighten as she hung up the phone!

Basking in the satisfaction with the acts of compliance received. The Lioness jumped up on the couch and pawed Roxanne to stroke her into a purr. Roxy pulled a long, satisfying hit off of Roxanne's cigarette. On the exhale, laughter mixed with the Lioness droning rhythm of a purr filled the air. Polluting Roxanne's reality with images of getting what she wanted. The queen began shaking with laughter while she guided the fantasy of her ambitions. *Into the land of new and exciting things!* But as they left the planet, Cynicism voiced. "So soon after

Scarlet's accident!" escaped from Roxanne's lips with an attempt to consider her children. Nevertheless, when she was unable to visualize their faces, let alone their needs. Roxy shrugged off the negative vibes and replaced them with thoughts of her first acquaintance with Mr. Stallino as the Trio blasted out of the atmosphere.

CHAPTER 3

TRANSFORMING

The Lioness guarded the week away by keeping the unwanted episodes of negative turbulence at bay while Roxy encouraged Roxanne during the wee hours.

"I feel so tired, yet very anxious!" Roxanne admitted to her most prominent companions, the Yeoman's, pushing the wind into her sails.

The Lioness's nose was in the air, smelling the hunt for Roxanne's weaknesses. Heightening her need to protect her boundary when suddenly, the Lioness turned and chased Roxanne down the trail that trapped her in a circle of isolation with Roxy.

That's okay, girl. If you need rest, just lean on me! Roxy would tell her in the beginning. But as each day ticked away, Roxanne's clock honed to erratic heights.

By five-thirty on Thursday morning, Roxanne had prepared two casseroles and a lunch for Steven. Wrote a letter to Spencer. Smoked a pack of cigarettes and drank a six-pack of Pepsi in the crowded room. Where her entertainers spun on the turntable, and her companions danced and bounced about the room.

When the children rose with the sun, Roxanne's anxiety heated her feelings with an abundance of overwhelming emotions.

And when the children crowded her space, demanding nurturing from their Mama, they found that she wasn't available.

Instead, the imposter offered an obstinate stare before she got up and walked away without an instinct for the well-being of Roxanne's children.

Mama's substitute chained smoked while driving the children to school. She glanced in the rearview mirror to find Roxanne's boys whispering to one another and forcing Roxy's paranoid thoughts of retaliation to shoot daggers at them. But the artillery bounced off the force field that temporarily protected them.

Double drat! Roxy exhaled before turning her attention back to the road and the droning sound of the tires.

A few minutes later, Roxy began tapping her nails on the steering wheel keeping rhythm with the melody that wooed her from the radio. At the same time, Roxanne's children interrogated her about her new job. Roxy turned the radio up louder to drown Roxanne's children. *Who the hell's idea was it to go to school way out here anyways?* Roxy complained as she pulled into the school compound without noticing the children had been baffled and gagged in silence. Their eyes, wide with confusion and maybe even a bit of fear, stared down on Roxy. Making her feel some obligation to explain, although she couldn't disguise the hint of annoyance.

Nothing would really change. Everything is going to be great! The invader attempted a sincere smile for the children's benefit as she pointed to her cheek, just like Vanessa used to do to Roxanne, demanding kisses before letting them out of the car. Not a second passed before the last passenger door closed did Roxy's annoyance shove the transmission into reverse. Nearly backing over Roxanne's scattering children frustrated

Roxy's patients. *Damn, kids, how many times has their Mama told them?* she growled.

Watch for cars! Roxy yelled out the window before she sped off with her fist waving in the air at the children.

Roxy exhaled into the mirror to find Roxanne's pleading eyes beckoning. But Resistance sucked the nicotine from the cigarette before exhaling a plume of smoke that filled the car. And when the cloud of smoke lifted, Roxanne was speeding down the freeway.

Driving toward Corona, actually, approaching the off-ramp. Confusion washed over her as she mindlessly crossed the lanes on the freeway with her foot on the break. A horn blasted awareness in her direction as she made a quick final swerve and made the Corona exit. Fear rushed her into a bombardment of Anxiety as she questioned her actions. "What the heck?" she stated as she raised her middle finger, as an afterthought and went to shove it out the window.

Her fingertip caught the roof and sprang into a backward bend. Causing a throbbing pain to signal her mind, something was amiss. While unclear Desperation, laid its weight on the horn, Roxanne quickly scanned the rearview mirror, hoping to find the hidden secrets.

"Where have I been?" she inquired the image of the Lioness, grooming herself with satisfaction. A wave of uneasiness sent her to inquire about the time. "Shit!" Panic, rushed into her muscles. "Where are the children?" polluted her instincts. "They're late for school!" danced contrary to the rhythm of the Lioness's desire.

Nervously, Roxanne turned her eyes to the rearview mirror to find a sudden surge of relief when she realized she was not truly alone. But was now accompanied by both of her companions in the reflection of the mirror. The discontent Lioness heavily panted, pacing back and forth, feeling restless. Or maybe she had grown short of patience for Roxanne and her swinging back and forth. *She'd be better off if she remained in the abyss!* The Lioness softly bit and teased Roxanne into play until her fears fluttered away. "What I like…" Roxanne paused for a moment. "Is the feeling that has manifested in me the last couple of days!" Roxanne winked a thanks to the purring Lioness and to the vision of the new and improved Roxanne before continuing to council with the ones that devourers her conflicts and sets her high on the throne of her newfound royalty.

"That's a good thing, right?" Turned her question into a smile in the rearview mirror. While a hint of a new conviction enhanced her eyes as she firmly pronounced.

"If a job calms the static. That must mean it's essential for me!" Roxanne concluded as she pulled into her designated parking spot in the apartment garage. "Essential for me … essential for me!" she hummed until her supportive companions jumpstarted her heart to a faster beat.

Roxanne sat in the car attempting to make a complete to-do list when she was startled by a rapping on the back door of her Cadillac. Anxiety fretted and taunted Roxanne as she wrenched her neck into a severe spasm. She spotted an acquaintance who believed she was Roxanne's best friend. "I don't have time for her!" insisted Roxanne.

Devour that insolent bitch! Roxy insisted with a chastising crack of a whip, causing the Lioness to spring from her lair and chase Roxanne out of the car, past the annoyance and up the stairs to pack clothes for her three children.

Thoughts of saving time raced through her mind as she put the last of the children's cloths into the overstuffed suitcase. Words flowed from her mouth in a manner that expected someone to disapprove. "I could send the bag with Steven in the morning," she assured the audience as she struggled to lock the overstuffed baggage. "So, he can take the children straight over to Tina's without coming home for the children's bag first!"

No sooner had she finished stating her perspective the companions protested a rebuttal. "Who cares about saving Steven's time?" stopped Roxanne in front of the coffee table, where she pulled a cigarette from the soft pack. *This is all about you and what you need.* Her fan club encouraged. "Old habits are hard to break!" Roxy chuckled at her host. Roxanne bowed graciously with that idea as she lit the cigarette and headed toward the kitchen.

Roxanne began humming a familiar tune that she and Steve once considered to be their song. While she followed the old familiar steps of a dance, she had performed a million times throughout her lifetime. It was called *satisfying everybody, else!*

"All he will have to do is heat them up!" Roxanne smiled with contentment in her ability to perform. "I can care for my family—and satisfy my needs also!" she said as she blindly fished for items in the fridge. Suddenly consumed with a growl that turned to words of resentment. *He can fix his own damn meals!* The companions insisted to the mounting frustration that rode Roxanne and hampered her ability to retrieve the last items from the refrigerator.

They need to learn to care for themselves! The Lioness chewed the ear that Roxanne waved a hand at, attempting to signal, a break in the conversation so she could turn her collected thoughts to glance at the contents of the icebox.

Two Dutch ovens sat on the bottom shelf. A stuffed lunch bag sat on the top shelf with her husband's name written in her script. Roxanne straightened her posture as her hand fluttered to her chin in thought. *Hmm ...* She scratched her head, searching for the information. *When did I, do that?* The question blew into the thick cobwebs in her mind.

But when the answers evaded her, she shrugged it off. Calmly, she looked at her watch. She decided she had enough time to straighten the house. And to take a long bath before her hair appointment. Roxanne made her way through the house looking for things to straighten up.

But everything was already in order. Again, she tried to recall doing her duties. But when it didn't automatically come to her, she approached the bathroom and opened the door. Steam from the hot bath crept its way into her confusion and clouded any clarity to her unanswered questions.

She sat in the tub, waving at the billows of steam that carried away any concerns of not being able to remember fixing her husband's meals—or cleaning the apartment to a sparkle and taking the children to school. The only emotion that was too heavy to be carried away with the mist was her Desperation. *I hope the children are at school?* she fretted, for only a minute. "I need to prove to myself!" she said aloud as she slid down into the tub, stopping when the water touched the tip of her chin. "And the world!" Spouted with a powerful resilience that caused ripples to form into waves, cresting up to Roxanne's lip.

"I can take care of my family duties"—again rippled the waters—"and hold down a job!" Caused tidewaters to nearly rush over her head. The current, attempted to pull her out to sea. Instead, the threat spanned out and dredged up the discouraging words from the conversations with Tina and Lisa.

"They'll see, everything is going to be marvelous!" Roxanne sang in an inflexible tune while competing with her companions during her bath and dressing session. Which had been titled "Debate" because Roxanne kept swaying back to the well-being of others and the dance, she had rehearsed for so many years.

"Spotless!" sounded with expectation. "The way, I was forced to keep Mother's house!" prickled Roxanne's flesh with goose bumps. Nausea burned into the crevices of her mind. "A marionette with severed strings attempted to join her in the selfless dance. But he needed just a little help? Raising the pitch of the static and stoking the fire, where opposition burned. Shooting sparks into Roxanne's direction, quickening a blaze under her feet, and pushed her out the door.

Roxanne stood tall and defiant, outside of the apartment, in front of the closed door. She was breathing deep while a warm, gentle breeze defrosted the prickles of old memories. She blew smoke from her nose And when the thick substance cleared, a new persona kicked the dirt from under her feet while Roxanne glided down the stairs and slipped into the car.

Diffidently, Roxanne glanced into the smile that reflected into her overwhelmed expression from the rearview mirror. Noticing the prominent dark circles that had taken up residency under her eyes since the second day of her daughter being in the hospital had now nearly faded to a normal skin color. She ran her long fingers through her hair and agreed with herself, she needed to get her hair colored. So, the gray that had come in since that horrible day would not make her look older than her twenty-six years of age.

Everybody in agreement? Roxy queried with a wink into the mirror as Roxanne lit a cigarette. Drawing the first hit long and hard while she opened a Pepsi and turned the radio up, excessively loud, before pulling out of the parking space.

The Trio settled on a beehive hairdo, with long ringlets caressing the jaw bone in a deep-auburn color. "For her first job since coming to California!" The thought of this compressed the hostess's heart, igniting an explosive laughter that shuttled Roxanne and her companions into the hair salon.

The Lioness padded in circles just inside the door as the stylist was pulled into the direction of the charismatic disposition that blew in the door. Roxy held Roxanne's hand out in a manner, expecting the servant to bow and kiss the queen's hand.

Instead, the hairstylist accepted Roxanne's hand and slowly spun her.

"You are going to be a treat!" she finished into Roxanne's spin that came to a slow stop in the face of her physical transformation.

After a lukewarm shampoo, massage, and conditioning, Roxanne was escorted to a luxurious throne. The hairstylist pumped her spirits up into the center of the mirror until the reflection presented our hostess sitting like a queen as she pronounced her needs and wants with precise determination.

The stylist locked eyes with Roxanne's reflection and smiled with sincere gratitude. "I would be honored!" She twisted into a woman's curtsy.

"To provide you, a queen's pampering!" The ladies, words enticed a tickle to flutter a giggle from Roxanne's stomach. And when the stylist quickly released her hold on the chair, Roxanne's giddiness took flight with the butterflies.

Roxanne was ushered into the yoke of the compulsiveness that closed her eyes.

"Do your magic!" fluttered up to the stylist's ears as she began gingerly massaging color into "Her Majesty's" hair. Then she took the extra time to caress a deeper relaxation into Roxanne's transition. The stylist slightly pulled the sovereign's hair as she finger-combed the dye into Roxanne's hair, causing the Lioness to arch her back before stretching out long and lean in the pool of sunshine on the floor.

CHAPTER 4

ROXY

Stage-bright cam lights, each one a different color. Flashed off and on in the abyss where Roxanne was isolated. Causing her heart to flutter when images of her dreams and ambitions appeared, each in their own spotlight. Anxiety encumbered Roxanne's space, making it hard to breathe.

But Roxy was there to encourage her charge. *Seek the adventure of the surprise behind the blindfold!* Roxy enticed in a calming tone.

A deep but subdued roar came from the direction of the Lioness as the stylist took a few minutes fluff-drying Roxanne's hair with a towel that danced over her eyes, capturing her in darkness and then releasing. Capturing. Releasing. Capturing and releasing. Nervously, Roxanne laughed at Roxy, who was busting a gut. "Oh my God, I'm loving this!" roared loud enough for God himself to hear.

Roxy really wanted Roxanne to have the full experience of her transformation. But she found it necessary to leave Roxanne in the cues, where darkness kept her restrained. It was there she was safe, considered innocent, while the companions did the queen's bidding. When Roxy slid back into the transformation throne, another subject inquired about her choice of beverage. As the stylist began to comb and clip different lengths into Roxanne's new persona before rolling it up into big curlers.

Roxy thought of bringing Roxanne out of the dark as the stylist busied herself with eyebrows, then a facial. But Roxy, was enjoying, Indulging in the well-deserved freedom she had been waiting for so long, caused her to bat a wink into the mirror, as yet, another subject performed a manicure on the queen's nails. She was sipping on her second Pepsi and smoking a cigarette while she silently watched in awe, the transformation from the old repressed Roxanne.

"To the new and improved, get what you want!" Roxy bellowed out in a cloud of smoke, verbally stating the first words spoken, in nearly twenty minutes. And as she puffed away at the last cigarette from the pack, the last curl bounced and fell perfectly in place at the collarbone.

Curiously, the Lioness rose from her catnap. Stretching her lean, muscular legs as she padded slowly around the distinguished creation that sat atop the throne. The Lioness leaned into Roxanne's leg and rubbed her entire body against her host while Roxy glided her hand firmly down the Lioness's back, causing the friction to initiate a roar of approval. A blushed smile of gratitude brightened the room during the initiating union, where the Trio bonded in self-satisfaction for the approved reflection of Roxy, who was the splitting image of Roxanne's new makeover.

The entourage was dancing with all the beauticians who had enjoyed sweating their brow for the queen, who now stood in front of a full-length mirror, staring at herself! Awe swayed her into adjusting her crown! The Lioness continued to chatter a low-deep cat call of approval.

Bravo! Bravo! stated Roxy, clapping her hands.

Did the stylist. just take a bow! Flashed a suspicious thought through Roxanne's mind, where tattered cobweb cluttered the spaces that she now, begun searching since stepping out of the dark. Leaving behind any recollection of how she got here. Or how long she had been there. The information continued to remain elusive as she looked into the reflection of the mirror. Giddiness, pushing her shoulders into a shrug as her hands' landed on its guided destination, palms down, on the new hairdo. Bubbles of surprised excitement floated through her body as Roxy reached a conclusion. *"It's indeed, a hair fashion, only a prominent lady would wear!"* "Enticed her, to pat, every part of her new creation as sarcasm chewed her ear.

For each second Roxanne hesitated, to agree, several of her excitement bubbles exploded and vaporized into a deadly toxin that strangled the union of self-satisfaction.

"Not very practical!" Exploded through a choking cough from Roxanne's abyss, aimed toward the Lioness with resistance. Roxanne stretched out the curl that dangled at her neckline. Mindlessly, she poked at the curls that were fixed to the top of her head.

Hesitantly, the Lioness circled around the stylist, who gasped with confusion. Stalking up behind Roxy, with impatience fraternizing with her temper. Causing the Lioness to react with claws of five, sharper than razor blades. Intolerance bit into Roxy, with fangs built to devour. Focusing her attention on the matter, she should be controlling. Roxy took flight from the clutches of the piercing authority of the prominent personality. Just as the Lioness whipped her tail, slapping a blindfold over Roxanne's eyes, and rushed her with compulsive thoughts. "I want to drive out to Home Gardens, take a look!" she finalized before sucking nicotine from a wet cigarette butt. "It's a small community ... like we used to live in!" Roxanne informed her companions with a disposition that eased the Lioness.

Roxy slid Roxanne into an illusion of her children laughing and romping in the yard as they built childhood memories. When Roxanne's mind shifted to the thought of her children at school, she checked her wristwatch. Which reminded Roxy, she wanted to change that school situation ASAP.

Considering how far away it is! Said Annoyance, with a sigh.

"There are only a few months of school left!" Roxanne firmly made her final decision. "Next school year, the children would go to the school in our new community!" stated the queen's newest command.

"Excuse me?" said the beautician to Roxanne's reflection, which flushed with compromised priorities.

Three hours later, Roxy held her head high and walked out of the beauty salon with a new confidence, feeling and looking better, than any other time in her entire life. She sat in the car, admiring herself in the mirror, turning her head in every angle as she giggled with delight. She loved the transformation, giving her a whole new sense of individualism and made her feel, *on top, of the world*! Roxy's screech, raised Roxanne to giddy heights, made Roxy and the Lioness to look down, from the top of the world. "This is a good thing!" filled the air with persuasion, as she traveled toward her destiny.

CHAPTER 5
TOP OF THE WORLD

Roxanne puffed a cigarette to life while pulling off the freeway into the quaintness of Home Gardens. She bebopped along with the rhythms that blared from the speakers as she cruised through the community. She drove up and down the streets inspecting the residents and seeking out their appeal. Roxanne, pulled up to a middle height woman with dark hair and a bit over weight, whom was standing, in front of the house across the front of the school. Deciding, to get out and greet the lady, Roxanne went to open the door. But before she could get a firm grip on the handle, the Lioness jumped out the window and rushed up to the lady. The Lioness smelled her from, a good foot away before she coughed and reared back on her heels and spun pack about three-feet before folding her body onto her legs. The Lioness ears pulled back; her eyes slanted, tail switched, back and forth. Roxy climbed off Roxanne's lap, where she had ben co-piloting, all day. She straightened the queen's attire before she stood erect and held her head high with a complacent smile faking her disposition as she extended Roxanne's hand and greeted the lady

"According to what's her name; the school, efficiency is top grade!" Roxanne stated, as she stroked the Lioness. Roxy piloted the car, two-blocks down the main street and made a turn toward the south, onto a street named "Brentwood!" Roxanne, introduced to the companions, who chattered her into temptation, now fell silent for a long moment. "Brentwood!" Again, it rang with high hopes.

"Brentwood ... Brentwood ... Brentwood!" The Trio's chorus filled the air as the they slowly prowled their new territory.

Halfway up the gradual incline, the Trio spotted their lair with a sign that read, FOR RENT, which forced the car to halt in front of the house that resembled the house on the cul-de-sac. *Where the sun shined brighter than any other place in the world!* The Trio chorused a rhythm that slowly slid them, out of the car. They were shielding their eyes from the intensity of the sun. As a smile spread across Roxy's anticipation. Confidently, she nodded her head before joining the others. The Trio turned a contemplative look up and down the street as the Lioness set out to walk the perimeter. Sniffing the air and the things that had been dominated before her arrival. She scratched, rolled, and rubbed every inch of that perimeter before rejoining the group. Purring into the smiles of her co-conspirators, before they each instinctively and simultaneously turned their noses to the sky. The sun warmed The Trio's faces as they sat in council until forming a majority vote. "The sun also "shined bright" here!"

Along with her supportive entourage, Roxanne peered into the windows of a four-bedroom, two-bathroom, two-car garage house. "This is perfect!" Roxanne assured her companions, signaling Roxy's shrill laughter of excitement. *We're standing, under a lucky star!* Appeased the Lioness enough for her to cease her prowl. "Yep ... this is definitely it!" the Trio finalized. They were peering through the sliding glass door while they each panted from the pleasure of their successful hunt.

Roxanne floated toward the front of the house in a wondrous daydream that collided with a man. A stark reaction tempted the Trio to scatter. Instead, Roxanne offered a nervous laugh. "Oh man, you scared us—I mean, me!" she offered as she watched the Lioness take a pouncing stance behind the elderly man.

"I'll size him up!" The Lioness chattered to her pride, assuring them she would defend their queen. Again, Roxanne laughed. But this time, she was full of confidence as the group recollected themselves. And the host of the Trio stuck her hand out, in a greeting fashion, in the man's direction. "I'd like to rent this house!" Caused the creases in the man's face to crack into a warm smile. "Would you know?"

The Lioness quickly sprang up and began deliberately stalking around the man's quizzical disposition. "To whom should I talk?" Roxanne asked the man, with blue eyes that had been hazed by age. "Ma'am, that would be me!" he assured her, emphasizing his words with a tilt of his baseball cap in her direction.

"I own this house!" he said while raising a hand that clutched a full key ring and shook it into her anticipation. "Let me show you the house?" An alluring tone rang through the air when the cylinder of the lock released its hold, and the man waved Roxanne in.

The older gent began to explain that the place was just exceptionally too big now that the children had moved away and with his wife not being well. His voice drifted while his eyes reflected a sadness that bled from his heart and painted his eyes red. *Well, it's a beautiful house!* Roxanne coddled his personal feelings.

"Your family must have ... many precious memories from living here?"

Her words seemed to lighten his burden as a smile once again lit his eyes with life and the memories of loving his wife. Whom he had carried over this exact threshold on the day they had married, and together they raised four children in this house.

The older gent continued to jabber his fond memories into Roxanne's direction as he and the Trio walked the rooms together when suddenly, the ill-patient Lioness turned to the man and severed his memories with Roxy's steady bluntness. *This house is perfect!*

Roxanne blushed in a heated moment, finding it still necessary to fondle the man's receptive nerve.

"It has been very well taken care of, and it holds a family-oriented spirit!" Roxanne looked directly into his eyes for the first time.

Well, take it! Roxy said with an abrupt coldness. Roxanne shyly added, "We hope—I hope to restore a family orientation for my children!" caught her up in a daydream of clean communities, where scores of children played in the homes, yards, and streets.

Roxanne shook the man's hand, sealing the deal to rent this wonderful house in this pleasantly radiant neighborhood. Roxanne thought of her children and how happy they were going to be. While Roxy wrote his phone number down. "I am going to discuss it with Steven!" Her mouth slammed shut, caught in an error. "I mean my husband. His name is Steven!" Roxy smiled. "Anyways, he will call you to work out the details!" Roxy said.

"No later than this weekend!" Again, she looked him in the eye and the man's pleased smile. He made an ushering gesture with his hand toward the front door;, and when they stepped into the warm sun, he turned and locked the door. "So you, your husband, and your children will be residing in the house?"

Roxanne didn't think it necessary to explain about her entourage as he walked her across the front yard and opened the car door. "Yes, sir!" Roxanne said without a hint of doubt in her mind as she slid into the car.

It was when Roxanne pulled up to the stop sign at the end of the street, her abundance of luck toppled her cup. Spilling the contents from her eyes as laughter gripped her gut. "Finding the perfect place and, to top it off, the owner being there at the exact same time!" Wiggled her butt with excitement. She looked at her watch before again looking up at the sky and decided, "The sun is so bright. I have to wear my shades!" she sang as she slipped her sunglasses on.

CHAPTER 6

STATE OF AFFAIRS

Scenarios of manipulation flipped in the matter of a slideshow viewing. Projecting consideration of how to bait her husband onto the subject "of moving!" Roxanne mumbled, each ideal, that crossed her lips, over and over.

Repetitively piercing the Lioness until she took on a "no-tolerance stance."

Slyly, the Lioness slid by. Leaning her slick body just out of reach of the coaxing hands. Before pouncing her annoyance into the air and landing on Roxy's lap. Enforcing the intent of the Trio's pact, made months ago, while Roxanne sat speechless and indecisive; In the jungle of what, she wasn't sure? She only watched and learned the dance of the companions. Listening to their consuming words until the abyss howled with laughter

He'd do anything to make his young emergent queen happy!" Feather tickled Roxy's fancy into flight and sent her hurling down into Roxanne's persona. Wiggling nice and deep into their much-loved hostess until she had full control.

The cool and seductive Roxy exhaled a hit of marijuana into the review mirror and smiled. Sucked in another hit. Exhaled… sucking in another hit, way deep. Little bellows of smoke escaped from Roxanne's spasming rejection that forced a hand to cover her mouth; Trying to pull the smoke and Roxanne, deeper into the wiggle dance, created by the Lioness's tickling influence. Back and forth it brushed Roxanne's tender spots on her neck and face in play, like a feather. A giggle came out in a big puff of smoke, clouding any clear vision of a sane reality.

The tail-feather swooped her neck… Up and down strokes put goosebumps on her flesh. Fluttering across her cheeks, tracing the distinct jawbone from the right earlobe. Slowly, very slow, making trail across Roxanne's lips until finding the left earlobe. The feather paused, breathing seductively. The Trio sweated, in the excitement of the feather, dominating its opponent and swooping down onto Roxanne's collar bone, where it teased with temptation. Down, down, down to the breast bone, The feather lightly touched and swept the cleavage, which heaved with admiration; As Roxanne emerged and joined the party in the smoke-filled car, howling with laughter as they headed down the freeway.

Where the days are long….
And the nights are strong…. Yelled the Trio at the top of the lungs.
Alligator lizards…. in the sky.

Roxanne sucked the nicotine from the long white cigarette that quivered between her teeth. Not the usual place she held her habit, but these days, "Nothing is as… it once was!"

Persuasive words coursed the feathering trail, creating a friction to spark the combustibles under the mirth. Plumes of black smoke, grew thick, obscuring Roxanne's reality when laughter clapped in the abyss, rolling up… Visibly shaking Roxanne and pushing the unwanted out the exit. "Everything's going great!" sang Roxanne.

Steady as she goes! Roxy sang in reply.

The Lioness kneaded Roxanne's heart with an encouraging, self-satisfying caress. When Roxanne spotted the children playing by the dorms, Roxy blew the horn. Only to draw the children's attention. Wanting to relieve her host of any undue stress caused by those children. Never in a million years, did she think, the unruly brats would spin around and dart into the dirt road without looking.

A surge of panic froze Roxanne's heart as fret pulled her from the car.

"Hey, watch for cars!" rushed from her as she stepped in front of her boys and delivered a halting hand to each of their chests. Sending them to the ground, where they bounced and then fell into a sprawled-out position, their eyes wide with a mixture of confusion and bewilderment.

Stevie slowly came up to a sitting position before leaning his weight back on his elbow-locked arms and blew an admiring whistle. But Mark's head was spinning for recognition of the woman who stood above him. She looked like his mama, but different... much different.

Roxanne wanted to sweep her baby up and cuddle him with an instinct that still burned inside her. But Roxy churned the course by slapping Roxanne on the ass—*That's not the plan!*—stung Roxanne's hide and snuffed out that flame.

"Gee, Mama, you look great!" Turned Roxanne's head in every direction as she fluttered her fake long eyelashes at them. "Thanks, I feel great!" she offered with a spin of her new persona while she wished they could see the change from the inside, also.

The boys were caught in an enchanting stare, only for their mama's beauty. The strong firm tail, switched. Ears radaring the scrutiny that challenged their queen. Heavily, the Lioness padded around the threat before taking a seat behind the boy's; Mouth open, tasting the air... Saliva, dripping from her fangs. *The better to smell you!* she chattered.

When Scarlet and Lisa's kids walked by Roxanne, they showed no sign of recognition before they slipped into the car. But her own boy jury, watched her suspiciously. Hardly did they recognize her! And they wondered, why suddenly, the extreme change. Before the Lioness snatched each boy by the back of their shirt, luring them into a phantasm, as she tossed them into the back seat of the car, their eyes clouded with admiration. Their hearts, warmed by the memories of her nurturing.

On the drive toward Norco, the secret burned in the kingdom of Roxanne. Creating an unattainable whirlwind of happiness blowing into the children, the queen's announcement. "I got a big surprise, for my kids!" Her voice rang with a suspenseful energy that pulled her boys close with anticipation. "What is it, Mama?" Roxanne's boys chorused in harmony.

"I've been thinking… Hope carried the suspense. Roxanne looked into the mirror. Curious eyes half paid attention. "About moving!" lured their attention. She glanced at the rearview mirror, to view the enthralled faces of her audience.

"Can we have a yard instead, of a dirt field?" echoed her boys' pleas.

Of course! exclaimed Roxy with a tone of annoyance, which chastised the demeanor of the questioner. While promising to slash the throat of anyone who might be thinking of questioning her, or her motives.

Although Roxanne lay back in the lair with the Lioness, filtered from any reality that might detour her. Her reflection beamed at the children from the rearview mirror. A sudden surge of confidence washed over her as they confirmed they were on the same track as her.

"The house has a huge yard!" she sang toward the heavens, a tune that caused the boys to go wild. Their howls of excitement cut in at the appropriate moments as Roxanne explained the details of the house, the neighborhood, and the small community until they pulled up in front of Lisa's house.

CHAPTER 7
MANIPULATION

The assurance of self-pride came over Roxanne as she stood up from the lair of the Lioness. Knowing for a fact, the Lioness and Roxy, had just sprung a surprise attack. Giving her the confidence to think she could do this on her own.

"Does Dad know?" flowed from the back seat in the tone of a female commentator. Roxanne spun in her seat and fretfully looked each child in the eye before continuing. "No ... nobody but the six of us know!" Roxanne shot Carolyn a challenging look as she continued. "I ask, all of you not to say anything to anybody until I've talked to Steven!" Her voice filled the air with a command as the children began to pile out of the car. "Okay... pinky promise?" Roxanne called out to the scattering children who defied her, completing the contract she had stipulated.

Roxy flew from the car, sprinting ahead of the young racers, and met them at the door. With a finger pressed against her lips in a hushing motion.

That brief moment of silence lasted long enough to roast Roxanne's almond eyes into a dare that challenged the children. "Momma, we're home!" Carolyn daringly called out while defiantly brushing by Roxanne and her companions and darting to the back room where Lisa performed the sweatshop work, of ironing clothes,

for families that could afford to pay to have someone else do their tedious but necessary tasks.

Lisa's ears picked up on the frequency that magnetized the iron and thrust her arm spastically, down and out. The spasm had the iron temperature set on cotton, pressed firmly down, on some fat man's worn briefs. Disgust, and maybe even some envy, burned in the pit of Lisa's stomach when Roxanne, her companions, and the children piled into the already small and stuffy room. The beads of water that streamed down Lisa's face and dripped from her chin and onto her breast bone was clearly unexplainable at this point. And did not register to the group of on lookers. No empathy rose in the Trio's circle as they looked at the pitiful vision of Roxanne's mentor. Standing over a steaming iron with her hair up in curlers. Looking hot, tired, and a bit frustrated. But the clue came to the Trio from Lisa's increased exertion and reputations of the aggressive back-and-forth motion. Lisa was a lot more than a "bit" irritated. The Trio decided as the Lioness circled Lisa smelling the promise of a hunt.

We don't care! Roxy nudged Roxanne. Who was playing tug-o-war with self-satisfaction and compassion?

The more Roxanne resisted in that game of Narcissism, the more she could feel her courage fade, with the disapproval of her companions. And although she really didn't want to hear it, she imagined, the answer to the question she hesitantly asked out of respect.

"What's up, Lisa?" Sent a chill crawling up Roxanne's spine as Lisa turned and fixed her aim into Roxanne's eyes. She contemplated, letting go of the repressed shot. Instead, a look of disapproval creased Lisa's face. Roxanne's courage shivered like a rabbit trapped in its den. Not breathing. Anxiety, screaming … flickers of advice, blinding her.

Lisa's mind raced, searching for her true emotions. Suddenly, the damn of the repressed cracked. Beads of water turned to hoodwinked oppressions, crashing into the violent seas of madness. Threating to drown those who can't save themselves.

Lisa couldn't control the charged emotions that created an electrical current in the water. "Okay, let's be honest!" Lisa suggested, but Roxanne stood fixed in her spot, looking void. "I feel abandoned … since the day your family moved from the street where our friendship had begun!" Lisa put great effort into selecting her words before she opened her mouth to express herself. "Your actions … … I don't know!" Lisa set the iron in an upright position, just short of scorching the briefs, and came around the ironing board.

Lisa stepped up to Roxanne, trapping her in a corner. Closing the circle, the Lioness had sprayed as her perimeter. The sirens blared, causing Roxanne to clasp her hands to her ears. Until the companions pulled the staggering Roxanne back from the predator.

That will be consumed if it becomes a threat! The Lioness assured the stabilizing Roxanne. "Look at you … what's shaking?" Lisa dared question the host of the hostile companions in such a manner.

In turn, Roxy stood tall as the Lioness attentively smoothed her attire and her hairdo. Giving Lisa ample time to prepare, another jab. But the assertive Roxy put her hand up in a stopping motion and took a step into the circle-shaped boxing ring.

"If this has anything to do with neglecting my children and my husband, I've already heard it today!"

The Trio's stare, held Lisa in contempt.

Lisa's jaw fell open like a boxer who's derailed by a severe blow that he neglected to duck and cover from. Staggered by this charlatan that resembled her dearest friend, who stood just inches from Lisa's waving arms. The Trio watched, strutting their defensive body language. As Lisa's emotions fell futile into the flood of water that had now begun to disburse. "Everything will be great!" Exclaimed the interloper as she disappeared from the room and headed toward the front door.

"Don't be angry because I found something better than ironing clothes!"

Roxanne shot over her shoulder, hitting a nerve and wounding her once–best friend.

Lisa's already-listless self-esteem felt crushed. Churning coals of smoldering anger and striking fire under her step as she rushed up behind the brazen Roxanne.

"I am not mad because you got a job!" Lisa shook the molten words loose from the foundation of her sentiment. "It confuses me ... makes me mad as a hornet!" Lisa declared to Roxanne's back. "I no longer recognize, my best friend!" rushed from the pit of her womb.

Roxy laughed with disdain in her tone that visibly shook Roxanne's body. "If you were any kind of friend, you would be happy for me and support my decision!" She said as she reached the door.

Lisa anticipated Roxanne to walk out, never to be seen again. Unexpectedly, her former friend turned with an expression of hostility plastered on her face. "You, are like everybody else, in my old life!" Shot fiery darts from Roxanne's burning eyes. "You want *me* to fail!" shook loose Roxanne's restraints.

"You want me, to be trapped like you for the rest of my life!" Roxanne opened the door at the end of her well-pressed words and strutted out, wearing a self-satisfied smile as she approached the car where Roxanne's children waited. Leaving disbelief, to shake the Trio's adversary. Stunning her and trapping her in a paralyzed position. Lisa fought to pronounce the words that rushed from her mind. Only to find those words trapped behind her choked throat and quivering lips.

Tears of frustrations, welted Lisa's eyes. Pouring out the pain of emptiness as she watched Roxanne get into her car and drive away without looking back.

Roxanne checked and rechecked her reflection in the mirror as she drove the three blocks to the fire station, where Steven was pulling a twenty-four-hour shift.

She could not wait to show her husband the extraordinary transformation that had taken ahold of her in such a short period of time. The beaming smile of the Trio reflected in the mirror when Roxy insisted that Roxanne's oldest boy, announce her entrance. The other two children could ride her train as she proudly paraded for her prey. *To get... what she wants!* Her strut became cat-like. Her chemistry was tantalized by sleekness and determination. Laced with confidence, she would stop long enough to wiggle her tail. She would entice them by licking her paw; seductively slow, she would smooth herself. Again, she would lick her paw with consideration before she turned the dampened paw to her face and slicked her hair back.

Roxy turned a daring eye to the children, who carried her expectations. She slowly batted her eyelashes at them, a wink without consideration for anybody, including them. The Trio watched as the oldest boy walked through the door speaking words that sounded, rehearsed. The children had smiles plastered to their faces that had been fixed and powered by Mama's apathy when the entourage pushed through the door.

The crowded room reeked of testosterone and a sorted mixture of aftershave, sugared doughnuts, and coffee. Fell silent as she cat-walked her strut. Parting the crowd like the Red Sea. Firemen, Police personnel and the Grand Marshal released the long bellow of a sailor's whistle. Pride lifted Steven from his chair as the room went wild with applause and respectful catcalls.

When the last of the spectators parted, Steven was there, to proudly claim what was his. He extended his arm to accept whatever she was about to give him. Roxy's eyes burned confidently when she placed her hand in his. She licked her lips wet with the juices of unruliness. The

Trio leaned into their prey and bit into his lip. Steven pulled his lip from her clenched teeth to lick the wound of her foreplay. He extended her arm out, looking up and admiring her on the way back down. His loins growled with enough power to spin his delight into him. Pulling her close, taking in the softness of her heaven's scent. He exhaled, breathing heavily in her ear. "You are a beautiful woman!"

MEOW! the Lioness warned. *Search him for sincerity!* Flicked her tail as she swatted at his attempt to play with her. "You've never said those words before!" Scratched at him suspiciously.

Steven instinctively guarded himself for a moment while he attentively cared for the slash she had created in his confidence.

"Why now?" She hissed.

Steven smiled into her question, took her hand, and took a couple of steps back. Before spinning her like a top, her colors blended and swirled-spinning and swirling the hand of her new persona. Admiring her, until she became giddy. Her giggles filled the air.

"Look at you—you've grown into the most beautiful, strong, confident woman I've ever seen!" he confessed. Roxanne spun into him, squeezing him like a teddy bear as she squealed. "You have always been, my biggest fan!" she acknowledged before planting a long, wet kiss to his wanting lips.

Hot dogs and beans for eight was a bit overwhelming for Roxy, what with having to care for someone other than herself. She hated to cook, and she didn't like Mothering Roxanne's children. That's why the children were sent outside to play with Sparky. Because Roxy was struggling to "stay in character!" She didn't care for a moment; the children were protected and considered off-limits.

Steven cleaned up the dinner aftermath while Roxanne and her companions stood next to him. She whispered, purred, and licked her prey, teasing him as he washed the dishes. His smile was wide. His mouth released a laughter, of giddiness. Roxy leaned her body across his chest and sealed her lips to his. Steven's bubble bounced across the room, gleefully floating, without care. *I think it would be a good idea to move to Home Gardens!* Roxy maliciously popped his bubble.

Steven ducked in sarcasm. "Shit ... where did that come from?" He said after he received a shot of disapproval from the Trio of critics. Who hesitated for a moment while contemplating the best reasons they could think of? "It's the halfway point...." Twisted Steven's eyebrows. It has a big yard...." Caught his interest. "The kids will love it!" came at him in a rush of conviction.

Steven smirked as he wondered what Home Gardens was in the middle of. "We'll go look at houses when we have time!" His suggestion held no real priority; mostly, it was only an attempt to appease her.

"I already found a house, and I really want to live there!" the Trio rushed their manipulation into Steven, full force. "Well, you have been busy today?" Steven said as he watched Roxanne rummage through her cluttered purse.

"The house is big and beautiful. Very well taken care of. Ironically, the owner of the house was there!" she finished as she pulled the number from her purse. "The nice man agreed to rent the house to us!" Roxanne added as she handed the phone number to her husband, avoiding his perplexed look.

Roxanne and the companions toyed with him. Purring his doubts away while seductively kissing and biting his tender lips until he became responsive. "You'll love it!" She cast her spell of promises with a nip of his ear. She slid the desk phone with one extended, well-manicured, finger. A flash of light caught the glitter of gold from her new charm bracelet, shooting Steven in the eye, with hypnotic powers that encouraged him to make the call.

The Lioness's parading began to wear thin the prejudice prowl where contempt laid with Annoyance. The magistrate hissed at Roxy's giddiness and optimistic delusion while the Trio listened to the one-sided conversation.

When Steven winked, the tone of his affirmative words began to blow Roxy's bubble of delusion to great heights. Encouraging a flirtatious Roxanne to lie across the desk. She stretched her lean legs, one to each side of Steven, squeezing him firmly.

Steven lifted his eyes from her panty-covered crotch. Meeting her approach with a smile and a quick lick of his lips. Roxanne almost blushed and recoiled from Roxy's efforts, but the Lioness stiffened Roxanne's back with a snip of persistence that caused their host to reach out and begin twisting Steven's hair around her finger. Causing the room to purr during the act of Ceremonial symbolism of wrapping him around her finger.

Steven grabbed Roxanne's thigh with his free hand, pulled his tempest closer to him. He took in a deep breath through his nose, smelling her sweetness as he closed the deal with the man on the phone. He dropped the receiver into its cradle with a successful stance. The Trio tugged single strands of Steven's hair with a sense of satisfaction, smiling at his need to please Roxanne.

As an onlooker, Roxanne had no expression of her own. She only fretted and wrung her hands. Until the Lioness jumped on Roxy's back, causing her to collide with the non-compliant Roxanne and pushing her into Steven's wanting arms.

The Lioness confidently chattered in the midst of a heavy purr. Liking the idea that Roxanne was already disconnected from Steven. She really had no feelings but animosity for him at this point. And as Steven held his love in his arms, a tremendous quake trembled their world, and as Steven's heart slid down his sleeve, the Trio calculated their game score.

"Everything's going my way!" she whispered.

"Our way!" Roxanne submitted a retraction that created a crack of laughter to conceal the Trio's selfish intent.

CHAPTER 8

NEWFANGLED THINGS

Her excitement about all the new things in her life, which are about to blossom, had kept Roxanne from a deep slumber and found her in the kitchen preparing breakfast for her children. The aroma of the apartment danced with cinnamon, bacon, and a hint of blueberry. Roxanne filled glasses with fresh-squeezed orange juice as her sleepy-eyed children trailed in one at a time from their bedrooms.

"Good morning, babies!" she chirped, like a happy mother bird in song.

Stevie plopped down on the couch. "Today, is the first day, of many new things to come!"

The children rubbed the sleepy dust from their eyes, blindly returning Mama's smile.

"I fixed us, a celebration breakfast," She joyously sang out to the children who looked to one another for a clue before returning their confused stare on Mama?

A sudden jolt of anxiety rose from Roxanne's stomach and rushed her words. "Please, sit down and eat!" Mama barked before retreating to the kitchen. The boys gave Mama's sudden mood little recognition as they began to crowd the table and devoured the scrumptious food without a care in the world.

Scarlet picked up her glass of juice, pretending to sip the citric substance while she curiously observed Mama's demeanor over the rim of her glass.

Roxanne was pacing in the small kitchen, talking to herself, when she suddenly felt gored in the small of her back. She spun around to retract the object that was slicing her in half to find Scarlet's scrutinizing eyes, singeing her soul.

Doubt quivered Roxanne, toppling her as she spun her back into Scarlet's reproach. The Lioness prowled with the challenge from Roxanne's nine-year-old daughter. *Let's eat her!* the Lioness suggested, padding a half-circle around the girl, then sprang up onto the table and lay down in front of Scarlet.

Feeling forced to endure another line of negative inquisition, Roxanne's heart skipped a beat. As she approached the table where the judges sat, prepared to threaten her survival, static rose in the chambers of Roxanne's mind from the pressure of yet another grand performance, being in high demand.

These three, being her toughest critics, since Vanessa! Anxiety counseled Roxanne's shaken confidence.

The Lioness's tail switched and snapped with irritation. A low growl came from the abyss before she sprang from the table and nipped Roxy in the small part of her back. Insisting, Roxanne stand for emancipation.

"So ... have you thought of any questions?" Roxanne glanced a curious eye to each of her boys before she shifted a dead stop on her target and shot a daring look into her daughter's eyes.

"Why do you ... look so beautiful, Mama?" Mark inquired as he attempted to wink. Instead, both of his eyes shuttered.

A smile curved his mama's lips as she began to explain her favorite topic. "Today, I start my new job. I want to look perfect! Roxanne shrilled with a willful laughter as she sprang up from her seat to adorn her attire upon her captive audience. This is my first job in almost ten years!" Roxanne's breath caught in anticipation.

"I am very excited ... and really looking forward to it!" She selfishly admitted while Mark's eye's swirled with admiration, and his head nodded in the rhythm of her words. Mama soaked up his attentiveness with a piece of toast, smeared with the fresh preserves, of her children.

"Who'll... take care of us?" The question from the party crasher shattered Roxanne's celebration. Causing her shoulders to drop and the light dimmed in her eyes. Waves of static crashed in her mind while instinct told her to cuddle the child. But Roxy and the Lioness wanted to brush him off as an irritant when Roxanne's hand shot out, with the force of a mother's instinct, to touch her youngest son's face tenderly. Again, she began explaining the redundant information.

Once again! Stabbed out Roxy's statement with any lack of self-control.

"You, your brother, and your sister will be going to your Aunt Tina's for the weekend." Then she assured her suspicious-looking children, "On Sunday, your dad and I will come and pick you up!" Rushed from her mouth, like a promise.

Roxy elbowed her hostess, drawing her attention to the perplexed look on Scarlet's face. *Just... ignore her!* insisted the Lioness into Roxanne's growing hesitation. Instead, Roxy's head snapped in Scarlet's direction. *Do you have something to say, young lady?* came out razor-sharp.

Scarlet squinted through calculating eyes for what seemed like a lifetime. Her body convulsed from the piercing shards of ice that shot from her Mama's mouth and forced "No!" from Scarlet, although her mind spun in a whirlwind of questions, like... *who's Aunt Tina? How far away does she live? Would we, be safe there? What's an auntlant?* The question swarmed without answers until fear overcame Scarlet, forcing her head to drop down on the table with her eyes closed.

She slipped through the tunnel of a light sleep to find reoccurring flashes of Troll-men, dancing around her bed, where the smell of whiskey and cheap cologne consumed her. The Trolls began laughing and lapping their long, sticky tongues at her before they pounced on the bed. A violent convulsion of an unknown reality shook her, awake with fear. The Trolls were real—and not only monsters that caused her to cry herself to sleep at nights.

Mama attempted to ease the tension in the room as she wrung her hands with contemplation. "There are only two weeks until the May Day ceremony!" she chirped like a happy mother songbird again. "So ... on Sunday. On the way home from Aunt Tina's, we will take Scarlet shopping for a new dress and shoes!" she proudly announced.

Stevie abruptly pushed back in his chair, arms folded across his chest and his face turned beet red. Roxanne looked to Roxy and the Lioness for encouragement, knowing that she was soon to endure her oldest son's daily stance.

"That's not fair!" he shouted as he shot up from his chair.

"Ever since her accident, everything is all about her and for her!" he steamed.

Although, Mark was too young to understand most of his older brother's words. He could relate to the feelings he sensed from his brother's words.

"Yeah ... that's not fair!" Mark shouted, then stuck his tongue out at his sister before both of the boys spun out of the room with the force of a tornado.

Roxanne turned a smile, laced with the stare of insanity, into her daughter's dismayed expression as the Lioness took out after the boys. Roxy began to laugh hysterically into the situation before she plopped down on the couch and lit a cigarette.

Don't make me! she said on the exhale. Roxy took another long drag from the cigarette. *Eat you!* She stated over her shoulder in a tone that ricochet throughout the apartment.

Scarlet ducked and dived from the violent waves that intended to instill fear in the household. Fear, glued her to her seat. She could not physically move. The only cover she could find was the shelter she found in her folded arms. She burrowed deep into the privacy and safety of the foxhole on the kitchen table. Her tears collected into a puddle, where she swam in confusion while searching for answers in the dark depth of her short memory.

Scarlet sat adrift on that now-pond of tears, where unanswered questions swirled her emotions. She did not understand why she had to be the May Queen or what that meant. However, she did know both of her brothers were mad at her again. Because once again, Mama has singled her out, burned Scarlet's fuse.

"Mama always made the boy's feel, less important than me!" Rushed out in a whispered breath as Roxanne reached across the table and gently squeezed her daughter's shoulder. The startled girl abruptly pushed away with enough force to break the hold of the glue. She stood up, facing one of the three persons who existed in mama.

She aspirated a breath of disgust before she spun away from her aggressions and ran to her bedroom, finalizing her disapproval, by slamming her door and shaking Roxanne's nerves. "That girl sure has become very defiant, lately!" Roxanne uttered softly through the heavy panting that turned to a growl as it coursed from the Lioness's den.

Maybe she needs a good spanking? the Lioness suggested.

Roxanne shuddered with laughter. However, her mind spun in confusion as to what had just happened. "I would never, hurt my children!" Roxanne stated with a resilient defiance as she pulled back her shoulders, with her daughter's untouched breakfast in hand.

Whatever the problem, the kids, will survive whatever life hands them! The Trio assured the council. *They will adapt! T*he Lioness panted confidently.

Scarlet raised her face from the softness of the lavender quilt atop her unmade bed, now soaked with tears of frustration. "I don't want to be, the May Queen! I don't want, my brothers to be mad at me!" she screamed into the pillow that threatened to suffocate her. "I don't want to go to Tina's, and I don't want our mama to go to work!" Scarlet was feeling numb in isolation. She sat wearily with discontentment on the edge of her bed when suddenly, Mama opened the door. "Are you ready to go?" she chirped happily.

A sudden rumpus in the hall caused a rush of anticipation to vault Scarlet from the bed and sprint past mama, who acted as if nothing had happened. Scarlet landed in the hall to greet her brothers and offer them her radio as a peace offering. But the boys looked at her like she was an alien before they sent her and the radio crashing to the floor as their howling laugher turned to mimic her cry.

When Scarlet opened her eyes, the boys had disappeared; only their mimicking cries lingered in her vulnerable state of affairs. She lay there on the floor, feeling crushed. She rose to a sitting position, wiping tears of disappointment from her eyes. "Maybe the boys have a right, to hate me?" she attempted to reason with her anguished soul. Although her foiled attempts at fitting in, trying to make peace, not complaining, and being a good girl, left her to question her already-turbulent mind.

"How am I to make a stand, in such a chaotic place?" Where she doesn't remember belonging. And where confusion, numbness, and loneliness consume her days.

Roxanne came out of the bedroom to find her daughter's face red, her expression sulking.

Now, what's wrong? blared Roxy's irritation, startling Scarlet into a stiff stance.

"Nothing's wrong!" Scarlet said. A good-long minute passed, each contemplating the other. Mama held a daring stare, roasting those darkening eyes. But Scarlet harnessed her fear as a rush of anxiety pulled her atrociously past Mama before a gravitational pull sucked her out the door and into the parking garage.

Scarlet stood just inside the parking garage with a smile that warmed her heart as the boy's laughter filled the space. Until envy bit, at her heart, as she watched her brother's smile in the embrace of brotherly bonding, that had been sealed, with a high five.

"Why can't you achieve that?" Haunted Scarlet as she reached out to open the back door, but her efforts were in vain as her brothers began taunting her.

They pointed their fingers and bounced on the back seat, hard enough to rock the whole car. Alligator tears welled in Scarlet's eyes as she grabbed the doorknob and began violently attempting to shake it loose. She pounded on the window with desperation as she cried. "Please... unlock the door?"

But they only laughed harder and louder.

"Please ... please!" Scarlet uttered, with quivering lips smashed against the window.

Roxanne was met with her daughter's screams of distress as she stepped out of the apartment. She sounded wounded and surely would have died if someone did not help her. Causing static to raise its volume in Roxanne's mind as she flew down the stairs to find her boys inside the car. They were making faces and laughing at their sister behind closed doors and rolled-up windows. Scarlet's wounded existence was pressed against the car, with tears smearing the windows and her hands gripping and shaking the door handle while her crackling voice pleaded tiresomely. "Please, let me in?"

Rage seized Roxanne as she pulled her daughter away from the car. "Just get in, the front seat!" Mama spewed.

Scarlet's startled reaction insisted, "The doors are locked!"

Roxy bent down and peered at the boys in the back seat with their red-stained eyes and faces that were no longer laughing. Their eyeballs shook with fear as they stared at this woman, who sailed on a frenzied wrath and shot smoke from her nostrils.

"Unlock, this fucking door!" the Lioness commanded while Roxy pointed at the lock on the other side of the rolled-up window.

Stevie urged his younger brother to unlock the door for the imposter as he took cover in the far corner of the back seat. No sooner could Mark unlock the door than Roxy flew over the back seat, slapping both of the boys. "How dare you, upset your Mama?"

"Can't all of you, just be nice?" Roxanne fought for control as chastising words slid past the cigarette that bounced between her lips and Roxy, who continued hitting Roxanne's boys. "All of you, just need to deal with it!" bit the Lioness. "I don't ever, want to hear crap like that again!" the defender finished while Roxanne's body suddenly froze. Her eyes were fiery beyond recognition. Black as coal, obstructing any of her former priorities and clouding anything that inconvenienced the queen. And with the blinders fixed in place, Roxanne shifted her body toward the front window and slid down behind the steering wheel. She sat silent as she inhaled a cigarette long and hard, noticing she was experiencing a sense of satisfaction.

Roxanne leaned forward, turned the ignition of the car to auxiliary. Calmly, she rolled down the windows, allowing the pungent smell of fear to escape its enclosure.

She butted the cigarette, then turned the radio up. Jimi Hendrix was blazing in the airways. "Are you experienced?" he asked her directly, leaving her to ponder the question as she lit another cigarette. "I'm getting there!" she decided on the exhale, halfway through her cigarette.

She went to put the car into reverse when she caught a glimpse of the reflection in the rearview mirror. Suddenly the static grew, questioning her surroundings.

"I thought, I was alone?" Enticed her to sneak another peek at the reflection in the mirror. Sure enough, the children were clutched in the grips of Roxanne's companion's ranting.

"See how nice and quiet it is?" she offered while noticing that the blaring static had calmed to a warm, whispering breeze. Roxanne smiled down at her wide-eyed children, exhaling the last hit of her second cigarette into her daughter's face.

"All of you, sitting so quiet and proper," Roxy said.

Pleasant... little subjects! The queen agreed.

Children... tender... tasty... vulnerable! Tantalized the taste buds of the prowling Lioness who licked her wanting lips.

CHAPTER 9
ANTICIPATIONS

S teven sat around the table drinking coffee with the relieving shift at the fire station, where he usually participated in shooting the shit for hours with the guys. But this morning, the conversation didn't compare with the anticipation of making love to his beautiful wife.

He swallowed the last drop of his coffee, glancing at his watch before he picked up his bag of dirty clothes and some dishes that were rinsed free from the dinner he had brought from home. Steven smacked his lips, recalling the aroma of the mouth-watering flavors of the delicious liver and onions that his wife had prepared only for him. "No one else in his little family would even consider eating the delicacies, let alone put it to their lips," he thought out loud as a special feeling warmed him with his next whispered thought. "My beautiful wife prepared a meal, only for me!"

He grew with the pride that a confident man holds when he has been bestowed with having the perfect family! "She must, love me— yes, indeed. Yes, sirree!" he sang to himself as he walked out the back door of the fire station with a jounce in his expectant strut. He crossed the parking lot with Roxanne's promises burning through his bloodstream. He could feel himself harden with the thought of his wife naked and wet as he tossed the dirty clothes and the dishes across the seat of the truck, jumped up on the runner, and slid in behind the wheel. He reached down and turned the key, permitting the engine to come alive while letting go of its harnessed growl. Before succumbing to a purr of bridled vibration that pumped Steven with a stockpile of satisfaction.

He chuckled at the animalistic sounds that came from the fine-tuned engine.

"Yeah, baby, I am going to do the growling, you the purring!" Steven grinned seductively as he looked over his shoulder. He began to slowly release his hold on the clutch, allowing the truck to begin backing up. "I told you, everything would work itself out!" He laughed out loud as he shoved the shifter into first gear.

Listening as the engine growled with its transmission in gear. But its clutch held to the limit. Harnessing her power. She screamed with passion, begging to be released.

But not until he was satisfied did Steven hit the Ready button, signaling the clutch to release its hold slowly. The tires squealed into a spin, grabbed the pavement, and pulled the road under its wheels. "I love this truck!" chuckled his heart.

Steven felt playful, excited when he pushed the clutch back in, revving the engine until she screamed. He pounded his chest with pride, over a successful conquest. He stood firm on the clutch. He was heroically howling as he released the pressure of his foot. The truck jumped forward, screeching and burning rubber into the blacktop. He fought the fishtailing rear end while laughing defiantly as he tamed the bitch that possessed the beastly truck. Riding her until he had complete control of not only the truck but also his life. Deciding it would be the most appropriate time for a bottle of wine, a warm bath, and a long, slow romp in the hay. Topped off with a long nap, with his beautiful naked wife lying up against him.

Steven pulled into the local country store, which was in front of old Sam's house. Sam being a friend of Steven's father, had known Steven since he was a young lad. Nearly knee high, Steven thought, as he left the truck idling and ran in to find Sam stocking shelves. "Just in the nick of time, son!" Sam's words caused the anticipating Steven to sigh with impatience squeezing his testes that were rearing to go.

"I guess these old bones don't stretch as far as they used to?" Sam admitted as he and Steve traded places while making small talk about the job, the store, and the families. Steven stocked the items that were too heavy for Sam to lift above his head.

"So, how's the little lady?" Steve smiled into Sam's question with a gleam in his eye.

"I have a hot date planned with Roxanne today!" He chuckled as he put the bottle of wine on the counter. "Yeah, none of the ninety-eight-cents-a-bottle stuff, no, not today!" he told Sam. "Today, I will spend a whole two dollars for this special occasion!" Steven assured his mentor before ending with a heated smile that blocked the excitement that coursed through his veins, pounding tribal rhythms on his heart. His testicles groaned with anticipation that looped visions of him ravishing Roxanne.

Steven raced toward his castle, where his queen awaited him with the lusciousness she had promised to award him. He thrust the transmission into second gear, slowing the beast he rode, and pulled into the parking garage of the apartment. A smile assured his longing needs when he saw Roxanne's car in the garage, although parked cattycorner.

He looked at his wristwatch. "Great … the kids have been gone for quite some time now!" he stated as he jumped down from the cab of the truck like a knight in armor brandishing his sword, he imagined with the bottle of wine in hand. He stuck his chest out with the exhilarating adventure, pounding his warrior drum as he began ascending the stairs. Floating in the daydream of his happy kingdom when he noticed his castle door breached.

Dread flooded his dreams as the smoke signaled a warning. Steven could hear the whacking of the machete, slashing at the vines of his anticipations, causing his branches to quiver. The slayer took his final blows while Steven pushed open the door, sending most of the vines crashing into the acidy pits of disappointment.

Internal cursing gripped Steven's large intestine, setting it ablaze with anger. Confusion swarmed him and buzzed at his ears as he scanned the apartment. The place was demolished; clothes, toys, dishes, blankets, and pillows were scattered throughout the house.

Upon receiving the assumptions his mind settled on, the last of the vines that suspended his remaining dreams snagged his heart and pulled it into the pits of his smoldering stomach.

Steven stepped over and kicked the things out of his path as he trudged through the apartment. Listening for any signs of life as he made his way into the hall. He caught a breath in hesitation as he pushed open the door of his marital room to find Roxanne sitting in a trance on the edge of the bed. And on the floor at the foot of the bed, his children set quietly, watching their mama.

Steven's rage boiled up from his churning stomach until bellows of smoke rose from the dark pits where the vines of his dreams and his heart boiled to a pulpy mush until spewing words of jumbled thoughts. "What the hell's... going on?" he insisted. Steven maneuvered careful steps around his children until he stood directly in front of his wife but neither her body nor her mind responded to his presence.

Steven bent down to look into Roxanne's eyes, which were as dark as his abyss these days and as haunted as his family's reality. "Roxanne, what's wrong? What happened? Roxanne?"

She did not answer. Only her lips quivered, and her body shuddered as she fought to be released from the hypnotic state she had been sucked into. Steven turned a precarious expression to his children as he considered them guilty for their mother's state. "Nothing's wrong!" She finally spoke. "I just don't feel good!" The lie was blurted abruptly from her pressed and dry lips. Her black eyes became alert and began softening to a warm almond color.

Relief began washing over the boiled mush and cooling the coals of Steven's charred heart as he readjusted his blinders. He then turned his attention to his children long enough to bark orders at them. "The three of you—go clean up the house!"

Their dad's order caused the children to scrambled to their feet, trampling over one another in fear of the icy tones and the havoc that lurked, meant the belt would be flying in their direction.

When the children were out of sight, Steven sat on the edge of the bed and took Roxanne's damp and trembling hand. Attempting to comfort her with a sense of safety, assuring her, he is her knight in shining armor… Her King.

"What happened here?" Steven searched for answers. But Roxanne only shook her head for what seemed like the lifetime of Steven's patience while she attempted to dislodge the muddled information from the ringing chambers of her mind.

"I'm not sure," Came out in sobs. "All I can remember was having a terrible headache. My body was shaking. I felt weak and fatigued." Her words rushed out as she tried to recall leaving the apartment. But when she couldn't grasp the recollection of her memory, she gasped for air. Preparing to state the information Steven wanted to hear, but the Lioness growled and bit Roxanne's tongue.

Steven settled for the only relieving solution he could grasp from behind the blinders. "Babe, you just lie back down and get some rest!"

He stroked her shoulder. "Don't worry. I will take care of everything!" he promised.

Roxanne looked to Steven with a hopeful expression. She searched for his determination and ability. Roxanne reached out to touch her husband's face, but the Lioness swatted her hand, causing Roxanne to recoil.

Her eyes were dull, distant, and empty when she laid her head into the cradling comfort of the pillow, which smelled of heaven. "Thank you!" she uttered from her red-stained lips. Steven gave her a warm smile as he gently and tenderly tucked the blanket around her thin-framed body. He stood there for a brief moment, watching, waiting for any other comfort he could give her. But she lay there, still as a timid mouse. Her eyes closed. Her breathing was shallow but consistent. "Just rest, my beauty!" Steven whispered, brushing the hair from her face. He turned to leave the room when he heard a faint "I'm sorry!" coming from the direction of the bed.

Steven paused for a moment, reflecting on his dashed anticipation of their lovemaking. "That's okay, babe… Just get some rest. So, you'll feel better!" cinched Steven's blinders, even tighter, when he turned and shut the door.

The main purpose of the blinders being cinched so tight was to cut the blood supply to his brain, keeping him in a submissive pattern. But he did notice the front room was nearly cleared of the debris that hampered his walk earlier. He picked up the bottle of wine waiting on the coffee table and carried it to the kitchen, deciding to hide it in the back of the cupboard. "Next time!" he promised the bottle of wine, a date to be honored. Steven stood just inside of the living room, watching his children pick up the remaining tatters of their nightly crusade.

He thought of rendering the third degree to his children, but when he opened his mouth, "When you have finished, we will go out for breakfast," forced itself from his voice box. "Are we going to school today?" The children's voices echoed in chorus.

"Not today!" was all their dad said before he walked out of the room, and the boys slapped a high five. They quickly returned to the task of cleaning up the rest of the mess they had made. While their mama's physical body lay in a state of null and void.

Scarlet felt overwhelmed and void of clarity as to what had happened. She could hear Stevie challenging their youngest sibling. "Bet yeah!" trailed into her room as Scarlet closed the door. She lay down on the bed, snuggling into the sun-caressed blankets. Pondering the situation of the reality she had been dropped into. She had no alarming senses, in the middle of the night, when she sat on the floor, at the foot of her Mama's bed. She had no feelings at all for this lady, who fought demons in her sleep. Scarlet remembered considering her brothers, who slept curled next to their beloved Mama. Scarlet really had no feelings for them either. "Sure, I'd like to have a bond as they have with anybody!" But she couldn't think of anyone.

CHAPTER 10

BLINDERS

Scarlet found her dad on the floor with the boys piled up and weighted down with one led leg. Steven looked up from the crushed pile. To find his daughter's face painted with an amused smile, but her eyes were swollen with sadness. He returned her smile just before he released a caveman's grunt that signaled victory. Only then did he raise the leaden weight from the boys. Scarlet suddenly received a charge from a compulsive thought. She took a huge step forward and leaped. Suddenly the pile scattered while she was in midair, in the form of a perfect swan dive. She hit the floor, hard and solid, knocking the wind out of her and rolling her onto her back. The boys attempted to ignore Scarlet's agonizing moans, until they could no longer contain the combustion that came rolling out as their fingers pointed in Scarlet's direction. Scarlet quickly searched in vain for her defender. But when there was none to be found, her resilience swiftly raised her from the floor and stood her in front of her brothers. She swung at them. Choice cursing words impacted her wailing arms. Mark stepped behind his brother, taking cover from the bombardment. Stevie stepped up to his sister's fortitude and shoved her with all his might.

Scarlet stumbled backward until she lost her footing and fell into the same spot she had just risen from. Scarlet just lay there, with her neglected emotional needs forming puddles in the crook of her arm. "Sis, you can't lay there all day!" Steven informed his daughter as he came into the front room of the apartment. Scarlet peeled her tear-stained eyes from the blankets of her sulking area, she turned a look of disgust to the one they called dad.

With Steven's blinders snuggly affixed, he did not see Scarlet's puffy red eyes. But he did offer a smile into her humiliation. She reached her hand out to him, begging for a helping hand. But his blindness missed that one also when he turned from her and called the children to order.

Steven inspected his children, not only for grooming purpose but also to see if they suffered any long-term effects from last night before he honored them.

"All of you did a good job taking care of each other and keeping an eye on your mama!" His voice shook out the words as he gestured them to sit at the dining table. There in front of dad, sat a pen and a pad of paper, waiting for him to write down the instructions he gave his children. "This is my work number, and this is your grandparents' phone number!" The children watched as he wrote in big capital letters and bold numbers before looking up at his children.

"The next time something like this happens, I want you to call me. If you can't get a hold of me, then you are to call your grandparents." His brows twisted tighter with each serious word before he encouraged his children to follow him to the phone. Where they watched him tape the paper to the wall just above the phone.

"Is mama… okay?" the boys chorused.

"Your mama is very tired. She needs to get some rest!" Steven assured his children as he turned the conversation. "That's why we are going out for breakfast!" he screeched in play, poking the children into a shrill laughter. Fearful of picking open the scab that lay over the affliction his babies had endured. He again decided not to ask any questions. Instead, he quickly opened the door and pushed the noisy children out, with him in tow.

CHAPTER 11

SUGARCOATED

Steven and his three children raced down the stairs, heading toward the parking garage. Stevie and Mark were in the lead, nose to nose, when Stevie reached out and touched the car with enough force to push him into a winner's dance as he cheered himself on.

Mark stuck out his tongue while pushing his brother out of the way. Stevie was laughing at him when Mark opened the car door, taking the shotgun seat before he pushed the button that automatically locks all the doors. Mark howled at his brother from behind the safety of the locked door, at his brother's unavailing attempts to get into the car.

"Hey, what are you guys doing?" Scarlet rushed up to the car with Dad in tow.

Stevie turned his back to the window, placing both hands behind him. He gave his brother two middle fingers that could not be seen by anyone else. He held a nonchalant expression, "Dad, Mark's a bad sport!" he moaned.

Steven said nothing to the instigator; instead, he shook a ring full of keys at Stevie's tattling. Which motivated his oldest son to move out of the way with a plan to punch his brother. Steven tapped on the window and gave a smile that automatically unlocked the door. Stevie slid into the back seat, sitting directly behind his brother. He mustered up all his strength and kicked the seat. "What was that... a flea?" Mark said, loud enough for all to hear. But Dad chooses to ignore any conflict that may be going on between those two. But Stevie flinched when his dad put his arm across the front seat, looking over his shoulder, and began to back out of the parking spot.

Questions, of last night's events continued, attempting to pull Steven's blinders off. As he kept a vigilant eye on his children, monitoring them to see if they showed any trauma to what had happened last night. If anything, had happened? Retightened the blinders. However, he was curious about the events that may have taken place. But it's those, kind of things, you just don't speak to your children about.

Steven watched young Stevie in the back seat taking apart an old alarm clock.

"That boy was always taking things apart," he mumbled over his thoughts. Suddenly, Mark's telepathic talents. Burned into Steven, causing his eyes to cast down to his youngest son, whose eyebrows were knitted in contemplation.

The seriousness of Mark's demeanor lightened with a smile for his dad's sake and brightened his rosy cheeks. Steven returned a reassuring smile as he reached out and rubbed his son's red hair. "What's up, son?" Steven inquired. Mark shrugged his shoulders as gloom washed over his face again, knitting his eyebrows into a frown.

"Is mama... going to be okay?"

Steven shifted a funny look at his youngest boy. "Of course, she will be okay... she's just tired!" His words seemed to convince Mark, turning his concerned expression back into a smile as he began nodding his head.

"Groovy, man!" Mark insisted while continuing to rock his head to a rhythm only he could hear.

Steven turned his eyes to the rearview mirror to see his daughter, nearly the splitting image of her mother, but different. Her green-hazel eyes were enhanced by the reddish complexion, speckled with freckles. And her thick red hair could have been inherited from him. From day one, when Steven saw her red curly locks—a sure sign of his family traits—it left little doubt in his mind that she was his own. A sudden cringe of guilt clutched his scrotum over retrieved memories of when Roxanne was pregnant with Scarlet. "Well, it's a damn good thing she was born with red hair!" Punched a reminder of Roxanne's words into his solar plexus.

Steven stole another look at Scarlet, recalling Roxanne's newest revelation. Insisting, their daughter is different since the car accident. She had loudly testified during one of their frequent sessions behind the closed bedroom door. But when Roxanne stepped close to him, "She might be an imposter!" her whisper informed him. For a brief moment, Steven did contemplate Scarlet's apathy these days. As if nothing bothered her. Unless you stepped on her toes, that is. Steven scrutinized Scarlet, reflecting on how she seemed, not to be concerned about her mama's condition. His brows burrowed, contemplating his oldest. She doesn't seem concerned… dug his brow even deeper. Steven could tell something was bothering the girl, but what… Cinched the blinder, even tighter.

Finally, he pulled into the parking lot of a family-owned diner. He wiped at his sweating brow with a hanky he had pulled from his pocket. "Are yeah ready for some really good pancakes?" Sent the children into the blaring sound of joy. They piled out of the car and ran to the door of an establishment that had been owned and operated by a husband and wife team who were dear friends of Steven's parents.

CHAPTER 12

DREAMS OF FATE

Roxanne stood inside the chambers of the abyss, feeling giddy and fretful, all at the same time. The Lioness lay at the emerging queen's feet, gnawing on her tempest bone. On the black walls of the abyss, film strips reveled, how bright the Trio's future could be; If their charge, continued to comply.

Roxanne tossed and turned into a deep sleep; at times, she danced with excitement and happiness. But during the times she was overwhelmed and questioning, Roxy sat on her lap with ultimatums. *Either you're a willing participant"* She gave a smile before she raised her arm with something clutched in her hand. At that moment, all that had become constant in the chambers sounded. *We will take you hostage!* Released the items clutched in Roxy's fist, leaving a gag and a blindfold dangling from her pinched thumb and forefinger.

The predestined hostage fretted with the only stance that she had. She bit her lip until blood trickled down her chin when she decided with her faltering efforts and courage. "Where are the children?" Caused the Lioness to crack the bone she had been gnawing on. Roxanne, feeling fatally wounded, could not compete with the blindfold that slapped over her eyes and the gag over her mouth. Her only hope of finding the children was to drop to the floor and, hopefully, crawl away without being seen. But as she finished that thought, the chastising and persistent crowd jumped on top of their host.

Roxanne struggled to breathe with the weight of an elephant on her chest. And when she had only one breath left, she pulled that breath deep inside her and held it with all her might. The Lioness had noticed Roxanne's face turning purple and her eyes bulging.

An aggressive and demanding chatter drew the weight away from the chest of the hostage. Roxanne released the depleted breath, sucking fresh air into her lungs. But before she was replenished entirely, the bough of the abyss collapse on top of Roxanne and knocked out her breath, expelling one word from Roxanne. "Uncle!" was the word that loosened and removed the bondage; balloons dropped from the heavens in the Kingdom of Roxanne.

Those who had sat their will atop of Roxanne were now tenderly lifting her up—adorning her. Tenderly cleaning her. Replacing her rugged threads with a fine gown of purple, made of silks from the Orients. They placed a gold crown atop her head, but the scepter was withheld until her vows had been sworn.

With the Lioness on her right and Roxy to her left, they walked her toward a magnificent throne. Roxanne touched the glory of her crown as she rose up onto the first step. Desiring a hands-on view of the throne that was to be hers, she daringly took the second step. But when her hand dropped down from the gold crown and reached out to touch the red crushed velvet fabric that covered the queen's seat, Roxy snatched her hand and spun her to overlook the Kingdom of Roxanne. The whole kingdom was dancing, jesting in jubilant times, and toasting their newfound freedom. Roxy and Roxanne stood on the queen's platform, nodding their heads. Laughing and smiling while entertaining a perfect queen's wave.

Many balloons rose toward the heavens. All different colors of souls sang praises to her as they floated higher than she could see.

She blocked the confetti that fell from way up there with one hand. While maintaining a distracted queen's wave for the soulful balloons, ascending into the metallic paper. Aspiration insisted, fanning the heat—that flushed the queen's face when they turned to the party on the floor, in the kingdom, of soon to be, entirely Roxanne's.

The flight of the overwhelmed butterflies tickled Roxanne's stomach. While a pleased Roxy, laughed with her charge as Roxanne wavered toward the throne. Roxanne picked a piece of transparent confetti from the air that created a narcissistic reflection; enticing Roxanne to stick her tongue out, in a sacrificial manner. Roxy chuckled with delight as she plucked the image from Roxanne's fingers and placed that blotted with acid paper on her waiting tongue.

Roxanne stood there, back straight, her head held high as the bright light from the confetti radiated all around her and lit a room that had gone dark. Her black irises lit up with glee—dancing her into the depths of her commitment.

The clicking of crystal glasses hummed a victory song for her. Sweeping her off her feet, swooping and swirling her, into Queen Roxanne.

Speech, speech! All the colors demanded. Suddenly, a cat caught Roxanne's tongue. Fret spotted the blinding white with splotches of brown. Black drizzled, Anxiety. "What does a queen say to all those?" She reached out an arm. Stopping on pictures of her children that burned in her eternal fires.

Leaning all her weight into Roxanne, the Lioness spun her away from the pictures of all the things, their onus, still cherished. Roxanne stumbled into Roxy, who quickly propped up, the diligent hostage to face her. Roxy put her fist between them and opened her hand. The powder that glistened in Roxy's palm captivated Roxanne for a few moments. But when Roxanne began to turn in search of those important things, Roxy blew the magical powder into Roxanne's face.

An overwhelming disgust, filtered through Roxanne's body, as the red of Fear drizzled onto the platform. Being dumbstruck made her dizzy, then a little nauseous. Before the intoxication of the dust levitated her from the stage. She began to float through the masses of the soulful balloons and over the crowd of peasants while laughing hysterically. The butterflies danced with her gleefully, encouraging her to loudly profess the statement that had put flight under her feet. But as tattered as Roxanne's spirit was, she fought to hold on when she slammed her mouth shut on the laughter that tried to push the words out that the kingdom wanted to hear. Crestfallen butterfly wings began to fade, due to their vain exertions, struggling with their last-ditch efforts; Attempting to carry the soon-to-be queen back to the podium, where Roxy and the Lioness waited. Roxanne battled with the butterflies until she remembered to perform her queen's wave for the cheering crowd, initiating her loss of ground, and lightened the load for the butterflies. They had lost many due to the dissolving wings before giddiness, blew a bubble underneath the precious cargo. The bubble wavered with weight; it crested to a height and then would fall, allowing the peasants to give it buoyancy with their personal efforts of delivering their hostage in front of the strongest, most compulsive companions in the kingdom!

CHAPTER 13

CROWNING

When Roxanne looked up to those who struggled for her soul, they could see a swirl of emotions battling inside of her. The chatter of the Lioness could only be heard by Roxy, who copied the command. And when Roxanne searched her for an interpretation, Roxy blew a handful of the magic dust all over her.

Roxanne sat on the queen's platform, watching the dust quickly, absorb into her pores. And when the last trailed into an open pour, a queen effortlessly rose from the ground. She graciously gave a confident smile and waved the strong arm of the queen in the kingdom of Roxanne.

The Lioness winked at Roxy, signaling her to get the ceremony started.

They had their hostage right where they wanted her. Honestly, they didn't care!

If she, had to be induced to break her sane side. Actually, if they could keep her sedated, it would make it simple! But the Lioness liked a good chase.

And as long as they could get her to commit now a little time in training and instruction, she would make a magnificent queen.

Roxy stood close to Roxanne in the center of the queen's podium. The Lioness circled the hostess and came upon her left side and took her place beside her queen. The peasants crowded and encircled the platform, chanting for the future of the kingdom.

Roxy untied the scroll of the kingdom. She looked Roxanne in the eye and winked. Both she and the soon-to-be-queen watched the loosened scroll slowly drop to the floor. It rolled, slower than it had fallen, across the podium. It continued to unroll all the way across the platform. When it finally had reached the end of its mostly blank length, an appointed individual carrying a silver tray with a burning candle and a stamp of royalty took his place next to Roxy. Roxanne stared down at the one carrying the tray. "He looks familiar!" She questioned herself. Roxanne watched his shifty eyes. The tray trembled in his nervous hands. Suddenly, she loathed that person. The queen stepped over the scroll and quickly rushed up to the one who enticed her to kill. She daringly circled her prey until coming to a complete circle, stopping nose to nose with him.

She could smell his lacking consistency of pleasing, the queen. She sensed he couldn't be trusted. "Who are you?" she demanded in a thunderous tone. Blown a few steps back from the force of her storm. The tray holder looked to the Lioness. Who was drooling, over the control, the soon-to-be-queen was showing!

"I was summoned, Your Majesty!" he meekly stated.

She leaned into him, so their noses smashed together. The heavens rumbled when she opened her mouth. "What is your, fucking name… Is what I want to know!" Spanked him in the back of the head. He looked for an escape, but the crowd of colored balloons began to pop. The angry souls that once floated harmoniously in their own delight splattered their colors all over him. Making him an easy target as he recoiled behind Roxy. Who began laughing hysterically.

Go ahead, tell her! she insisted.

Tell her! Tell her! Tell her! chanted the crowd when Roxy stepped to the left, exposing his insecurities. And leaving him face-to-face, with the queen, whose eyes had turned to coals.

CHAPTER 14

KINGDOM

The male subject, who may end up a sacrificial lamb before this was over, bit his lip until he drew blood. Alerting the Lioness with an alluring, tantalizing aroma.

The queen grew annoyed with the one who remained in front of her. He stood there timid as a mouse, biting his lip. Until the pool of blood dripped, first to the bottom lip. Finally, the pool of blood ran down, filling the crevasse of his tightly closed lips. Huge droplets fell to the tip of his chin and splattered on Steven's chest. The aroma of the wound promised a good hunt. As the scent shaped itself into a shaft and hooked the Lioness by the nose; Leading her into a parade of circling the prey.

On her third advancement toward her long-waited moment, she lifted her front limbs and came to rest them on his shoulders. The Lioness licked him, slow and hard. Serrating his flesh with her jagged tongue, pulled her back, mouth open. She breathed in the scent of her desired hunt. Drooling, burned his taste into her memory. Replacing her immediate wants with a hopeful thought; Of eating Steven, someday soon.

The peasants' chant became hostile with impatience as the left side of the kingdom led, "Tell her!" Then the right side would back that up with "Already!" shouted repetitively, gaining great momentum that threatened to plow him over before the queen had her say. Busting a gut, Roxy had never seen a sight, such as Steven's lips moving-silently; Being too weak and mortally frightened, to be heard over the commotions in the kingdom.

The queen took in a deep breath that pulled her shoulders back. She raised one foot off the ground, and as she released a manic scream, she slammed her foot down.

The kingdom trembled. Fire shot from her nostrils, torching the ground under her soon-to-be-tasty treat. Suddenly, the man was tied to a stake and prepared to be slow-roasted. "My name is Steven!" he professed in a room that had fallen silent.

His tears of hopelessness dropped from his eyes and sizzled on the hot coals. The spit turned to a slow roast, clicked a twelve-count, above the hot coals while the ceremony continued. Again, the Trio took their position at the podium. The Lioness stopped in front of Roxanne during her passing by to take a stance next to her. Slowly, the Lioness licked with pride, from hand to elbow, the arm of the soon-to-be-queen. Expectation, carried a tray that held a dagger when she stepped up to the podium.

Roxanne gave a happy and content smile to the crowd before she performed a perfect queen's wave. Roxy took two steps forward and turned to face the perfect contestant. She batted an eyelash at Roxanne and smiled.

Miss Roxanne, thus far, you have shown your great strength and qualities of being a perfect queen! But your commitment has to be long-lasting and loyal!" Roxanne shook her agreeing notion to Roxy, the Lioness, and the crowd of emotions. *"The test of 'denounce and loyalty' must be passed! Before you receive, the crown of the kingdom!* Roxy instructed her while

Determination walked up on the stage and handed Roxy a remote. 'Determination' then took a stance with its buddy 'Expectations' behind Roxanne, who smelt roasting flesh in the air.

Let the test begin. The answers, denounce, or maintain your loyalty to the pictures on the screens. You will be scored by your hesitation and indecisiveness. And of course, your answers have to jive with the kingdom! Roxy could see nervous sweat beginning to bud on Roxanne's forehead as she wiggled in her spot. While the band blew the Kingdoms anthem through their horn instruments. Roxy pointed at Determination, gesturing for the magical dust. Expectation escorted, Determination, to the front of the podium. Where they turned facing each other. Expectation, held its hand out.

Determination poured magical dust into the accomplices' hands. Then Determination laid his own hand out in a cupped formation, filling it with dust.

The conspirators turned toward Roxanne as the band reached the final notes of the anthem. Anticipation ran up onto the podium. Spun around, then curtsied. Impatience cartwheeled across the podium, kicking up a whirlwind that landed in the piles of magical dust. Inpatient's twisted and turned, creating a fierce wind that pushed the powder straight into Roxanne.

However, the soon-to-be-queen withstood the sudden storm that failed in dragging her away. But it did leave her, a heavy coating, of multicolored powder.

Roxanne admired the sparkling colors of the perfect-fitting attire. She closed her eyes, snuggling into its softness, inhaling the seduction of the kingdom's fantasies.

When Roxanne opened her eyes, they were on fire. Her head raised with confidence. A rod of steel straightened her back. Roxy knew she was ready, caused Restraint, ordered off the podium. But Restraint waved the blindfold hopefully, for participation. Roxy scowled before looking over at the roasting sacrifice, named Steven.

Slap it on him. He's. going to need it! She appeased the bonding companion into a dance that led up to the sweating man.

"No, no ... Please, Roxanne!" he pleaded as the blindfold was cinched tight.

The kingdom ruffled its feathers into the pleas of the sacrifice pushing them away from their desires. The breeze caught Roxanne's neckline, causing her to giggle. She slapped a knee with humor as the giggle turned to a thunderous laughter.

Are you ready to receive the crown of the kingdom? Roxy entertained a question she already knew the answer to.

"Hell, yeah!" Roxanne gasped, replenishing the oxygen she had spent on laughing.

Roxy began to explain the directions of the test. But Roxanne held up her hand, nearly smacking Roxy in the head. She caught another breath in her heaving chest. "Get on with it!" she commanded the kingdom.

Roxy clicked the remote that allowed pictures and scenarios to appear on the screens. The first was *Consider the kingdom, above all!* Roxanne contemplated on things more important than her kingdom. When she couldn't find any, her shoulder voluntarily shrugged. The second, third, and fourth were scenarios of a selfish existence. Without consideration for anybody or anything that would come between the kingdom's happiness. Acceptance ran up to the podium. She began a cheerleading support system for the queen. When the cheers were complete, Acceptance turned toward Roxanne and gave her a big thumbs-up before exiting the podium.

Roxy looked to the Lioness. They both knew this was the toughest part of the test, and they hoped Roxanne was still fully coated with magic dust.

The Lioness batted an eye at Roxanne as she rubbed up against her. Roxanne smiled with confidence. "I got this!" she assured her two strongest companions.

Roxy again clicked the remote that exposed a span of pictures that reflected her first encounter with Steven, and every time, he mishandled situations.

Without consideration, she quickly answered, "We are going to eat him!" And with the second most important subject dealt with, they moved to the last and hardest subject.

Pictures of Roxanne's children filled the screens.

Roxanne stood there emotionless; her expression dull. She batted her eyelashes, trying to recollect who these children were and how exactly they pertained to her. The kingdom was silent, nearly quaking, and threatened to crumble.

Well, Roxanne, what's your answer! insisted Roxy.

Roxanne laughed, busted a gut, slapped her knee, taking the remote from Roxy before clicking the off button.

"Where's my crown!" she insisted, raising her scepter high with a strong arm of a Queen.

Printed in the USA
CPSIA information can be obtained
at www.ICGtesting.com
LVHW040718261023